Body Narratives

Body Narratives

Writing the Nation and Fashioning the Subject in Early Modern England

Susanne Scholz

First published in Great Britain 2000 by
MACMILLAN PRESS LTD
Houndmills, Basingstoke, Hampshire RG21 6XS and London
Companies and representatives throughout the world

A catalogue record for this book is available from the British Library.

ISBN 0–333–76102–2

First published in the United States of America 2000 by
ST. MARTIN'S PRESS, INC.,
Scholarly and Reference Division,
175 Fifth Avenue, New York, N.Y. 10010

ISBN 0–312–22783–3

Library of Congress Cataloging-in-Publication Data
Scholz, Susanne, 1966–
Body narratives : writing the nation and fashioning the subject in
early modern England / Susanne Scholz.
    p.   cm.
Includes bibliographical references (p.   ) and index.
ISBN 0–312–22783–3 (cloth)
1. English literature—Early modern, 1500–1700—History and
criticism.   2. Body, Human, in literature.   3. Politics and
literature—Great Britain—History—16th century.   4. Literature and
society—England—History—16th century.   5. Nationalism—England-
-History—16th century.   6. Nationalism in literature.
7. Imperialism in literature.   8. Sex role in literature.
9. Narration (Rhetoric)   I. Title.
PR428.B63S38   1999
820.9'35—dc21   99–33529
                                                 CIP

This book is printed on paper suitable for recycling and made from fully managed and sustained
forest sources.

10   9   8   7   6   5   4   3   2   1
09   08   07   06   05   04   03   02   01   00

Printed and bound in Great Britain by
Antony Rowe Ltd, Chippenham, Wiltshire

For Gisela and Gisela

Contents

Acknowledgements

My first thanks are due to Tom Healy and Gesa Mackenthun, who have fundamentally shaped my understanding of Renaissance texts, and to Bernhard Klein, who has been a source of information and inspiration. Without their wit, criticism, and friendship, this book would be much poorer. For their unfailing encouragement and support I want to thank Gisela Ecker and Gisela Engel, to whom this book is jointly dedicated. I would like to express my gratitude to Klaus Reichert, who supervised the thesis from which this book derived, and whose open-mindedness and generosity provided the climate in which my work could take shape. Helen Hackett kindly allowed me to read relevant parts of the typescript of her book at a crucial stage in my work. I also wish to acknowledge my debt to Andrea Maihofer, who has influenced my thinking about power and gender probably more than she knows. I am grateful to the members of the *London Renaissance Seminar* 1993–4 and the *Zentrum zur Erforschung der Frühen Neuzeit* in Frankfurt, and to the *German Academic Exchange Service (DAAD)* for awarding me a scholarship which gave me the opportunity to complete my research in the stimulating atmosphere of the British Library, the Warburg Institute, and Birkbeck College, London. Thanks are also due to the members and library staff of these institutions. For sharing their knowledge, time and enthusiasm, I want to thank Dagmar Gleditzsch, Ina Habermann, Margaret Healy, Lesley Johnson, Conny Lösch, Christian Schmitt, and Peter Sillem.

Finally, it remains for me to thank the 'person-without-whom', as someone has so aptly called the indispensable figure in the background, Christoph Pabst, for providing strength and support, and much besides.

A Note on the Text

I have, as far as possible, retained original spelling, but have silently expanded contractions, given modern equivalents of obsolete letters, and modernized punctuation where necessary. When quoting from classical and medieval texts, I have used modern translations, or early modern ones when the argument required it.

Introduction

'Bodies,' writes John Donne, 'are ours, though they'are not wee',[1] summarizing a central tenet of modern subjectivity: 'we' are separated from our bodies, and though we possess them, they are no constitutive part of our 'selves'. In contrast to this apparently modern notion, throughout much of the period covered in this book, man was conceived as 'a little world made cunningly',[2] as a microcosm of a greater order which contained all parts of creation in condensed form and thus constituted God's likeness in the flesh. Its 'medical' configuration, the humoral body, was conceived as in constant flux, with insubstantial margins and inseparable links to all parts of the creation. It seems, however, that what is now regarded as an opposition between disembodied and microcosmic versions of the self was not conceived as contradictory at the time, and the more or less unproblematic coexistence in early modern England of different ways of conceptualizing the body is aptly illustrated by the fact that both the above quotations derive from one and the same poet.

Recent findings about the history of the body have alerted us to the fact that bodies were perceived differently in the early modern period. It is by now almost a truism that different historical times conceive of the same item in different ways, taking recourse to culture-specific patterns of description. In the case of the human body, however, the insistence on the historical and cultural contingency of our descriptive categories seems to contradict not only our perception but also our own experience of our bodies. While we (depending on our ideological locations) more or less emphatically embrace the idea of the fundamental historicity of cultural categories, we only hesitantly accept the idea that our body, this most 'natural' basis of human experience, could be similarly historical. Historicizing the body means deconstructing the

1

implicit nature–culture dualism that traditionally prevails in historical description, which assumes the human body to be the unchangeable substratum on which culture and history imprint their traces. Taking the historicity of the body seriously demands that we abandon this nature–culture dualism that is also, somehow, an inside–outside split, and that we regard it as the effect of a certain descriptive pattern that emerged at a specific point in the history of Western cultures. But the conception of the body as perceived and thus *written* differently in different historical or cultural settings still retains the idea of a natural, prediscursive body. 'Historicity' here also implies that the body in different historical periods was 'produced' differently, by normative discourses that did not get imprinted on its surface but which, as Judith Butler insists, structure the very shape in which the body materializes and then proclaim the result to be 'natural'.[3] Thus it is my intention to demonstrate how the human body was constituted differently from today in various discourses in the early modern period, how they effected and 'produced' the body as the 'natural' base of our thought about historical change.

The early modern period is traditionally regarded as a time of important social, political, and economic alterations, and likewise as the beginning of an epistemological shift during which the universalist notion of order which made sense of the phenomena of the world by way of a hierarchy of analogies and correspondences gave way to an *episteme* that we see, at least in part, as the beginning of our own ways of generating meaning. On a very abstract level, this epistemological shift could be described as the tendency to sever the ties between microcosm and macrocosm, as an impetus to isolate worldly phenomena and internalize their meaning instead of attributing signification from the point of an overarching structure of correspondences held in place, ultimately, by God. This shift in the epistemological framework of things effected all kinds of alterations on various levels of early modern cultures. One of the outcomes of this shift, and one which is not usually perceived by those that have analysed it[4] as completed before the eighteenth century, is the development of a medical discourse of the human body. Certainly, the human body had been the focus of 'medical' attention before that, but it had not been the object of a discourse, by which I mean a set of texts, practices, institutions, forms of knowledge, ways of thinking, feeling, acting, and social power-relations, all of which constituted the body as an object of a scientific gaze quite separate from its 'possessor's' location in the world and society.[5]

Arguably, this is not the way in which bodies were constituted in the Renaissance; and yet some aspects of early modern ways of seeing the body can be thought to be adaptable into later 'scientific' discourses about the human frame. I am quite aware that this can be construed as a teleological argument, and am convinced that we cannot escape the teleologies involved in describing early modern approaches to the human body in the light of our own thought about our bodies: any gaze into the past can only render its otherness in terms and categories provided by our own location in history. But besides the inevitable teleologies which come with historical hindsight, there are others that result from our seeing only the 'progressive' element in early modern discourses about the body, which then conduce to a view of Renaissance 'science' as inevitably leading to our modern ways of describing the body. Retaining the awareness that many options coexisted at this point in history in turn raises the urgent question of how and why certain paradigms became hegemonic, while others disappeared as not telling the truth about the body of man.

The destabilizing effects of a historicization of the body for our own cultural discourses become quite evident when focusing on the gendered body and the description of sexual difference. In the microcosmic paradigm, so Thomas Laqueur tells us, there could be only *one* body, the image on earth of the one God, and this body, whose pure idea resided with God, existed in two possible versions which were differentiated according to their degree of perfection.[6] The male body version, due to its heat-induced purity, was nearer to the divine ideal, and was thus conceived as the norm, while the female version was characterized by its deficiency in heat. Heat was also the factor that led to different body morphologies for men and women: it 'forced' the male genitalia outward, while the female remained inside. Evidently, this way of making sense of what could be perceived on the surface of the bodies was gradually replaced by a mode of description that rendered the female body as fundamentally different from that of the male, a difference that was later thought to be essentially linked to body morphology and proved by the science of 'anatomy'. Although I agree with Laqueur that this process of differentiation did not develop into a separate 'female anthropology' as a result of an essential sexual dimorphism before the late eighteenth century, I do not share his contention that the early modern period described female bodies exclusively in terms pertaining to the male normative body. Even if the microcosmic paradigm was still called upon to authorize 'medical' observation, female bodies were more and more subject to special scrutiny, focusing on their generative capacities. And although this may be a way of making sense according to a natural teleology that tied in perfectly with a microcosmic paradigm, it definitely meant that female bodies were perceived, described, and finally constituted as different. The one body that had accommodated both sexes gradually developed gendered emphases: while in the male microcosmic body, godlikeness shifted from the body to the mind, the female microcosmic body became uterocentric, a dissociation that was only at one remove from discourses conceptualizing male and female bodies as insurmountably different.

The fundamental change in the 'order of things' that occurred in the early modern period in Europe had tremendous repercussions on all levels of early modern culture and society. In the area of socio-economic organization, early modern England experienced enormous alterations and restructurings concerning urban development, banking and trade, and increase in manufacturing, with a concomitant demand for credit and capital. On the demographic level, too, things changed rapidly; inflation and unemployment caused a breakdown of rural community structures and a gradual restructuring of the social order that entailed a high degree of social instability. In addition, the Reformation effected a reorientation of the single believer away from a community-centred belief towards an unmediated, intimate relation with his or her God, a move which strengthened a feeling of personal responsibility that carried a strong individualizing impetus. Rapid social change enabled groups and individuals that had previously been excluded from social and political agency to enter the field of social action, which generated tremendous anxieties about perceived hierarchies in Tudor England. In the domain of political order, overarching power structures such as the Holy Roman Empire or the Universal Church had disintegrated through the impact of political struggles for sovereignty and the Reformation, leaving a power vacuum that was soon to be filled by the universalist claims of sovereign states and separate religious confessions. Thus on the socio-political level, too, the ties were severed that had previously united the European political 'universe' under a single power. The sovereign states and also the communities inhabiting them – and this especially applies to the diasporic community of Protestant England – felt the need to counter the loss of an unifying ideological structure by individual integrational concepts that would provide them with a feeling of belonging and significance. In the words of G. R. Elton, 'A national unit came to be, not the tacitly accepted necessity it had been for some time, but the consciously desired goal.'[7] In England a concept of nationhood emerged that aimed at ascertaining the country's imperial stature and that would serve as an integrational concept of loyalty modelled on, and yet in contradistinction to, earlier claims for an overarching European unity. Providing the individuated members of the body of the former *Societas Christiana* with an ideological centre, the collective identity could refashion itself as a 'universe' in its own right: the 'realm' of England became an 'empire'. The models within which these claims and self-definitions were voiced largely derived from older, often decidedly monarchical, discourses and images which were redefined in accordance with the new social and cultural constellations. In this context, the English 'nation' did not develop in the form of a nation-state but was articulated within the confines of a dynastic, quasi-absolutist state, with specific implications for its distribution of political agency as well as its forms of representation. Among these, the medieval model of the King's Two Bodies retained a prominent place, but was reworked to match the requirements of the current situation. In its Elizabethan use, it merged the juridical fiction of the 'crown', which comprised the synchronic, horizontal dimension of the corporation, head and body of the body politic in the present, with the notion of 'royal dignity', conceived as a diachronic, vertical, one-man corporation which guaranteed dynastic continuity.[8] The union of these two concepts in the person of the monarch enabled an appropriation of the traditional organological body metaphor, but with an absolutist bias: in the Elizabethan body politic, the head had absorbed the body. In its conjunction with images of the Queen's virginity, it linked a fiction of continuity through time with an image of territorial integrity; it envisaged synchronic and diachronic stability in the image of the Queen's inviolate body. Obviously, this constitutive fiction drew on a concept of the human body as a microcosm of the larger universe: only if the body of the ruler could be metonymically linked to the universe could it symbolize divine order on earth. As such, the ruler's body is different in kind from the bodies of his or her subjects, and gender is of no consequence here. We will see how the disjunctive impulse of both scientific thinking and nation-building gradually interfere with this integrative image of organic wholeness and take it to its semantic limits in the cult of Elizabeth I.

It has been argued that the English nation in the sixteenth century came into being not as a conscious political concept, but in the form of cultural productions, and pre-eminently of texts. Richard Helgerson has claimed that 'nation-ness' in sixteenth-century England was mainly articulated in language, and that those who envisaged it were also those who were most affected by the dislocation of the old order and social status. Being members of an élite by virtue of their humanist education, but with no access to state power nor participation in courtly politics, 'these poets sought to articulate a national community whose existence and eminence would then justify their desire to become its literary spokesmen'.[9] In historical narratives, chronicles, chivalric romance, history plays, and topographic descriptions these 'younger Elizabethans' sought to draft a political entity that would acknowledge their abilities and assign them a position of power within the cultural system. In that respect these authors of the 'nation' were by definition at variance with an absolutist sovereign and a dynastic state which had proved unwilling to accept of their services in more than cursory fashion. Nevertheless, much of this 'national' sentiment was voiced in the genres and imagery of courtly panegyrics, assigning to the Queen an ambiguous position as the focus of a loyalty that was ultimately bound to transcend her. The authors of the texts I have selected for my readings of English nation-building in early modern England, Edmund Spenser, Walter Ralegh, and Philip Sidney, to name but the most prominent ones, were Elizabethans of the younger generation, born around 1550, who were intensely dissatisfied with their social status as well as the politics of the establishment and the position it assigned to England and Protestantism, and who felt the need to change this by drafting their versions of national greatness. Edmund Spenser's *The Faerie Queene* in particular, appearing in two instalments in 1590 and 1596, took the challenge to write England's imperial stature seriously by virtue of its epic form as well as its Arthurian contents. As a self-declared national epic, this most sustained attempt in English Renaissance literature to write the 'body' of the nation by writing (or rather, scattering) the body of the Queen also testifies to the difficulties besetting the enterprise of providing coherent narratives of England's greatness in a courtly context presided over by a female monarch.

The implications of a definition of 'nationhood' as being constituted primarily through language, and of the nation as a narrative, are obvious.[10] Requiring a focus on the performative aspects of the medium and the impossibility of closure inherent in any kind of textuality, the idea of the nation as a narrative shifts our analytical focus from historical and sociological methods of investigation to textual ones, including the 'textual strategies, metaphoric displacements, subtexts and figurative stratagems'[11] which structure the national narrative. As Saussurean linguistics has taught us, language does not function referentially, and rather than merely reflecting an extratextual reality it constructs its objects. Additionally, these poets' quasi-didactic visions of national identity were meant to be translated into social practice. So if, as Helgerson claims, 'England writ large' was the goal of various discursive communities' endeavours to articulate versions of English nationhood,[12] thereby constructing a cultural system on which the loyalties of Englishmen and -women could focus, how do we define the relationship between these texts, social and cultural practices, and courtly politics?

As Benedict Anderson reminds us, 'identity... because it cannot be remembered, must be narrated'.[13] His by now classical definition of the nation as an 'imagined community' has opened up the possibility to conceive of national identity as originating from a representational process taking place in the medium of language. This does not mean, however, that English nationhood remained a textual affair. The reciprocal concern with the 'textuality of history' and the 'historicity of texts'[14] which has been practised for almost two decades under the name of 'cultural poetics' or 'cultural materialism' in Renaissance criticism has made us realize that literature is one domain of cultural production that is inextricably linked with other fields of cultural production, and with the social power structure, in that it reflects and likewise creates social reality. It is the reality of the imagined that is at issue here: through its implication in a web of power relations that pervades the cultural system, textualization is not merely a fictionalizing process that mimetically reflects an extratextual reality, but is intricately linked with social and cultural power structures. Elizabethan attempts to imagine Englishness articulated the differentiating ideology of nationhood in the discursive communities of literature, law, religion, history, and economy, not only in the texts they produced but also in their cultural practices and institutions. What their cultural texts have in common is that they are structured according to a narrative logic, that is to say, they organize their subject matter as a chain of causally connected events teleologically moving towards the goal of full realization of national autonomy within a linear time scale. In this context, literature and history occupy special positions because they enable visions of the nation's past which can be taken as utopian views and aspirations to future greatness. Again, the 'nation' as imagined in various texts and images is productive of certain practices, institutions, ways of thinking that are by no means fictitious, but are real. In telling stories of origin and destination, these texts determine the political actions and cultural practices of the present.

Drawing on the seminal work of Norbert Elias,[15] who has convincingly demonstrated how, in the early modern period, individual and
collective bodies were being shaped in a dialectical relation, and of
Mary Douglas,[16] who has shown how a culture's way of imagining
itself in the image of the body is inextricably linked to its norms of
individual body behaviour, I argue that social and somatic formations
emerged in a relation of reciprocity in early modern England. Both
body and nation were imagined as contained, independent structures
controlled by an inner core that could be described as an internalization of God at the centre of the new identity formation. In the chapters of Part II will attempt to trace the emergence of this pattern of
identity formation in early modern texts about bodily comportment
and individual behaviour. In these discourses, focusing on personal
and bodily demeanour, the subject's body was constituted as a product
of culture, purged of its instances of corporeality, which were reconceptualized as 'nature'. At the same time, this entailed a severe devaluation of femininity as identified with corporeality. Bodies were being
'produced' through the performative reiteration of cultural norms
concerning bodily demeanour, gestures, dress, and other instances of
(not always conscious) self-fashioning, as having one of two possible
genders. Thus I contend that, in the texts analyzed here, emphatically
gendered bodies were constituted as early as the 1590s, implying that,
at that early date, subjectivity was almost exclusively located in the
male body. As Foucault has argued about classical 'techniques of the
self',[17] only he who is able to achieve a certain self-relation that is
coded masculine, only he who has taken himself as an object of ethical
scrutiny, who has gained control over his inner 'nature', exterritorializing part of himself as 'other', can rightfully claim to be called a
'subject'. This self-government is isomorphous with political concep-
tions of government, both being predicated upon the domination of an
– often feminized – other within the self: 'governing oneself, managing
one's estate, and participating in the administration of the city were
three practices of the same type. … The master of himself and the master
of others received the same training.'[18] To be a man was (and is) no
natural, biological, or anthropological given, but the result of a complex
historical process. In regard of his body constitution and self-relation,
fashioned by both cultural discourses and power structures, the subject
emerged as inherently masculine. In this concept of gender performativity, agency inheres in a process of reiteration that produced subjects
who in turn claimed to be the originators of their actions, but who in fact
drew on norms and discourses beyond their own making. The literary

and didactic texts analysed here – the quest for Temperance in *The Faerie Queene*, Hoby's translation of Castiglione's *Cortegiano*, as well as the host of courtesy manuals current in sixteenth-century England – not only mirrored but also, by providing images of perfection and accomplished virtue, *produced* the subject's new body in accordance with the demands of social, economic, and political discourses. As writing constituted one of the modes of self-fashioning, subjectivity as it emerged from the literature of the time assigned a certain function to the female; the female beloved, in the prevailing Petrarchist mode, was instrumentalized to constitute male authorship/*auctoritas*: the scattering of the female body guaranteed the wholeness of the male subject. Thus I investigate the uses of images of the female body in relation to masculine identity formation which are also relevant for the collective identity's imaginings of the dangers besetting it from inside and from without. It is my contention that the narrative of the nation is matched, on the level of body politics, by disciplinary discourses on habitus, gesture, apparel, and speech. Again, performativity is a major issue here, translating textual prescription into body practice, thus effecting a body formation that is constitutive not only of individual but also of national identity.

The obvious linkage in Elizabethan courtly panegyrics of social and somatic formation is, of course, the 'virginity' of the Queen. I propose to read Elizabeth's 'virginity' as a political metaphor which, as many commentators have demonstrated, tropes the integrity of the island realm in the inviolability of the Queen's body. Focusing on the microcosmic, divine, perfect, *and* female body of Elizabeth-as-England, courtly panegyrics envisaged the nation as a paradisiacal territory safe from encroachment by its enemies, yet always under threat: a nourishing and autonomous, if fragile, locus of peace and plenty. Yet while the paradoxical combination of virginity and fruitfulness – as well as the Edenic associations of the place – render this as a highly aestheticized, quasi-otherworldly *imago* that structured human endeavours for collective identity on earth, the notion of the territorialized female body nevertheless drew on the Queen's body as a physical entity. In a (decidedly absolutist) pictorial overlap of the Queen's natural and political bodies, the collective body of the nation was given 'a local habitation and a name' in its identification with the royal body. This reading of the political implications of the Queen's inviolate state must not, however, exclude from sight the image's somatic referent: Elizabeth's 'virginity' is no dead metaphor. On the contrary, the moral state of virginity and the bodily practice of chastity were at the centre of disciplinary discourses focusing on the containment of the female body, and as such they had a decided impact on actual bodily comportment. It was not only the containment of the Queen's body that mirrored and, in a way, guaranteed the nation's integrity: this was, in turn, to be reflected in the closure of every woman's body. This preoccupation with drawing and fortifying boundaries took place on various levels of early modern English society, and it surfaces in the pictorial representations of Queen and nation.

So far I have argued for the reciprocity of social and somatic formation in the constitution of modern identity. How does this relate to what I have stated before about the historicity of body perception and constitution? Though the body image has a long tradition of depicting a unity of diverse elements, it is by no means a static universal of political theory, but is closely linked to cultural discourses and the respective community's way of imagining itself. Thus it is important to analyse *which* features are being chosen for representation in the respective body image: it is by no means coincidental that Elizabethan depictions of the national community put special emphasis on the body boundaries and stressed its fortification and defensiveness. Yet the ongoing shift in body paradigms also affected representations of the Queen and nation. Images of wholeness and spiritual as well as physical perfection clearly drew on a microcosmic paradigm, rendering the sovereign's person as divine guarantor of social order. Alterations in this way of generating meaning were necessarily also reflected in the political body image. While the strong emphasis on body boundaries in the earlier images already pointed at a loss of organic coherence and unifying power of the sovereign's body, which could provide stability only by means of enforced closure, in later representations the femininity of the Queen's body became a problem. In the chapters of Part II I discuss the gradual replacement of representations which draw directly on the virginal body of the Queen by images which render her in the form of disembodied, transcendent goddesses, as a corollary of these shifts in body perception and constitution. Different body paradigms were at the base of different forms of representing the Queen and nation, and gradually the connection of femininity and corporeality undermined efforts to depict the nation in the image of the Queen's body. The female body emerged in various cultural discourses as a particular, porous, penetrable entity that must be rigidly policed in order to contain its potential subversiveness. It was rendered as an instance of the 'other', and was used in this sense, for example, in representations of the indigenous peoples of the New World. In readings of Spenser's versions of England's 'Irish quest' and Walter Ralegh's description of his voyage to Guiana, I demonstrate how the shift in body paradigms was made meaningful in the course of new discourses on anthropology, through which gender difference as based on different body morphology and colonial otherness emerged simultaneously, one authenticating the other and *vice versa*. In representations of the nation we witness a change in the meaning of the signifier 'virginity' which prompts a shift in emphasis from the feminized territory to its complement, the male subject called upon to defend this vulnerable and precious entity. Male agency moved into the centre of attention and the national imagination sustained the notion of a 'band of brothers'. Here again, various cultural discourses went hand-in-hand in the production of a new subjectivity that was predicated upon a certain self-relation which enabled political and social agency. At the same time, the conceptualization of the female body as a commodifiable object deprived it of its capacity to symbolize paradisiacal perfection and wholeness.

The reciprocal relation of individual and political 'body' was not merely established on the level of ideal images, however. Discourses of the nation and panegyrical literature in praise of the Queen shared a metaphorical field and largely overlapped, both producing images of perfection and completeness which should be comprehended not necessarily as praising the *status quo*, but, as Philip Sidney pointed out, as ideals to be aspired to: 'For as the image of each action stirreth and instructeth the mind, so the lofty image of such worthies most inflameth the mind with desire to be worthy, and informs with counsel how to be worthy.'[19] Interestingly, in this form of what Helen Hackett has described as 'Protestant panegyric',[20] the nation comes to be incorporated with the Queen's body. By providing an image of divine wholeness that was to be achieved in the future, the textualized body of the Queen thus contributed to the national narrative, in that it rendered the nation as eternal and its territory sanctified. It also provided an image of perfection for the individual's endeavours at proper bodily comportment in accordance with social and cultural discourses. On the fictional level it promoted the idea that the national community was somehow a natural and organic, if vulnerable, entity; while on the social level it was translated into a body practice that, via certain disciplinary discourses, constituted a special habitus and perception of the actual human body that made the single person fit to be a subject of the nation. In both cases the body image was productive of strategies and practices which structured the emergence of national and subjective identity. In both cases, identity formation emerged not as a static act but as a 'citational' process that involved continuous reiteration. Linking the concept of the nation as a narrative with the notion of performativity structuring the materialization of the body, I will try to establish the connection of body and nation in a way that accounts for their reciprocal constitution: both narrative and body practice are citational processes that depend on permanent reiteration, allowing for a certain degree of agency even if the discourses within which identity formation takes place have always already determined the options available. Writing the nation and fashioning the subject can thus be understood as performative practices that produce identity by reiteration and imagination; that is, as a narrative or a practice. The conceptionalization of nation- and subject-formation in this vein makes clear that closure is never to be achieved, that this constitutes an open-ended process. Imagining the nation and imagining the subject('s body) emerge as reciprocal and at the same time unfinished performative processes, not only on the textual but also on the social level.

Part I
The Subject's New Body

1
Well-Tempered Bodies:
Self-Government and Subjectivity

In his magisterial study, 'The Civilizing Process',[1] Norbert Elias has argued that in the course of the early modern period the human body was subjected to a disciplinary process during which it emerged as a fortified structure in control of its affective and emotional impulses. He especially emphasized the diachronic dimension of the modern subject, whose emergence he described through changes in behaviour observed over a long time-period covering the twelfth to eighteenth centuries. Elias understood the gradual changes in bodily demeanour as an effect of increasing psychic constraint, concluding that the 'civilizing process' was due to the repression of 'natural' drives under the pressure of new models of social organization, such as the absolutist court and state. It is here that I part company with his ideas, for even though the behaviour changes which he attested and amply demonstrated from courtesy books certainly testify to the emergence of a 'new' kind of subjectivity, they should be explained as effected by renegotiations in the various discourses that contribute to the formation of the self and his or her body. Rather than believing in a 'natural' and universal core of the self which is then increasingly repressed by the requirements of culture, I want to describe the subject wholly as a product of social and historical discourses. As Linda Gregerson has claimed, the Tudor subject 'was always a crux and an interpellation of power';[2] that is to say, was subject to, dependent on, and, in a way, produced by a centre of power beyond itself. At the same time, the fluency of the concept of reiterative identity formation allows for several combinations of behaviour models resulting in various, and by no means coherent, subject positions.

Thus a major reorganization of the human frame, which emerged coextensively with changes in the political configurations in the early

15

modern period, can be traced in the behaviour instructions and courtesy books of the time. Behaviour manuals were mainly preoccupied with the question of how to translate 'abstract potential' into 'concrete historical embodiment',[3] how to inscribe a catalogue of virtues such as those provided by the writings of St Paul and Augustine and the moral philosophy of Aristotle, Seneca, and Cicero[4] on the surface of the body. This notion of *se facere*, deriving from classical, especially Stoical, sources, constituted part of the educational programme of the humanists in which a rhetoric of the self was translated into certain techniques of the self and body practices. Besides opening up a gap for self-consciousness in the most immediate sense of the word, this performative remodelling of the body entailed a domestication of affective impulses which were accorded the status of 'nature' to be disciplined by 'culture'. A self-relation was established in which the self assumed the positions of both subject and object of this ethical discourse, a relation, so Foucault reminds us, that is coded as masculine.[5] The inherent opposition of 'nature' and 'nurture' establishes gentlemanly behaviour as a practice in which the future gentleman needed to be trained. The behaviour manuals, usually written for the use of boys in grammar schools, thus provided a guideline for the drill these would-be gentlemen had to undergo in order to emerge as courteous subjects, while classical texts, as well as the quest for temperance in the *Faerie Queene*, afforded models of the desired result. This also implies that gentlemanliness was not exclusively reserved for boys born into the gentry or aristocracy, but was also for those who intended to become gentlemen primarily by 'nurture' (incidentally, like Edmund Spenser himself), allowing for a certain degree of social mobility. In their conjunction of teaching and practical exercise, courtesy, gentlemanliness, and temperance did not remain contemplative exercises, but affected and were in turn structured by large-scale social, political, and economic developments. Since social success increasingly depended upon the subject's control of his inner 'nature', which manifested itself in his dominion over his body, conduct books for would-be gentlemen focused strongly on the proper bodily comportment that was the indispensable precondition for gentlemanliness.

In his popular *Book of Nurture* of 1550, Hugh Rhodes delineates the gentleman ideal in a way that joins bodily containment and inner virtue in a discourse of proper humanity:

> A stil man is a castle, and keepeth him from woe
> A busie tung oft his fraend maketh his fo

A gentleman unstable is follie
Shamful life in anie man is ungodlie
A gentleman should be merciful by his natiuitie
Liberall and curtesie, and ful of humanitie.[6]

As we shall also see in Spenser's description of the Castle of Alma, only the body that is reframed as a castle is able to contain all the virtues befitting a gentleman and to represent them on the body surface. In this context, the idea of measure emerges as a central guideline of the reiterative process of inscribing virtue on the body. One of the most popular conduct books of the sixteenth century, Giovanni della Casa's *Galateo*, in an English translation by Robert Peterson from 1576[7] (dedicated to the Earl of Leicester), offers prescriptions for 'moulding' the body and thus fashioning a gentleman subject which accord to a large extent with Spenser's imaginings of the temperate body. The *Galateo* advocates discretion and measure as the central guidelines for behaviour, claiming that 'for the healthe of the Soule' the youth has to learn how to behave courteously:

> I meane what manner of Countenance and grace, behoueth a man to vse, that hee may be able in Communication and familiar acquaintance with men, to shewe him selfe pleasant, courteous, and gentle: which neuerthelesse is either a vertue, or the thing that comes very nere to vertue. (1)

No essentialist claims about the courteous gentleman's inner disposition are being made here: what is at issue is how to 'show' oneself to be 'pleasant, courteous, and gentle', with no implication that the subject might have 'that within which passes show'. The main aspects of bodily demeanour contributing to this demonstration of gentleness are identified as gesture, apparel, and countenance, which can be read as 'a language or discourse which creates rather than simply regulates, the categories of bodily perception and experience'.[8] From the subject's performance in regard to these bodily utterances, conclusions about his or her character can be drawn. As Anna Bryson continues, 'This representational view of manners implies a sense of the continual interpretative gaze of a social audience, deducing character from external signs.'[9] Gesture, apparel, countenance, and speech would thus be the central parameters along which to establish (the appearance of) gentlemanliness, and the major courtesy books of the time, the *Galateo*, Erasmus' *De Civilitate Morum Puerilium,* and Hugh Rhodes *Book of Nurture* dedicate large parts of their texts to the disciplining of these bodily utterances in order to make their bearer culturally intelligible as a gentleman.

The question of apparel is dealt with at great length by all authors of courtesy manuals, and like the other parameters of body habitus, it is constituted and defined in a highly gender- and class-specific way. Erasmus calls apparel 'the forme and fassion of the bodye. And of this apparayle we maye coniecture the habyte and apparayle of the inwarde mynde' (B3ᵛ). As such, what the gentleman wears is by no means accidental; through his apparel, he partakes in a system of signification that assigns to him a certain place in the social order according to his outward appearance. In his brilliant analysis of sumptuous male display in early modern England, David Kuchta has argued that male sartorial splendour was not necessarily eyed with suspicion or associated with effeminacy, but that within the predominant 'semiotics of masculinity' 'wealth should correspond to worth' and 'material fabric and social fabric resembled one another'.[10] This implied a denigration of social upstarts who could afford sumptuous dress financially but not in terms of social status, while aristocratic males – due to their social position – could display rich fabrics and sumptuous array. Dress as a signifier of social rank was thus ideally to be brought in line with the signified of a man's position, and, as Kuchta remarks, 'to presume that material signifiers made the man was to destroy the hierarchy of analogies so central to Renaissance masculinity.'[11] The obvious need to issue sumptuary laws (those regulating the richness of apparel according to social status) derived from the need to keep this hierarchy of analogies in place. The decision as to whether the relationship between a man's clothing and his status was natural or artificial was, however, ultimately referred to the sovereign, who, by legal means, naturalized the coherence between social and material fabric, virtue, and beauty. Nevertheless, the problem remained that dress, just like gesture, demeanour, and speech, is a manipulable signifier whose signified is invisible, so that the desired coherence cannot ultimately be verified.

Especially as regards the gender specificity of apparel, the instructions of the *Galateo* are adamant, another point that contributes to the argument that it is the body's outward 'dressing' rather than an 'inward', 'natural' core that separates male from female bodies:

> For, a man must not apparell him selfe like a woman: that the Attire may not be of one sorte, and the person of another: as I doe see it in

some that weare their heads & their beards curled with bodkins, and haue their face, and their necks, & their hands, so starchte and painted, that it were to muche for a girl, nay, harlot, that makes a merchandize of it, and sets her selfe to the sale. (108)

Similar warnings about the gender specificity of certain gestures and a certain way of moving the body are issued by Della Casa and others; again it seems that the masculinity that is inextricably linked to gentle-manliness must be established via a certain code of behaviour that accords with the contained body. When Della Casa inveighs against 'musing, niceness, daintiness' (27) as demonstrations of self-love, and concludes, 'Let us therefore leave these soft and wanton behauiours to women' (29) and, even more conspicuous, when he demands 'I would not yet have a man go so softe and demurely, as a maide or a wife' (111), he produces a behaviour ideal for men as separate from that of women, but in no case does this include any notion of essentiality. These are acquired forms of bodily demeanour which, being codified in a culturally specific way, establish a different 'grammar' for male and female body 'languages'.

In terms of the class specificity of bodily demeanour, too, the instruc-tions are very precise. The *Galateo* claims that proper greeting is only requested for gentlemen and not for merchants (51), and Erasmus, who is rather anxious to establish a class-specific body, states that

It is also all of the carte to shake the head and caste the busshe, to coughe without a cause, to hem or reyche, lyke wyse to scratche thy head, to pyke thyne eares, to snytte thy nose, to stryke thy face, as a manne that wepeth for shamefastnes, to scrubbe or rubbe thy necke, shrugge or wrygge thy shoulders, as we se in many Italians. (C8^r)

Besides gestures and apparel it is the visage or countenance that is subject to strict regulation in these texts, as it is considered to be a direct reflection of inward character or thought. Although they do not explicitly deal in physiognomy, the authors of the said manuals, espe-cially Erasmus, place special emphasis on the aspect of the face and its subjection to the will. Considering the eyes, 'the seate and place of the soule', he commands: 'Let the eyen be stable, honest, well set, not frownyng which is sine of crueltie' (A3^r), while at the same time, women were commanded to cast their eyes down in token of their modesty. Erasmus continues his instructions for the face by giving advice as to the proper posture of the mouth: 'Let not thy mouth be slopped, that is signe of hym that feareth to take the brethe of an other, nor let it not gape that is token of ydiot fooles but close the lyppes softe touchynge together' (A6ᵛ). His precept is reiterated in Seager's *School of Vertue*, a didactic text which summarizes many of Erasmus' ideas in verse form to be memorized by school children:

> Gape not nor gase not
>   at euery newe fangle.
> But soberly go ye
>   with countinance graue
> Humbly your selues
>   towarde all men behaue.[12]

The *Galateo's* instructions also aim at disciplining speech, counselling that the proper subject should neither be too talkative nor too silent and should speak with a moderate voice, not too shrill, not too low (86).

All courtesy books devote large parts of their instruction to the disciplining of what they conceive to be human 'nature'. Della Casa points out that:

> For albeit, the power of Nature be great: yet is she many tymes maistered and corrected by custome: But we must in tyme begin to encounter and beate her downe, before she get to muche strength and hardines. But most men will not doe so: but rather yealding to their appetite without any striuing, following it where so euer it leades them, thinke they must submitte themselues to Nature: As though Reason were not a naturall thing in man. But, Reason hath (as a Lady and Mistris) power to chaunge olde customes, and to help & hold vp Nature, when she doth at any time decay and fall. (97/98)

What is here generally called 'nature' is later identified as the human body, and especially what Bakhtin has called the 'lower bodily stratum':[13] 'Reason without custome and vse, cannot make an vnciuile bodie, well taught and courtious' (G100). The reiterative, performative aspect of this way of reshaping the body is evident in the recourse to 'custome and vse', and the disciplining of the body must start at an early age, while the body's 'nature' is still mouldable. Bodily excretions are the primary focus of concern, and they are regulated in a fashion that leads to their 'exterritorialization', that is, their exclusion from the contained body, and their subsequent 'reterritorialization' as private or 'privy' domain of special body regions, mainly the anus and the genitals. The evacuation of bodily substances by coughing, sneezing, vomiting, and excretion is consequently dealt with at great length, as is also the taking of substances into the body when at table. As the boundaries between body interior and the outside world are being reinforced, the orifices must be submitted to increased vigilance, and the processes of exchange between body and world must be governed and disciplined. Unsurprisingly, the imagery employed when dealing with behaviour at table and in relation to the 'privy' functions belongs to the register of animal lore, bestiality, and the grotesque.

Instructing his pupils and readers about proper behaviour at table, Rhodes, like Erasmus and Della Casa, constantly has recourse to images of feeding animals, especially pigs:

> Corrupt not thy lips with eating, as a Pig draffe
> Eat softly and drink manerly, beware ye doo not quaffe
> Scratch not thy hed or fingers, when thou art at meat
> Nor spit ouer the table boord, see thou do not forget
> Pick not thy teeth with thy knife, nor finger end
> But with a stick or some cleane thing, then do ye not offend
> If your teeth be putrefied, me think it is not right
> To touch meat other should eat is no clenly sight. (B1^{r-v})

Similarly, Della Casa admonishes his readers not to feed too greedily 'like swyne with their snouts in the washe, all begroined' (12), and concludes his lesson on table manners with the exclamation: 'Truly these beastly behaviours and fashions, deserve … to be throughly banished all places, where any honest men should com' (13). Honesty as identified with gentlemanliness is constituted as a class-specific virtue with a strong leaning towards the Protestant virtues of soberness and modesty. Erasmus also renders the unmannerly behaviour at table in grotesque images, drawing on metaphors of excess:

> Some cramme so muche in to their mouth at once, that both their chekes stand out and swell like a payre of bellowes. Some in eatynge slubber vp theyr meat lyke swyn. some snuff & snurt up the nose for gredinesse as though they were choked. (C3^{v})

The grotesque body is identified with animality, excessiveness, and untutored nature, and then metonymically linked to the people living in 'natural' surroundings, without the blessings of 'culture'. Erasmus thus provides the nexus between the beastlike greedy feeder and the 'carter', turning this connection into a major instance of negative identity fashioning; the gentleman must at all costs avoid appearing as a 'rustic':

> To thrust his fyngers into his dish of potage is the maner of carters, but let him take vp the meat with his knife or els his forke, nor let him not chose out this or that sweet morsel out of the hole dyshe, which is the propertie of a lickerus person but that which chaunceth lye towards him. (...) It is small honestie to giue to another that thou hast bitten of. It is al of the carte [orig.: 'rusticanum'] to dip or put thy bread againe into the dishe of potage that is gnawen vpon. Likewise to take thy meat out of thy mouth that thou hast chawed, & laye it on thy trenchour, is a lewde tutch. For if thou haue taken any morsel that can not go downe, it is maner to tourne thy head, & cast it priuely away. (C1^r-C2^v)

The 'rustic' way of behaving appears so degenerate that it is eventually compared to madness: 'This manner cometh all of the carte, and hath in a manner a resemblaunce of madnesse' (C4^r). Here, at a very early date, 'madnesse' is cast in opposition to reason, which turns men from 'foolish' nature to culture: 'We should be children still all the time of our riper yeares & in our extreame age: and waxe as very fooles with gray hoary heads, as when we were very babes: if it were not that reason, which increaseth in vs with our yeares, subdueth affections in vs, and growen to perfection, transformeth vs from beastes in to men' (G99/100). Grotesque imagery here not only renders the 'exterritorialized' parts as bestial, to be subjected to the government of reason; it also represents the gentleman as emerging from the matrix of the animal world which not only contains his body, this materiality which he shares with nature, but also women and the lower classes. The binary relation established here between nature, body, senses on the one hand and culture, reason, 'nurture' on the other eventually leads to the erection of a gentleman ideal that emerges through the dialectical devaluation of women and lower-class people as beastly parts of nature, not gifted with reason.

Class specificity is also implied when Della Casa speaks about the gentleman's demeanour when walking in the street: 'I would not have a gentleman to runne in the streate, nor go to fast: for that is for lackies, and not for gentlemen to doe. Besides that, it makes a man weary, sweate, and puffe: which be very vnsightly things for such men to doe' (111). Obviously, a gentleman can be identified by ambling with leisure in the street while those of the lower social echelons must move in a different manner. As Jan Bremmer points out: 'In classical and later times, ... the proper male behaviour in public walking required a leisurely but not sluggish gait, with steps that were not too small, with the hands firmly held and not upturned, the head erect and stable, the eyes openly, steadfastly, and firmly fixed on the world.'[14] Again there is nothing essential about this difference, which is acquired according to the model of classical behaviour rules which have found their way into early modern manuals on courtesy and civic virtue.[15]

Among the behaviour regulations discussed in courtesy books, table manners assume an extremely important place, since eating is an activity that takes place in a social environment as a public occasion, where the body orifices are in a delicate position and the individual feeder is under observation and called upon to prove his social status. Eating in a civilized manner is only one part of the exercise; the individual's gentlemanliness is put to the test when it comes to evacuating substances from his body in company, by coughing or sneezing. Della Casa provides a deterrent example of unmannered behaviour:

> So there be some kynde of men, that in coffyng or neesing, make such noyse, that they make a man deafe to here them: other some vse in lyke things, so little discretion, that they spyt in mens faces that stand about them: besydes these there be some, that in yauning, braye and crye out like Asses. (7)

Besides these obvious instances of evacuating actual substances from the body (most of which are gradually rendered as revolting and nauseous), behaviour manuals are also concerned with immaterial instances of the extension of the subject's body into space, such as sound and smell. Readers are constantly admonished not to speak with too loud a voice, not to sing with an 'untuneable voyce' (G6), and not to smell, either of perfume or of less pleasant odours. 'Belk neer no mans face, with a corrupt fumositie/Turne from such occasion, it is a stinking ventositie,' counsels Rhodes rather bluntly (B1ʳ). Scent is also frowned upon by Della Casa, and again the gender-specificity of these discourses becomes evident: 'You must not smell, neither of sweete nor of sower: for a gentleman would not sauour nastily like a begger: nor yet should a man carry a sauour and sent about him, like a harlot or whoore' (108). Smelling of perfume becomes an attribute of whores, and, as we shall see, of the court, the link being provided by the necessity to please to a degree that undermines the very idea of self-hood: courtiers, like harlots, 'make a merchandize' of their good looks and pleasantness. The respectable woman, in contrast, 'euer smelleth best whan she smelleth of nothyng'.[16] The major focus of concern, however, is undoubtedly the excretion process and its relegation to a private, secret domain. The *Galateo* counsels:

> Lykwise, I like it as yll to see a Gentleman settle him selfe, to do the needes of Nature, in presence of men: And after he hath doone, to trusse himselfe againe before them. Neither would I have him...when he comes from such an occupation, so much as washe his hands, in the sight of honest company, for the cause of his washing puts them in minde of some filthy matter that hath bene done aparte. (5/6)

Contrary to Erasmus' well-known instructions on the medical necessity of breaking wind, hygienic considerations are here subjected to notions of propriety. Similar to other unmentionable but unavoidable evacuations, like vomiting, excretion in general is cast as 'of nature' and consequently to be done in private: 'Go asyde whan thou must vomyte, for it is no rebuke to vomyte, but to vomyte of superfluitie is shameful' (E: A8^v). The action done in private, it seems, is non-existent in the public domain; not only the actual substances, but also the body parts associated with them, are being split off and cast as not really belonging to the subject's body. Moreover, these members are rendered as 'naturally abject': 'To disclose or shewe the membres that nature hathe gyne to be couered, without necessitie, ought to be vtterly auoided from gentyl nature' (E: B1^r). Della Casa makes a similar point:

> A man must not uncase himselfe, in the presence of any assembly. For it is a slouenly sight, in place where honest men be met together of good condition and calling. and it may chaunce he doth vncouer those parts of his bodie, which work him shame & rebuke to shewe them: besides that, it maketh other men abashed to looke vpon them. (118)

He concludes that these are things to be done 'alone in your chamber' (118). Erasmus even goes as far as counselling not to disclose the privy members when nobody is present, with the argument that the 'Angels always see us' (B1^r). His advice concludes – and it should be remembered that he is writing for boys in boarding-schools who also shared beds – 'Muche more we ought not suffer other to touche them' (B1ʳ). Thus it appears that excretions from the body became gradually unmentionable together with the body parts associated with them. The body was restructured in a way that disclaimed the existence of these parts in public while approaching them, privately, with a sense of shame that in the course of time turned into nausea, a process which testifies to the actual material effects of these discourses and practices. Interestingly, readers are admonished not even to mention privy members and excretions, as if a ban on naming these things eliminated them from (discursive) existence: 'We must not only refraine from such things as be fowle, filthy, lothsome and nastie: but we must not so much as name them. And it is not only a fault to dooe such things, but against good maner, by any act or signe to put a man in minde of them' (G5).

What can be witnessed here are the first steps of the relegation of bodily functions to the realm of nature, and, via their gradual erasure from civilized discourse, to a domain disclaimed by consciousness, from which they reappear as a threat to civilized existence. It is evident that the form of subjectivity which is framed in these processes is not universal and epiphenomenal; on the contrary, it is produced in social, cultural, and literary discourses that contribute to the didactic manuals intent on teaching 'how to become a gentleman'. It is likewise evident that the subject 'produced' in these discourses is inherently male, and that the same kind of self-fashioning is not unproblematically available to women. What emerges from these texts is the image of a contained body in which every movement is subjected to control and in which everything that is 'fowle, filthy, lothsome and nastie' is relegated to the private domain. Only this body configuration is capable of mirroring the subject's inner virtue and performing it daily, for this contained structure is *per se* a demonstration of the subjection of 'nature' and its relegation to an invisible realm. The subject emerges as an allegedly self-styled product of culture, who has mastered all instances of 'nature' in his own body, and, by extension, in his household also.[17] Thus, rather than merely describing this most 'natural' basis of human existence – the body – these texts establish norms of what the body is supposed to be, to look, and to feel like for the early modern subject.

Processes of identity fashioning cannot take place without ideals to be aspired to, how ever unattainable they might be. One of the areas of cultural production which offers itself for drafting models of virtuous behaviour is, of course, literature. In its didactic functions of *prodesse et delectare*, Renaissance literature reflected changes in cultural discourses, and likewise affected them, by providing images and ideals for future behaviour.

In the literature of Edmund Spenser, 'gentlemanliness', as in the courtesy books discussed above, emerges as a quality that must be acquired. The gentlemanly self is not predicated upon an inner essence which unfolds in the course of time, but can be moulded and 'made'. The rhetoric and techniques of the self implied in this notion of *se facere* are most obvious in the quest for temperance in *The Faerie Queene*. Spenser's didactic purpose in writing *The Faerie Queene*, according to the introductory 'Letter to Ralegh' attached to the first instalment in 1590, was 'to fashion a gentleman or noble person in vertuous and gentle discipline'.[18] This often-quoted statement contains *in nuce* the central parameters of subjectivity as advocated by Spenser and textualized in the poem: the notion of '(self-)fashion[ing]' that has been so brilliantly examined by Stephen Greenblatt,[19] the social status of the subject so framed, and, more obliquely, also his gender: a 'gentleman or noble person', the ethical dimension of the enterprise, which is to teach how to become 'vertuous and gentle', and finally the notion of practice which inheres in the idea of 'discipline'. The subject-configurations proposed in *The Faerie Queene* can be comprehended as products of a civilizing process that fashioned not only the individual body but the social configuration as a whole. The reciprocal categories of self and community, I contend, depend on similar practices of identity formation.

In the fashioning of subjectivity, the virtue of temperance plays a vital part. Besides being one of the more body-centred virtues dealt with in the *Faerie Queene*, the focus on temperance also established the self-relation so necessary for the early modern subject. Spenser's concept of temperance follows Aristotle's only in so far as it treats the virtue as primarily related to the body.[20] For Aristotle, however, the concept merely denoted the control of bodily pleasures, while for Spenser, temperance commences with policing the passions and then emerges as a major 'technique of the self'. As a principal foundation for his gentlemanly ethos, temperance requires and produces a high degree of self-reflexivity: the acquisition and 'embodiment' of the virtue is accomplished by taking oneself as an object of ethical scrutiny. The passions and senses that must be controlled, that is, grief, vainglory, wrath, greed, and concupiscence, instances of what later came to be envisaged as 'inner nature', are in Spenser's narrative of continence frequently displaced outside the body and depicted as hostile forces besetting the quester's body. Making use of a 'chiasmic principle' in representation, as James Nohrnberg observes, 'a man in an environment here often stands for the environment in the man',[21] refashioning 'inner nature', via this displacement, as 'the enemy within', a process which constitutes a martial self-relation of the subject.[22]

The *Faerie Queene*'s quest for temperance commences with an image of original sin. The infant Ruddymane, whose parents have died as a result of their concupiscence, has steeped his hands in their blood, which cannot be washed off. Though the child is completely innocent of his parents' deeds, he carries the mark on his body, so that Guyon rightly suspects that 'high God, in lieu of innocence,/Imprinted had that token of his wrath' (2.2.4). Original sin, written on the body and identified with human corporeality, is thus the outset of the quest for temperance, and in spite of all endeavour the body's mortality sets limits to what can be achieved by the human self:

> Behold the image of mortalitie,
> And feeble nature cloth'd with fleshly tyre,
> When raging passion with fierce tyrannie
> Robs reason of her due regalitie,
> And makes it seruant to her basest part. (2.1.57)

Aristotelian notions of temperance are here complemented by Scholastic ideas about the impact of the passions on the use of human reason.[23] The passions and their locus, the body, are being identified with original sin, and the body's mortality is cast as a result of the Fall, which has also impaired the power of reason. Consequently, in this Christian constellation of body, reason, and sin, the human mind, contrary to Aristotle's notion of teleological development, is unable to come to fulfilment within worldly circumstances. For its ultimate redemption, it depends on grace. The Palmer accompanying Guyon throughout Book 2 is one of the poem's allegorizations of the power of grace; another one, of course, is Prince Arthur. In this context, Guyon's quest is part of an attempt to ameliorate the human condition in a way that leaves this merely 'physical' state behind; the infant here constitutes an image of 'nature', while the virtue that elevates man beyond this 'brute' condition must be provided by 'nurture'.

Besides the martial imagery of a war between the soul, mind, or reason, and the passions, the connection between the social discourse of temperance and the body that is to become a well-tempered one is established by the use of 'medical' metaphors. Many of the passions are described in terms of imbalance of humours or body heat, and even the name of the enchantress who is the very opposite of temperance could be read as a medical term: Acrasia / *a-krasìa*, in contradistinction to Guyon's *syn-krasis*, that is, healthy state of equipoise. The 'burning' passions of the body must be constrained in the course of the quest; the contained, impermeable, 'cool' body is its desired result. The link between martial and medical images is provided by the notion of regimen, which implies a militant conquest of the passions by reason aiming at the balance or restitution of body heat. The achievement of a poised body temperature is preceded by a fight of the 'fiery' passions with 'cold' reason, which is also often rendered as a conflict between nature and culture. The allegorical figure representing irascibility in terms of heat is *Furor,* one of the principal enemies of temperance. He is described as 'all on fire' (2.4.6) and his effect as 'whot emboyling wrath' (2.5.18); his traditional locus in the body is the liver, which is here identified as 'secret bowels' (2.6.49), denoting the seat of passion but likewise of lust. Spenser's use of medical imagery not only points to the body-centredness of virtue, but implies that regimen rather than conquest is the suitable pattern for dealing with the passions. Guyon's encounter with Furor is conceived in terms of an imbalance of heat unsettling all other functions, including reason:

> And sure he was a man of mickle might,
> Had he had gouernance, it well to guide:
> But when the franticke fit inflamd his spright,
> His force was vaine. (2.4.7)

Instructed by a 'sober Palmer', Guyon vanquishes Furor and binds him in 'hundred yron chains' (2.4.15). This conquest, however, turns out to be impermanent: later in the quest, Furor is unchained again and roams at large. The government of the passions, so the medical imagery implies, is a matter of constant vigilance and careful discipline which cannot be accomplished once and for all, but depends on the continual watchfulness of the subject. The Platonic image of the bridle therefore provides the dominant paradigm for self-government in the first episodes,[24] and Spenser's ideas on the subject's war against its corrupt 'nature' draw to a large extent on late antique and early Christian ideas about the virtues and the vices, as advocated, among others, by Augustine.[25] Spenser depicts temperance as an unceasing effort to steer the right course which is to be individually established by recourse to the Aristotelian 'middle way'. This 'performative' aspect of self-government conceptualizes the right way as the middle position on a vertical scale; in this concept of the body as a system of caloric exchange, a balance must be maintained between inanimate coldness on the one extreme and outbreak of fire on the other. In relation to the irascible passions, temperance thus emerges as the practice of the golden mean in the domain of the corporeal. 'The temperate man keeps a middle course in these matters';[26] thus Aristotle's precept here, which is shared by Spenser, as can be seen in the host of images drawing on the Homeric narrative of Scylla and Charybdis and also in his allegory of the golden mean, Medina. Placed between her two sisters, one of whom represents inadequacy and the other excess, Medina morally and spatially represents the middle position. The applicability of this harmony-principle to the body politic is suggested by Guyon's comparison of Medina and his Queen:

> This thy demaund, O Lady, doth reuiue
>   Fresh memory in me of that great Queene,
>   Great and most glorious virgin Queene aliue,
>   That with her soueraigne powre, and scepter shene
>   All Faery lond does peaceably sustene.
>   In widest Ocean she her throne does reare,
>   That ouer all the earth it may be seene;
>   As morning Sunne her beames dispredden cleare,
> And in her face faire peace, and mercy doth appeare. (2.2.40)

Body natural and body politic emerge as reciprocal categories, casting temperance as a principle of order that not only affects bodily pleasures but is also an identity-forming technique: the well-tempered body corresponds to the well-ordered state.

Apart from depictions of the vital principle of body heat and its excess or deficiency, there is a whole cluster of images drawing on medical regimen in terms of diet and hygiene. Moral deviations are represented as poison, infection, or ulcers, rendering passions and emotions in distinctly bodily terms. Obviously, the notion of equipoise includes both physical and moral aspects of body behaviour. The lesson of temperance is to 'learne from pleasures poyson to abstaine' (2.2.45); it is rendered as a purgational virtue, and as a medication which floods excess out of the body, leaving it 'purged from drugs of foule intemperance' (2.1.54). Sidney's dichotomy of 'erected wit' and 'infected will'[27] comes to mind when the passions are thus described as ulcers festering in the body and making it suffer from its own corporeality. It seems that, ultimately, corporeality itself is conceived as an illness which must be purged so that the subject can emerge as virtually bodiless. The intended 'purifying of wit'[28] accomplished by the internalization of government in fact amounts to a complete denial of the body. What remains is a fortified container that can be moulded according to the culture's requirements and can thus afford an appropriate locus of subjectivity. The ideal outcome of this process of restructuring the body is pictured in the poem's prime instance of the well-tempered body, Alma's castle.

As I have mentioned earlier, the ideals and configurations of body natural and body politic are interdependent, and individual and collective identity are framed by similar means. The most prominent instance of this isomorphism in the poem is the double reading that can be applied to the Castle of Alma-episode in Book 2, Canto 9. In this idealized version of the temperate body, the concrete corporeality of bodily processes is displaced to a private domain and thus, in its invisibility, disclaimed as non-existent. This displacement has frequently been understood as a representation of psychological processes of repression and sublimation, and has often been commented on as such.[29] Rather than reading Alma's castle as a reflection of the 'fundamental facts about the human condition',[30] it will be suggested here that the description of the 'castle' is part of a disciplinary discourse that (re)constructs this most 'natural' basis of human existence that it purports merely to describe: that of the human body. In its inevitable conjunction with the national community, this is also an episode that reflects the double time-structure of imagined communities (and identities), in that it presents a wholeness that is simultaneously always already lost and still to be achieved in a quasi-apocalyptic future.

Guyon's entrance into Alma's castle after vanquishing Furor, Pyrochles, and Cymochles, Maleger's 'army', and after having resisted the temptations of Mammon, certainly echoes the soul's entrance in Jerusalem at the end of Prudentius' *Psychomachia*.[31] Alma's body-castle thus suggests the ideal state of the subject's body as well as the fulfilment of a certain political vision of unity and integrity. In accordance with the refined ('sublimated') state of his soul or mind, the body has to meet certain requirements to be able to afford a suitable location for it. Consequently, the castle is announced as an image of the godlikeness of the human frame:

> Of all Gods workes, which do this world adorne,
> There is no one more faire and excellent,

> Then in mans body both for powre and forme,
> Whiles it is kept in sober gouernment. (2.9.1)

The idea of government or regimen appears as central to the mainte-
nance of the body in that state of blessedness, and one of the central elements of governance is the control of body boundaries: hence the strong
emphasis on fortifications. The strength of the castle's outer walls renders the polarity of interior and exterior very pronounced, and the use
of architectural metaphors ties in neatly with descriptions of the body in
medical writings as well as with representations of the inviolable body
of the Queen. While the outside of the castle is characterized by its
defensibility, the interior is remarkable for its orderliness. Proceeding
from the 'Barbican' (2.9.25) controlled by 'twise sixteen warders' (26)
through a sequence of 'rooms', Guyon and Arthur witness the digestion process at work. Spenser's description renders these inchoate and
in fact involuntary motions as controlled, orderly, and balanced:

> It was a vaut ybuilt for great dispence,
>> With many raunges reard along the wall;
>> And one great chimney, whose long tonnell thence
>> The smoke forth threw. And in the midst of all
>> There placed was a caudron wide and tall,
>> Vpon a mighty furnace, burning whot,
>> More whot than *Aetn'*, or flaming *Mongiball*:
>> For day and night it brent, ne ceased not,
> So long as any thing it in the caudron got.

> But to delay the heat, least by mischaunce
>> It might breake out, and set the whole on fire,
>> There added was by goodly ordinaunce,
>> An huge great paire of bellowes, which did styre
>> Continually, and cooling breath inspyre. (29–30)[32]

There are no transgressions, no instances of overabundance, no blur-
rings of boundaries in this description of digestion; every stage of the
process takes place in a different vessel, with a guard nearby to take
care of ongoing processes, which are represented as offices:

> The maister Cooke was called *Concoction*,
> A carefull man, and full of comely guise:
> The kitchin Clerke, that hight *Digestion*,
> Did order all th'Achates in seemly wise. (31)

Everything happens under the influence of temperance and in good order, every organ within this body functions in accordance with a common purpose in an almost mechanistical way and there is no waste, except for the remains of the digestion process, which are taken good care of as well:

> But all the liquour, which was fowle and wast,
>   Not good nor seruiceable else for ought,
>   They in another great round vessell plast,
>   Till by a conduit pipe it thence were brought:
>   And all the rest, that noyous was, and nought,
>   By secret wayes, that none might it espy,
>   Was close conuaid, and to the back-gate brought,
>   That cleped was *Port Esquiline*, whereby
> It was auoided quite, and throwne out priuily. (32)

Contrary to expectation, there are no grotesque images, here such as are usually found in connection with food, eating, and digestion, the domains of the grotesque.[33] Though it is still addressed as a godlike structure, the body depicted here is no longer the humoral body in which everything is in flux and in which the different body fluids can metamorphose into each other. Here, the thresholds between body and world have turned into rigid boundaries. Fluids and processes are being kept apart, and the orderly manner in which digestion happens seems symptomatic of an effort to represent even involuntary bodily processes as ruled by temperance. Apparently, the ideal result of a disciplinary discourse which reconstructs the self and his or her body in accordance with social and political changes is a fortified structure, a castle or, as the Port Esquiline-image suggests, a city. Not only, as Foucault has argued, is 'individual virtue … structured like a city',[34] suggesting self-control and an internal hierarchy of functions, but the subject's body and the body politic converge in the notion of regimen, which renders individual self-government as a precondition of public action and social responsibility.

The most prominent instance of the corporeal in the body are, of course, the sexual organs. We have seen before that, in conjunction with the liver, they are cast as 'secret bowels' (2.6.49) and as the locus of 'base' passions that have to be conquered by reason. The configuration of Alma's body, however, seems to imply that the ideal temperate body has no sexual organs at all, testifying to the immense purgational effort that has gone into this structure.[35] Considering the evidence of the courtesy books, it seems likely that, given the overall impetus to purge the temperate body from instances of the corporeal, the genitals too must fall victim to this purifying effort. As we shall see later in the quest, corporeality is displaced onto the female body version, to the bodies of Acrasia and her ilk. The contained body as displayed in the tour of Alma's castle thus emerges as inherently male, produced in the course of a quest for self-restraint. Instead of discovering the sexual organs on their tour through the 'lower' parts of this 'body', Guyon and Arthur suddenly find themselves in the 'Parlour of the heart'. In this innermost room of the body, 'litle *Cupid*', the traditional representation of sexual desire, is merely 'playing' among 'a louely beuy of fair Ladies', who are 'courted of many a iolly Paramoure' (34). Apparently, sexual desire is displaced 'upwards' to the realm of social interaction, and is thus elevated to the very centre of the body. This process, which could be described as 'sublimation', and which, as many medical texts emphasize, is the outcome of restraint in dietary matters (conversely, excess in food and drink result in uncontrollable sexual urges),[36] constitutes (heterosexual) desire in a socially acceptable form as the core of the material body. This definition of the subject's desire, which, as Miller points out, 'reinscribes libido as ambition',[37] also requires a new body practice, which is articulated in discourses of chastity and temperance. Thus the emphasis on fortifying the body under the regimen of temperance is complemented on the interior level by the 'sublimation' of sexual desire into the heart.[38] Again, the body has been purified in order to make way for a new kind of subjectivity, for which sexual continence becomes absolutely crucial. The body's economy of pleasures has been restructured in a manner that gives priority to purposeful generation in the service of civilization, as the completion of this vision in the Bower of Bliss will show. What is effected, however, is not a restraint imposed on some features of the natural body, implying that they are still existent, if repressed; what emerges from the image of Alma's body instead is a reorganization of the human frame that completely disclaims its instances of corporeality. Thus the body's 'natural' core, and with it unrestrained sexuality, are imagined as always already lost, constituting and perpetuating a nature–culture dualism at the centre of human 'nature'.[39]

The assumed reciprocity of well-tempered body and well-ordered state is even more evident in the head of the fortified structure. The 'turret of the mind' (44), separated from the more corporeal body parts by the ten steps of the spinal vertebrae, is the absolute sovereign over the lower parts, and also the locus of the body's godlikeness, an analogy that mirrors political hierarchies in the community it represents: the Queen is the 'head' of both church and state and the representative of the divine in the social order. This structure is occupied by three persons, inhabiting three separate rooms.

> The first of them could things to come foresee:
> The next could of things present best aduize;
> The third things past could keepe in memoree. (49)

Given the reciprocal relation between individual and political body- and identity-formation, it is not surprising that in *Memoree's* chamber Guyon and Arthur find accounts of the past, not of themselves, but of their respective communities: Arthur discovers the chronicles of England, Guyon those of Fairyland. National memory stored in the head of the temperate body thus reveals Alma's castle to be a representation of the individual as well as the political body in ideal form: well-tempered body and well-ordered state correspond. The chronicles stored in Alma's head deal with the early colonization of Britain and thus re-enact on the level of British history the 'civilizing process' that has been the focus of the quest for temperance.

After Guyon's vision of the goal of his quest in the house of Alma, he is fortified enough to face the encounter with Acrasia at the very end of Book 2. The conquest of the Bower of Bliss, as culmination and crucial turning-point of the quest, can only be attempted when temperance has already been established, at least to a certain extent:

> Now gins this goodly frame of Temperance
> Fairely to rise, and her adorned hed
> To pricke of highest praise forth to aduance,
> Formerly grounded, and fast setteled
> On firme foundation of true bountihed. (2.12.1)

The experience of conquering the Bower and its inhabitant reassembles and concentrates all vices, demanding vigilance, alertness, and the practice of temperance from the quester. The Bower of Bliss itself is not easy to find, and only after many dangerous encounters does Guyon eventually arrive at Acrasia's island, that 'sacred soile, where all our perils grow' (37). This place, set apart from other places in the double meaning of sacred and damned, reflects precisely the status of sexual pleasure in Spenser's concept of temperance. Guyon's dealing with sensual pleasures in this episode demonstrates that his newly acquired continence is always under threat from the dangers of the outside world. Resisting the temptations offered to him by Excess, Guyon cannot help feeding his 'greedy eyes' (64) on the spectacle of the two girls bathing in the ever-flowing well, with the effect that 'His stubborne brest gan secret pleasaunce to embrace' (65). Clearly, pleasure threatens the containment of the body and the carefully fashioned identity, but it cannot be completely erased, as it ensures social continuity. Here, as in the case of Mammon's temptation, the right use of the pleasures is at issue.

The Bower itself is described in such a way as to suggest excess, corporeality, concupiscence, and femininity, all of which threaten the quester's (masculine) identity. His reaction to its temptations is consequently resentment, but this resentment in the end deteriorates into downright violence. It seems that Guyon's capacities to resist in a contained way reach their limits when it comes to the bodily pleasures, possibly owing to the fact that these temptations aim at parts of his body that are exterritorialized from the frame of the contained body, and which consequently cannot be dealt with in a rational way. At a certain point the temptation becomes so overwhelming that the interior struggle between attraction and rejection must be displaced outside in a fit of violence; the alternative would be succumbing to lust. The point is reached when Guyon is confronted with the effeminate knight Verdant in a posture of post-coital repose. The signs of the knight's masculine identity have been erased by his giving in to lust; and, even worse, he seems completely unaware of his shame:

> His warlike armes, the idle instruments
>   Of sleeping praise, were hong vpon a tree,
>   And his braue shield, full of old moniments,
>   Was fowly ra'st, that none the signes might see;
>   Ne for them, ne for honour cared hee,
>   Ne ought, that did to his aduauncement tend,
>   But in lewd loues, and wastfull luxure,
>   His dayes, his goods, his bodie he did spend:
> O horrible enchantment, that him so did blend. (2.12.80)

This negative projection of the good subject is, of course, a dreadful sight for Guyon, who is so intent upon honour. Not only has Verdant relinquished his armour and weapons (an act that Patricia Parker constructs as a castration),[40] but he has given up purposeful toil for 'wastfull luxuree', has wasted not only his good name but also his bodily resources. As a consequence, even his bodily contours seem to have become unstable, as he is 'Quite molten into lust and pleasure lewd' (73). The contained body with its outer boundaries reinforced by armour is here constructed as masculine, while the softness, daintiness, and permeability of the skin are identified as feminine. The bewitching qualities of the Bower thus inhere to a large degree in its being a female space that effeminates every inhabitant; this 'femininity' is reinforced by associations with artfulness, purposelessness, and the fact that its pleasures serve as an end in themselves. Interestingly, the lewd knight, Verdant, is not depicted as fully responsible for abandoning his honour: it is the combination of the 'witch' Acrasia and the enchanting place that has led to Verdant's deviation, and he can easily be brought back to the right way. Being the paragon of temperance, Guyon, of course, manages to detach himself from the temptations offered, but still the threat is so imminent that it prompts the Bower's destruction. Both captives are led away in chains, but Verdant is lectured about his duties and his 'captiue bandes' are replaced by inner chains: 'But *Verdant* (so he hight) he soone untyde,/ And counsell sage in steed thereof to him applyde' (82). The identity which is fashioned by means of a rejection of all instances of excess emerges as contained, purposeful, and masculine. In the Bower, the stabilizing contrast between art and nature is blurred, and its pleasures are conceived as 'artful', while Guyon's intention of turning pleasure into socially acceptable use in generation emerges as 'natural'. Guyon's eventual destruction of the Bower of Bliss in an act of savage iconoclasm constitutes an original act of repression, based on the premise that full enjoyment of sensual pleasure must be denied in order for a civilized use to emerge:

> But all those pleasant bowres and Pallace braue,
>   *Guyon* broke downe, with rigour pittilesse;
>   Ne ought their goodly workmanship might saue
>   Them from the tempest of his wrathfulnesse,
>   But that their blisse he turn'd to balefulnesse:
>   Their groues he feld, their gardins did deface,
>   Their arbers spoyle, their Cabinets suppresse,
>   Their banket houses burne, their buildings race,
> And of the fairest late, now made the fowlest place. (2.12.83)

The similarities between this act of fashioning identity by destroying what threatens it and Artegall's violent actions in Irena's island at the

end of Book 5 again establish individual and national identity as reciprocal categories that are framed in similar processes and by analogous
strategies. In contrast to the other episodes in the quest for temperance, the destruction of the Bower of Bliss is a unique venture that
does not need to be repeated. It marks a climactic moment in the
quest, in which its fulfilment depends on a reversal of the virtue that is
sought for: by completely relinquishing temperance, Guyon establishes
a foundation for temperance once and for all, at least as regards the
sexual pleasures. Binding Acrasia, restricting the wealth of possible
pleasures to their social use in generation, emerges as one of the central
founding moments of identity as envisaged by Spenser, a moment
which, by installing 'unrestrained' sexual enjoyment as always already
lost, also seems tinged by a nostalgic longing for non-identity that
must be overcome at all costs. Unsurprisingly, not all of Acrasia's victims appreciate this act. Those who refuse to become 'human' again,
however, are addressed with the words 'See the mind of beastly man,/
That hath so soone forgot the excellence/Of his creation' (87). In this
final comment, Guyon's act of destruction is represented as laying the
foundations of a civilization that will re-establish the godlikeness of
the first creation.

2
Imagined Individuals:
A Body of One's Own

In contrast to post-Cartesian notions of selfhood, the early modern subject was effected by discourses and power structures beyond itself. He or she emerged from within a framework of domination, loyalty, and courtly dependence, and was interpellated, or brought forth, by various historically and culturally contingent discourses. At the same time, these structures of dependency were gradually challenged by discourses that claimed self-determinacy and independence from worldly relations. This did not, however, imply autonomy from all forms of order; on the contrary, worldly dependencies were being denigrated in favour of an exquisitely intimate relationship to God which, via internalization, constituted an interior that was seen as the locus of the divine in man. God and the interior self entered into such a close relationship that divinely sanctioned actions appeared as self-determined decisions of the subject. Apparently, re-definitions in the perception and configuration of the human body as they have been discussed before somehow offered themselves for adoption by the advocates of these notions. In this context, the *Faerie Queene's* quest for selfhood and its concomitant refashioning of the body provided a literary representation of the performative assumption of different subject positions through discourses and practices uttered on various levels of early modern societies, but with a decided emphasis toward the allegedly self-determined, Protestant subject. As such, it reflected changes in cultural discourses, and likewise affected them, by providing images and ideals for future behaviour.

In that context, Spenser's textualization of the temperate subject and the contained body provides a model of perfection against which the subject could test his or her own day-to-day performance of temperance. As in the images of national wholeness and self-sufficiency, the perfect 'body' could only be imagined in aestheticized form, with the implication that its wholeness was always already lost (in the fallen world in Spenser, through the entry into the symbolic order in modern accounts of subjectivity), but which nevertheless structured human endeavours for subjective or national completeness in a performative process. Obviously, this way of moulding the body as an index of one's social self entailed a high degree of theatricality. As Stephen Greenblatt has pointed out, 'Theatricality, in the sense of both disguise and histrionic self-presentation, arose from conditions common to almost all Renaissance courts: a group of men and women alienated from the customary rôles and revolving uneasily around a center of power, a constant struggle for recognition and attention, and a virtually fetishistic emphasis upon manner.'[1] Consequently, self-fashioning in its intentional and also in its unconscious forms must produce highly strategic versions of the self, depending on the respective social audience and relation to the central authority without which, as Greenblatt reminds us, no self-fashioning can take place in the early modern period.[2] If the correct forms of behaviour constitute a way of projecting one's character onto the surface of the body, and if, at the same time, the processes of civilizing the body emphasize a rigid separation between the body's interior and its mouldable, material outside, virtue does not of necessity show on the surface, but must be represented. Representation as a process which by definition draws on the impossibility of ever attaining truth or wholeness – a truth or wholeness that can nevertheless be imagined – is thus inscribed in the very structure of the *Faerie Queene's* vision of the perfect gentleman (and, by extension, the national community).[3] On the other hand, this representation entails also a disturbing degree of contingency, in that it depends on the subject's (imagined) relation to himself, to the centre of power, and to his fellow subjects. The insurmountable gap between signifier and signified affects the representation of the subject's inner 'self' on the body surface in so far as this purportedly 'natural' relationship is in fact staged, acted *as if* it was natural. Ideally, the capacity to remould his 'natural' substance, the body, in accordance with his internalized vision of the temperate, contained subject-ideal, reveals the subject's superior humanity and is conceived as a domestication of nature.

In fact, however, the individuals striving to frame themselves by means of such a 'masculine' self-relation lacked the autonomy to fashion themselves in that way. As can be seen from Elizabethan courtly writings, the existence of a female sovereign determined the narrow frame in which courtly self-fashioning could take place, and the predominant structure emerging from this was based on a 'Petrarchist' model. Patricia Parker defines Elizabethan Petrarchism as 'not just a lyric but also a dominant cultural form, a politicized lyric structure inscribed within the complex sexual politics of the exceptional rule of a woman in an otherwise overwhelmingly patriarchal culture'.[4] Interestingly, and in pronounced contrast to Spenser's own list of his literary forebears (he names Virgil, Tasso, and Ariosto), Ralegh's commendatory sonnet accompanying the first instalment of the *Faerie Queene* identifies Petrarch's *Canzoniere* as one of Spenser's literary models. Preoccupied as he was with his own position as a courtier-subject dependent upon the favour of the Queen, it had to be Ralegh who pointed out the strongly Petrarchan subtext of Spenser's envisagings of the perfect gentleman:

> Me thought I saw the graue, where *Laura* lay,
> Within that Temple, where the vestall flame
> Was wont to burne, and passing by that way,
> To see that buried dust of liuing fame,
> Whose tombe faire loue, and fairer vertue kept,
> All suddenly I saw the Faery Queene:
> At whose approch the soule of *Petrarke* wept,
> And from thenceforth those graces were not seene.
> For they this Queene attended, in whose steed
> Obliuion laid him downe on *Lauras* herse:
> Hereat the hardest stones were seene to bleed,
> And grones of buried ghostes the heauens did perse.
> > Where *Homers* spright did tremble all for griefe,
> > And curst th'accesse of that celestiall theife.[5]

Ralegh's anamorphotic equation of Laura and Elizabeth not only points at a culturally well-established model of literary subjectivity,[6] but also explicitly foregrounds the conflicts and strains of this model for a selfhood in which subjectivity is predicated upon desire and absence. 'Deprived of full presence,' Linda Gregerson summarizes, 'the lover writes.'[7] Ralegh's vision of the grave of Laura in the temple of chastity which is then replaced by the Fairy Queen, on whom love and virtue willingly attend, is thus just another vision of a fullness that is not to be attained on earth. The Fairy Queen cancelling out the dead Laura, however, poses problems of a different sort: in her identification with Elizabeth, she reverses the positions of lover-poet and beloved, and assigns to Petrarch a place of stasis and silence.[8] While in traditional

Petrarchan lyrics the lover writes his own unified self by scattering the woman's body in his text, the full and rather disturbing presence of the actual Queen is, in Spenser's poem, translated into scattered images. In any case, the evocation of the Petrarchist structure not only of the poem's modes of description but also of the courtier's subjectivity as determined and threatened by his relationship to the (female) centre of power points at one of the principal conflicts in the formation of early modern selfhood.

Domesticating one's inner nature, as I have argued, constituted a principal aspect of courtly self-fashioning, resulting in a rather rigid separation of the subject's 'inside' and the outside world. By opening up a split between inside and outside, the internalization of virtue and a specific behaviour ideal by ethical teaching and body practice also introduced a notion of contingency that (theoretically) enabled a strategic remodelling of the self based on the impossibility of verifying the coherence between inner virtue and outer behaviour. Among the models for male subjectivity that could be envisaged under the strictures and dependencies of an absolutist court, Castiglione's *Cortegiano*, translated by Thomas Hoby in the 1550s and published in 1561, shortly after the ascent of Elizabeth to the English throne, played an important part. It provided one of the dominant behaviour manuals for the courtier in the form of a series of fictitious conversations between various courtiers at the court of Urbino, in which the perfect gentleman and his training were imagined. The personages engaged in framing the ideal courtier in this text were well-known Italian noblemen and leading courtiers of the time, and Urbino had a reputation for being the most fashionable of Renaissance courts, to which the high degree of dissemination of the *Cortegiano* no doubt contributed. Similar to behaviour handbooks for would-be gentlemen, *The Courtier* gives precepts that focus on the courtier's outward appearance as visible in such items as gesture, demeanour, countenance, and speech: the court is conceptualized as a stage on which every courtier is continuously on display, and this is why these aspects of bodily deportment were considered to be of utmost importance. In one of the very first speeches dealing with the perfect courtier, Count Lewis explains his demands on the outward appearance of the courtier:

> And such a countenance as this is, will I have our Courtyer to have, and not so softe and womanishe as many procure to have that do not onely courle the hear, and picke the browes, but also paumpre

themselves in every point like the most wanton and dishonest women in the worlde: and a man would thinke them in goyng and standing, and in all their gestures so tender and feint, that their members were ready to flee one from an other, and their woordes they pronounce so drawningly, that a man would ween they were at that instant yelding up the ghost: and the higher in degree the men they talke withall, the more they use such facyons.[9] (52)

This description of the effeminate courtier draws on a specific nexus of gender and power that Joan Kelly has commented on in her classic essay 'Did Women have a Renaissance?': 'To be attractive, accomplished, and seem not to care; to charm and do so coolly – how concerned with impression, how masked the true self. And how manipulative … In short, how like a woman – or a dependent, for that is the root of the simile.'[10] Yet while the count mocks some courtiers who are overdoing their self-presentation, he does not discredit the overall structure of a patriarchal society which inevitably codes dependency as feminine; neither does he question the association of femininity with the manipulation of appearances. In fact, in his concluding remarks on the topic he even reinforces this nexus by introducing mercantile categories which render the effort to please at all costs in terms of an objectification of the body that is proclaimed to be against the 'nature' of masculinity; the commodified body, decked out to please in the absence of other means of power, is feminized: 'These men, seing nature (as they seeme to have a desire to appeare and to bee) hath not made them women, ought not to be esteemed in place of good women, but like common Harlottes to be banished, not onely out of prynces courtes, but also oute of the companye of Gentlemen.' (52) Nature and art are here intertwined in a way that is clearly rendered as manipulative and destabilizing for the social order. At the same time, one of the major courtly techniques of self-fashioning depends on a similar mixture of art and nature.

For the perfect courtier, intent on earning preferment and status at court, *The Courtier* advocates the assumption of a certain bodily demeanour, leading to the display of what he calls 'grace': 'And let this be an ornament to frame and accompanye all his actes, and to assure men in his looke, such a one to bee woorthy the company and favour of every great man.'[11] Grace manifests itself on the body surface and is 'read' as a sign of inner 'order'. This effect, however, is to be con- sciously produced by the courtier in a technique that Castiglione calls *sprezzatura*, which Hoby translates as 'recklessness'. *The Courtier* proposes as one general rule 'to eschew as much as a man may, and as a sharp and daungerous rock, Affectation and curiosity and (to speak a new word) to use in every thyng a certain Reckelesness, to cover art withall, and seeme whatsoever he doth and sayeth to do it wythout pain, and (as it were) not mynding it' (59). *Sprezzatura*, the technique of the 'as if', creates an effect of naturalness where there is art and training; it makes the courtier's 'grace' seem natural (as opposed to affected). *Sprezzatura* does not, as is often assumed, necessarily imply a Machiavellistic consciousness of the dissimulative possibilities inherent in this practice of the self, and strategic versions of subjectivity must not result from conscious self-fashioning, which would, quite anachronistically, presuppose an autonomous subject. The text, however, leaves no doubt that this is art pretending to be nature: 'Therefore that may be said to be a very art that appeereth not to be art, neyther ought a man to put more diligence in any thing then in covering it: for in case it be open, it loseth credit cleane, and maketh a man litle set by.' (59) In *The Courtier*, *sprezzatura* is introduced in relation to questions of physical ability such as dancing, horse-riding, and fencing. It is evident that this technique can easily be transferred to social behaviour, structuring social relations according to strategic considerations, and the inherent dangers of such a technique, in which nature and art are bound up to the point of indistinction, are obvious: *sprezzatura* creates the impression of competence when there is none or where there is no proof (62), and it blurs the boundaries between the 'real' and the 'affected' in a way that renders this distinction almost obsolete. Drawing on the conceptual separation of the inside and outside of the subject, it enables the courtier to stage a self that clearly prospers on the power of the eye to naturalize what can be seen as 'real'. The anxious question about the verifiability of the staged self, however, remains latent, and yet Joan Kelly's question as to the 'masquerade' of the true self may not quite get the point: *sprezzatura* is a technique that stages the self on the body surface, and while, at the same time, it can produce the idea of a true self that is in control of this performance, this is always challenged by the fact that power relations at court consciously or unconsciously structure this performance.

Though I would not deny the courtier a certain degree of consciousness and agency in his self-fashioning – as agency inheres, as Judith Butler has shown, in any reiterative, 'citational' process[12] – there are, on the other hand, discourses and structures in operation that determine and have always already determined his strategic options. This is due to the fact that the identity so performed has its determining power factor outside the courtier: 'the subject takes its shape from that which is outside it'.[13] The courtly 'I' thus always emerges as the materialization of the sovereign's power on the body surface of the subject, who nevertheless claims to be in possession of an interior self that is the originator of his actions. It is the special quality of *sprezzatura* that it also disguises the social conditions at its base, and produces a self that stages itself as free while in fact being highly dependent. *Sprezzatura* is a body-centred technique that serves to displace the implication of subjection onto 'nature': refashioning the body into a graceful instrument of the self casts the courtier's identity as a work of art, and subjectivity as the domestication of the materiality of the body. Ultimately, it renders this conquest as an act by which the self attains freedom while simultaneously disclaiming the existence of identity-shaping discourses. The (imagined) freedom that is represented as the base of self-fashioning is in fact its very effect, created in a movement that naturalizes the identity so framed as emerging from an inner core of the self. Interestingly, male *sprezzatura* is cast as completely different from female forms of manipulating appearances, and in that respect Castiglione's extremely misogynous disclaimer can be read as symptomatic of the anxieties inherent in a technique of self-fashioning that is predicated upon the very manipulation of appearances:

> All women generally have a great desire to be, and when they cannot be, at the least to appear beawtyfull. Therefore, where nature in some part hath not done her devoyr therin, they endeavour them selves to supply it with art. Of this ariseth the trymming of the face, with such studye and many times peines, the pilling of the browes and forehead, and the usynge of all those mane wayes, and the abydyng of such lothsomenesse, as you women beleave are kepte very secrete from men, and yet do all men know them. (79)

In women the effort to dissemble is clearly referred to the appearance of their bodies and faces, quite in line with a taxonomy that assumes a natural coherence of beauty and virtue founded upon the Platonic notion of the *kalon k'agathon*. Obviously, the norms structuring female endeavours here are not determined by the women themselves: the gaze of the social audience is clearly a male gaze. Not unlike the efforts of male courtiers, the women of Count Lewis's narrative seek to please in order to earn themselves a position within the courtly dynamics of power. It seems, however, that while the technique of intermingling art and nature, moderately used, is advocated as a means to ingratiate

oneself with the great, courtly women's endeavours to beautify themselves are generally associated with excess:

> Do you not marke how much more grace is in a woman, that if she
> doth trim her self, doeth it so scarcely and so litle, that whoso
> behouldeth her, standeth in doubt whether she be trimmed or no:
> then in an other so bedawbed, that a man would wene she had a
> viser on her face and dareth not laugh for making it chappe: nor at
> any tyme chaungeth her colour, but whan she apparayeleth her self
> in the morninge, and all the rest of the daye standeth lyke an image
> of woodde without movinge, shewinge her self onely in torche
> light, as craftye marchaundmen do their clothes in their darke
> lightes? (80)

The male courtier's self-fashioning by way of adorning himself with an
allegedly 'natural' grace and competence that clearly disclaims the
effort that has gone into it is praised, while female efforts to the same
effect are denigrated as manipulative and, due to female immoderate-
ness, blatantly fraudulent. Male *sprezzatura*, as Kuchta has pointed out,
is a 'created naturalness' which 'meant cultivating a political image
which accorded with a natural order, acting and dressing according to
one's sexual and social station'.[14] Female decking-out of the body in
order to beautify it is cast by Castiglione and Hoby as a case of *sprezzatura manqué*, but one that has not failed for lack of practice but for
inherent, quasi-'natural' reasons. Although *The Courtier* does not make
an explicit point of this, the contrast of the positive image of *sprezzatura*
when depicting the male courtier with the failure that characterizes the
only mention of women in this discourse of *sprezzatura* is symptomatic
of the overall drift of the argument and the underlying nature–culture
split. The female body and its association with excess and corporeality
here undermine women's endeavours to mesh art and nature in a way
similar to men, and this ascription allows the projection of anxieties
about the inherent dissembling character of *sprezzatura* onto women.[15]

Besides obvious bodily qualities such as gesture, countenance, and
demeanour, speech is, of course, important when fashioning a courtly
self, and consequently rhetoric plays a vital part in all courtesy books.
Analogous to *sprezzatura* in regard of bodily demeanour, rhetoric is a
technique that purportedly voices the ideas of an authentic, interior
self and displays them to a social audience, and, like body practice,
rhetoric can be learned through training. What matters in rhetorical

performance is not only what is said, but also how it is said, as *The Courtier* points out:

> And this do I saie as well of writing as of speaking, wherein certayne thinges are requisite that are not necessary in wryting, as a good voyce, not to subtyll or soft, as in a woman: nor yet so boysterous and roughe, as in one of the Countrey, but shrill, clere, sweete and wel framed with a prompt pronunciation and with fitte maners and gestures which (in my minde) consiste in certain mocions of all the body not affected nor forced, but tempred with a manerly countenance and with a moving of the eyes, that may geve a grace and accord with the words, and (asmuch as he can) signify also with gestures the entent and affeccion of the speaker. (70)

Speech must be supported by gestures and a certain body demeanour in order to be effective: hence the tenor of these instructions. As though in an afterthought, this eulogy of rhetoric performance concludes that 'al these thinges wer in vain and of smal accompte yf the sentences expressed by the wordes should not be fair, witty, subtil, fine and grave according to the mater' (70), leaving the disturbing impression that maybe the reverse argument would function just as well, that whatever is said in this perfectly stylized manner would appear 'as if' 'fair, witty, subtil, fine and grave'. Greenblatt argues that rhetoric is a major factor in producing the self as a work of art, in that it 'offered men the power to shape their worlds, calculate the probabilities and master the contingent, and it implied that human character itself could be similarly fashioned, with an eye to audience and effect'.[16] On the basis of the underlying dualism of art and nature, any form of speech is a work of art that purports to voice 'naturally' the subject's thoughts. More than any other aspect of self-fashioning, rhetoric blurs the boundaries between the natural and the artful: 'rhetoric served to theatricalize culture',[17] rendering the identities framed in these cultural surroundings highly artificial. This danger also affected all arts drawing on rhetorical devices and language in general, such as epic and poetry, a vulnerability of which many Renaissance poets and especially Spenser were painfully aware, and which they endeavoured to counter by various strategies.[18]

Although Hoby and other courtly writers strove to solve the inherent moral ambiguities of a dissimulative technique like *sprezzatura*, the line between *sprezzatura* and dissembling must ultimately remain fluid. Ideally, *sprezzatura* means the representation of a natural coherence of outside and inside, signifier and signified, in the subject, a coherence which renders him culturally intelligible as a gentleman or courtier. Since its sincerity is impossible to verify on empirical grounds, the possibility of (Machiavellistic) misuse always remains an inherent danger. The gendering of this discourse reveals women as structurally unable to perfect this major technique of self-fashioning operating within a 'semiotics (or teleology) of masculinity'. Women are rendered as anxious projections of the imminent danger of failed *sprezzatura*, which ridicules the courtier, and of the dissimulation and manipulative impetus *sprezzatura* entails. These projections seem to be grounded in the idea that women's dependencies are undeniably and unalterably evident (and necessarily so). This in turn enables the disclaimer regarding male courtly dependencies via the technique of *sprezzatura* itself: the imagined 'natural' dependency of women dialectically enables the dependent male subject to stage himself as free. The accomplishment of perfect courtesy hinges on the subjection of his inner nature and the moulding of the material reality of his body in accordance with his inner virtue. The extreme emphasis put on the body surface, and the fact that the courtier's actions are determined by a centre of power that is outside himself, however, prompts the question of whether the allegedly existent 'inside' is not merely an effect of the discourses and practices of self-fashioning. Within the reach of the court, this is to say, there is no masquerade of the true self, for the masquerade *is* the self.

Castiglione's is, of course, a highly pragmatic version of selfhood and courtly existence, and one that was certainly an influence on Spenser. For the latter it was criss-crossed, however, by discourses propounding a different view of selfhood, such as Protestant and humanist, especially Stoical, discourses. Spenser's version of the virtue of courtesy in Book 6 of the *Faerie Queene* thus differs considerably from Castiglione's or Hoby's. Linda Gregerson has emphasized the way in which Christian and monarchic, courtly and Protestant imperatives intersect in Spenser's model of subjectivity, and how the subject emerges under subjection of one structure or another.[19] Thus, in disclaiming dependency, the courtly subject does not aim for autonomy but opts for a reliance on divine rather than secular guidance. In Spenser's view, courtesy as a virtue that complements the other five virtues (holiness, temperance, chastity, friendship, and justice) in *The Faerie Queene* emerges as a technique which mediates between the more 'individualistic' tendencies of holiness and temperance and the social environment of the court. Although all Spenser's virtues somehow serve the political goal of fashioning a subject that stands in a relation of reciprocity to the national community, courtesy stands slightly apart from the others. It is definitely centred around a monarchic court, and its version of civility is less applicable to Protestant (later, bourgeois) forms of selfhood, due to its strong, almost 'natural' links with nobility:

> Amongst them all growes not a fayrer flowre,
> Then is the bloosme of comely courtesie,
> Which though it on a lowly stalke doe bowre,
> Yet brancheth forth in braue nobilitie,
> And spreds it selfe through all ciuilitie. (6 proem 4)

Courtesy is defined as the proper behaviour at court ('Of Court it seemes, men Courtesie doe call', 6.1.1) and the art of giving everybody his or her due in terms of favour and deference (6.2.1), and although the text insists that courtesy is a primarily aristocratic virtue it nevertheless needs training to unfold itself in accordance with the courtier's degree: 'gentle bloud will gentle manners breed' (6.3.2). In this it closely echoes *The Courtier's* notions of a seemingly natural coherence of social status and courtly behaviour. Calidore, the knight of courtesy, is an example of that proper mixture of nature and nurture that characterizes the accomplished courtier:

> In whom it seemes, that gentlenesse of spright
> And manners mylde were planted naturall;
> To which he adding comely guize withall,
> And gracious speach, did steale mens hearts away. (6.1.2)

Courtesy, in Spenser's concept, is a social competence that depends upon the acquisition of the virtues that have been the objectives of previous quests. Temperance in particular is eminently important, as the contained body and the domestication of the subject's inner nature are important preconditions for courtly behaviour:

> In vaine he seeketh others to suppresse,
> Who hath not learnd him selfe first to subdew:
> All flesh is frayle, and full of ficklenesse,
> Subiect to fortunes chance, still chaunging new. (6.1.41)

Calidore is a master of *sprezzatura*, to such a degree that it has in fact become his 'nature'. He has reached the perfect congruence of his 'natural' status and his acquired behaviour techniques, as manifest in his ability to 'beare [himself] aright / To all of each degree, as doth behoue' (6.2.1), including a valid assessment of his own place on the social scale. Calidore knows how to represent his superior humanity on the surface of his body, and this happy state of harmony induces all other courtiers to like him:

> Ne was there Knight, ne was there Lady found
>   In Faery court, but him did deare embrace,
>   For his faire vsage and conditions sound,
>   The which in all mens liking gayned place,
>   And with the greatest purchast greatest grace:
>   Which he could wisely vse, and well apply,
>   To please the best, and th'euill to embase.
>   For he loathd leasing, and base flattery,
> And loued simple truth and stedfast honesty. (6.1.3)

Interestingly, despite Spenser's insistence on the moral integrity of this paragon of courtesy, the description of his superior qualities draws heavily on a mercantile register. In a way, the web of dependencies reappears here in the form of mercantile images and undercuts the proclaimed independence of the courtier-subject: the necessity remains, for him as for his fellow courtiers, to 'purchase' the liking of the great, or rather, considering the ephemeral nature of courtly favour, to 'lease' it. Nevertheless, Spenser claims for his proper courtier a certain degree of inner freedom from the strictures of an absolutist court, creating a tension between the dependence upon an absolutist monarch, the implicit competition of the courtiers for the sovereign's favour, and the (masculinist) self-assertion of the subject effected by a religious discourse that proclaims a direct relationship of the self and God. While denigrating contemporary courtly behaviour as inadequate for reaching a harmony between the inside and the outside of the self, he takes recourse to ancient models, thus instrumentalizing the very incommensurability of the ideal and the real that is at the heart of his representational mode:

> But in the triall of true curtesie,
>   Its now so farre from that, which then it was,
>   That it indeed is nought but forgerie,
>   Fashion'd to please the eies of them, that pas,
>   Which see not perfect things but in a glas:
>   Yet is that glasse so gay, that it can blynd

> The wisest sight, to thinke gold that is bras.
> But vertues seat is deepe within the mynd,
> And not in outward shows, but inward thoughts defynd.
>
> (6 proem 5)

Again, the exception of the Elizabethan court is only established in an afterthought, in a comparison of Elizabeth with antique, 'plain' courtesy in the next stanza. Representations of the court in Book 6 are very ambiguous, providing images of divine harmony besides episodes which focus on the ultimate futility of striving for the 'shadowes vaine / Of courtly fauour' (6.10.2). The proem's often-quoted image of the sovereign as a fountain of power establishes Elizabeth as the divine well from whom all virtues unfold into the world and to which they also return:

> So from the Ocean all riuers spring,
> And tribute backe repay as to their King.
> Right so from you all goodly vertues well
> Into the rest, which round about you ring,
> Faire Lords and Ladies, which about you dwell,
> And doe adorne your Court, where courtesies excell. (6 proem 7)

This image of divine order is challenged later, however, by the fact that Calidore has his vision of the dance of the graces quite apart from court, in a pastoral setting. Celestial harmony can thus be imaginatively located in a place that is drafted in clear contradistinction to the worldliness of the court. Quite evidently, this disrupts the underlying Petrarchist structure which is latent throughout the Book of Courtesy. A discourse of masculinist self-assertion obviously contends here with discourses that insist on the 'creatureliness' of the Elizabethan courtly subject, establishing the court and God as two alternative, and no longer coextensive, centres of power. Whereas the creatureliness of the subject as an effect of divine power is never disputed, there is no proper integration of court and creation, and though Elizabeth may be exempted from the overall contempt of courtly ways, she is nevertheless not the integrational figure that a divinely ordained sovereign is called upon to be: in the Petrarchist logic of the *Faerie Queene*, she is a Laura rather than a Beatrice.

The Book of Courtesie's contempt for courtly life focuses mainly on the idea of 'forgery', and the mismatch between inward thought and outward appearance is seen as one of its principal dangers, undermining the legibility of the social order in outward appearance, including, of course, 'forgery' in language. Indeed, much in this concept of courtesy, also advocated as the 'roote of ciuil conuersation' (6.1.1), depends on the right use of speech. The main enemy of courtesy in this book, and one that cannot be vanquished in the course of the quest, is slander as pictured in the 'Blatant Beast'. The Beast, 'a Monster bred of hellishe race' (6.1.7) has been sent into the world 'To be the plague and scourge of wretched men' (6.1.8). Echoing the punishment of the Fall, slander embodies the gap between social rank and representation, signifier and signified. Rather than representing a single instance of slanderous behaviour, the Blatant Beast stands for the general possibility of forging speech according to purpose and audience, a possibility that undermines the credibility of all speech acts. It ultimately unhinges, in Foucault's terms, the natural relation between words and things, and introduces the necessity of representation which always includes the danger of manipulation. David Kuchta has pointed out, as I have mentioned before, how sumptuary law was an ultimately futile effort to keep the hierarchy of analogies in place by legal means.[20] Spenser's treatment of the Blatant Beast in the last completed book of the *Faerie Queene* reveals these endeavours to be in vain: though Calidore for a short time manages to bind the beast, it breaks free again and roams at large at the end of the book. The dangers of the beast are rendered in images of the monstrous and grotesque, in clear opposition to the contained body of the quester. Pursued by the monster with the thousand tongues, Artegall, who has first-hand experience of the beast, claims:

> But I that knew my selfe from perill free,
> Did nought regard his malice nor his powre,
> But he the more his wicked poyson forth did poure. (6.1.9)

Even those who are perfectly innocent can be afflicted by slanderous speaking, and when subjectivity depends to such a high degree on the right use of signifiers it can also easily be ruined by their wrong, forged use. As there is ultimately no possibility to verify this, the conquest of slander is of utmost importance. Slander, in Spenser's view, is a decidedly courtly vice,[21] and one which cannot be overcome within the confines of the sovereign's reach. It is at a locus beyond the influence of the court where knowledge about how to conquer it can be obtained. The hermit to whom Serena and Timias are referred, both heavily afflicted with the beast's wounds, counsels them to rely on their own wills: the power to overcome (or be impregnated against) slander must come from a 'within' that has no chance to unfold at court. The wound inflicted by the beast is identified as 'the poysnous sting, which infamy/Infixeth in the name of noble wight' (6.6.1), and constitutes a blemish on the social position of the subject that cannot be healed of his or her own accord. It is a wound that 'festred priuily', necessitating, for its redress, 'to be disciplinde/With holesome reede of sad sobriety,/To rule the stubborne rage of passion blinde:/Giue salues to euery sore, but counsell to the minde' (6.6.5). The hermit's Stoical precept is isolation and contemplation, 'For in your selfe your onely helpe doth lie,/To heale your selues, and must proceed alone/From your owne will, to cure your maladie' (6.6.7). He advocates a discipline that, via enforcing bodily containment, opens up a gap for the emergence of a self claiming independence from outward appearances:

> First learne your outward sences to refraine
> From things, that stirre vp fraile affection;
> Your eies, your eares, your tongue, your talke restraine
> From that they most affect, and in due termes containe. (6.6.7)

This, of course, stands in stark contrast to a courtly life in which all actions, speeches, and texts somehow emerge from and return back to the sovereign, as implied audience and oblique addressee. The hermit's patients, removed from court, are quickly healed and, since they must return to their social place, counselled how to avoid further affliction:

> The best (sayd he) that I can you aduize,
>   Is to auoide the occasion of the ill:
> (...)
>   Abstaine from pleasure, and restraine your will,
>   Subdue desire, and bridle loose delight,
>   Vse scanted diet, and forbeare your fill,
>   Shun secresie, and talke in open sight:
> So shall you soone repaire your present euill plight. (6.6.14)

Quite in accordance with the behaviour manuals for the perfect gentleman, and somewhat leaning towards a Protestant notion of sobriety, these behaviour instructions draft a vision of the subject as independent of appearances, as having an internal worth that is beyond worldly influences: obviously a Stoical concept. It is doubtful, however, whether they will be practicable at a Renaissance court. The hermit himself appears to be very critical of courtly life; 'weary of this worlds vnquiet waies' (6.6.4), he has left the court and taken refuge in a hermitage:

> The name of knighthood he did disauow,
> And hanging vp his armes and warlike spoyle,
> From all this worlds incombraunce did himselfe assoyle. (6.5.37)

Read in the light of the suspension of instruments in Psalm 137 that Patricia Parker has suggested for the reading of Verdant's and the *Shepheardes Calender's* 'suspended instruments', this abandonment of 'warlike spoyle' might constitute a gesture of defiance, a refusal to sing the sovereign's praise in the absence of any real access to power, and a model of a self independent of the court.[22] As such it is reminiscent of Colin Clout's breaking of his pipe in the 'April eclogue' of the *Shepheardes Calender*, where dependencies on the courtly lady and God are also contrasted by means of differently coded social spaces. Colin's refusal to sing for his beloved is merged, in the 'Maye eclogue', with a religiously motivated introspection, so that the self emerges as 'inter-pellated' by discourses issued by two conflicting centres of power.[23] In the *Faerie Queene* Book 6 the hermitage itself is established as a counter-locus to a court that entertains its courtiers with 'forged showes, as fitter beene/ For courting fooles, that curtesies would faine' (6.5.38). An extended personification of courtly dissembling is provided in Canto 6, and, unsurprisingly, it is embodied in a female figure, Blandina. Not only the etymology of her name, which assembles her almost foolish merriness (Lat. *blandus,* merry, soothing) and dissimulating speech (Lat. *blandiri,* to flatter), but also her characterization as inherently false are significant here. 'Sugared' speech can have harmonizing effects, and as such it has always fallen into the domain of female social skills, as being an instrument to win favour when there is no other means of influence:

> For well she knew the wayes to win good will
> Of euery wight, that were not too infest,
> And how to please the minds of good and ill,
> Through tempering of her words and lookes by wondrous skill.
>
> (6.6.41)

This display of temperance in speech, however, turns into a comment on courtly survival techniques, denouncing the speaker as inadequate in bringing signifier and signified into a stable congruence and accusing her of Machiavellistically instrumentalizing speech for her own, utilitarian ends:

> Yet were her words and lookes but false and fayned,
>   To some hid end to make more easie way,
>   Or to allure such fondlings, whom she trayned
> Into her trap vnto their owne decay:
>   Thereto, when needed, she could weepe and pray,
>   And when her listed, she could fawne and flatter;
>   Now smyling smoothly, like to sommers day,
>   Now glooming sadly, so to cloke her matter;
> Yet were her words but wynd, and all her teares but water.
>   (6.6.42)

Instead of congratulating this courtly lady on her temperance and self-control, both indispensable preconditions for *sprezzatura*, Spenser's text denigrates her on the grounds of fraudulence. Like many other female figures in the *Faerie Queene*, Blandina is represented as duplicitous and a threat to the social order. But unlike many of the others, who are decidedly dangerous anti-figures to some superior virtue, Blandina's dissimulation, in the kind of casual misogyny so well-known from the writings of the time, is attributed, at least hypothetically, to womankind in general:

> Whether such grace were giuen her by kynd,
> As women wont their guilefull wits to guyde;
> Or learn'd the art to please, I doe not fynd. (6.6.43)

The text states explicitly that courteous speech is an art to be learned, providing the link with courtly behaviour in general, and with the notion of fashioning a gentleman in particular. Spenser's vision of the proper behaviour of his gentleman at court obviously differs considerably from what he has shown us in the image of Blandina (and what would possibly have been Castiglione's view). Calidore, the paragon of courtliness, spends most of his quest outside court, and he even focuses his desire, the central moving force of a courtly dynamics based on a Petrarchist model of subjectivity, on a woman that is not the centre of courtly power. On the historical plane Walter Ralegh, as we shall see, had suffered exile and even imprisonment for a similar transgression. Yet far from being judged a transgressor, Calidore is allowed to develop his model of selfhood in a pastoral, anti-court surrounding, through his love for Pastorella, which ultimately leads him to a vision of divine harmony that is a decided antithesis of courtly life. At the core of this version of subjectivity is not the sovereign who inscribes her power in the minds and bodies of men, but a notion of freedom that is voiced not only for the (would-be) individual but also for the collective structure in which he lives. 'Each hath his fortune in his brest' (29), the wise Meliboe tells Calidore, and 'It is the mynd, that maketh good or ill' (30), to which he answers:

> Since then in each mans self (said *Calidore*)
> It is, to fashion his owne lyfes estate,
> Giue leaue awhyle, good father, in this shore
> To rest my barcke, which hath bene beaten late
> With stormes of fortune and tempestous fate. (6.9.31)

Though this is a version of independent subjectivity that is not sustained throughout the quest for courtesy, it at least temporarily imagines an individuality that claims freedom from exterior systems of meaning other than God. Its alleged 'naturalness' is the effect of a dissociation of free 'inside' and material 'outside' of the body under the influence of Protestant and Stoical discourses voicing contempt for worldly vanities and drawing on a new concept of interiority. From a rigidly Protestant point of view, courtly 'rites' must have looked like an act of external observance and of no importance whatsoever concerning salvation. For, while the absolute power over the subject of God and the sovereign could be analogized, the 'service' done to either could not. In Spenser's underlying polarization of worldly and divine power working on the subject, concerns for worldly preferment must ultimately be abandoned in favour of the exigencies of his relation to God. It seems that in this respect the *Faerie Queene* moves from a more or less sustained identification of church and courtly lady in Book 1 to a disillusionment with Petrarchist models of subjectivity, rendering the court as a place of corruption in counterdistinction to an integrity that is located in the subject's interior as inhabited by God. Though avoiding overt criticism of the Queen, this version of selfhood prospers on the dualism of the 'inside' and the 'outside' of the subject, but it defines this dualism differently from courtly discourses. It has become obvious that the contained body drafted in Guyon's quest for temperance is easily assimilable to discourses of individuality and self-determination, providing every subject with a body of his or her own.

Yet while in discourses of courtesy or civility the body served as a vehicle of interior value, while in its behaviour, demeanour, and gesture being the only means beside speech to prove this worth and to earn a social position, Protestant discourses emphasized the qualitative alterity of the 'interior' that is made possible, in the first place, by the contained body. For Protestant practice, it is the 'inside' that is mouldable and not, as in courtly discourse, already determined by social rank and one's position within a courtly dynamics of power. The Protestant's 'interior' is directly connected to God as the ultimate source of power, and this connection is so vital that it is sometimes thought that the 'inside' *is* God, or, as an early seventeenth-century believer put it, 'a little God sitting in the middle of men('s) hearts'.[24] This qualitatively different 'interior' is fashioned into a self by various means of inspection and confession that frame a subject different from the courtly self in various ways. As Alan Sinfield has pointed out, 'self-examination, self-consciousness, in protestant practice is not a by-product, or even a characteristic, but the goal',[25] in that it achieves an 'actualiz[ation] of interiority' that, in contrast to a courtly 'inside' that was determined by social discourses and thus was not really an inner space free from worldly concerns, gives it a certain degree of autonomy.[26]

It is obvious that the ethical self-relation and the concomitant bodily containment discussed in Chapter 1 were easily assimilable, in terms of ideology as well as self-technique, by a religious discourse intent upon framing a subject that claimed freedom from material, 'outside' considerations, and imagined itself as free under God. Even though Spenser can only provide a glimpse of this freedom of Protestant subjectivity, resting uneasily in Book 6 of the *Faerie Queene* beside discourses of courtly life that imply political and personal dependence, the idea of the free Protestant subject inhabiting a contained body can at least be imagined as the goal of human (should one say male?) endeavours.

3
Gendered Objects: Sexualizing the Female Body

The strategies of identity formation analysed in the previous chapters by no means resulted in a universal form of subjectivity. On the contrary, despite being introduced as a configuration of humanity, this form of selfhood was inextricably linked to specific body configurations and body styles, and it was gender- and class-specific. The subjectivity formation of men and women, despite claims to the contrary, was (and is) no symmetrical process. As subjectivity depended to a large extent on a self-government that was in itself coded masculine, women could not become subjects in the full sense of the word. Rather, an allegedly universalist selfhood emerged through the exclusion of materiality, corporeality, and 'nature', all of which were implicitly feminized. Masculine identity formation and the feminization of material nature are two sides of the same coin.

In the course of this process, bodies were being reconceptualized in a way that matched the requirements of this binary logic of identity formation: the human being about to become a subject was endowed with a virtually incorporeal body, while the non-subject was declared to inhabit a 'corporeal' body that was part of the 'natural' world. In so far as women could acquire the status of a 'self', they were regarded as inferior on a vertical scale of perfection, an inferiority owing to the fact that their self-relation was modelled on the masculine self-relation, and was thus not genuinely self-determined.[1] Even though male courtiers were by no means self-determined either, they were fashioned by discourses that produced the effect of interiority and independence, and one of the prime vehicles for this was the control of their bodies. The domestication of women's different bodies was declared to be necessary from a masculine viewpoint, even if it was eventually internalized by the women themselves. As a consequence they were not

57

simultaneously subjects and objects of an ethical discourse of selfhood, but only mediated subjects in so far as their behaviour ideal was determined by patriarchal power structures: the self-relation that characterized the subject remained invariably masculine.

This chapter will trace instances of this process, which, as I have argued before, was only just about to begin in Elizabethan times (and maybe it was precisely the reign of a Queen which arrested the process for a little while) in the literature of Edmund Spenser. His sonnet cycle *Amoretti* and its final *Epithalamion* both construct an ideal woman who complements (and thus enables) masculine notions of selfhood. The *Amoretti*'s idealized addressee incorporates three historical referents named Elizabeth, as the author points out: his Queen, mother, and bride. The *Amoretti* draw heavily on the conventional aesthetic and formal standards set by Petrarchism and Neoplatonism. On the issue of the lyrical 'I's relationship to the described woman, however, the sonnets part company with Petrarchist assumptions about the basic conflict between a God-centred and a man-centred universe as manifest in the tension between the poet's love of God and the love of his lady. As Alexander Dunlop has commented on the *Amoretti*, 'Conceptually Spenser is closer to Dante than to Petrarch, for he manages to integrate the love of his lady with the love of God.'[2] In addition, Spenser's 'beloved', in spite of her spiritual worthiness, is represented as an earthly woman. In his characteristic amalgamation of Petrarchan modes of aesthetic representation with Neoplatonist and also Protestant thought, Spenser manages to replace an unattainable, aristocratic, possibly married lady by a nubile maiden, probably of bourgeois or mercantile parentage. The image of his (threefold) Elizabeth thus serves the erection of a masculine selfhood in a different way from that accomplished by writing a Laura or Beatrice. His progression is not exclusively self-motivated as that of the Neoplatonic lover who instrumentalizes his beloved's beauty for his endeavours at a reunion of his own soul with divine perfection; nor does he acquire a sense of 'self' by means of a perpetual and ultimately irresolvable conflict between passion and transcendence. Instead, the *Amoretti* and *Epithalamion's* lyrical 'I' opts for a 'spiritualized earthly union'[3] conducing to a vision of social and cosmic harmony in the image of a 'large posterity' who eventually 'of blessed Saints...increase the count' (E23). In that respect, the 'I' emerging from these poems is not self-centred in a way that would leave the world and its orders behind completely; on the contrary, in his endeavours to attain an ideal of spiritual union in marriage, the lyrical 'I' is strongly concerned with the integration of spiritual and worldly order. This is not to say that the woman whose ideal image is praised here has any say in the discourses conceptualizing her, nor did the Protestant ideal of companionate marriage imply any improvement of the social situation of women in general. Rather, this was an ideal that redefined women's social role in accordance with a gradually changing concept of the female body and the requirements of a market-centred society.

Jonathan Sawday has pointed out the structural similarities between the aesthetic conventions of the blazon and the medical practice of dissection. 'Anatomy' not only denoted the dissection of a human body but, in the course of time, turned into a genre that aimed at the description of an object by a detailed discussion of its component parts: 'In England, the language of the blazon developed poetic tropes which were peculiarly consonant with an emerging "science" or knowledge of the body.'[4] 'Blazon', as Nancy Vickers reminds us, means to praise or proclaim, and can also have a heraldic meaning.[5] One of the earliest examples of the usage of the word in this sense is in the French collection *Blazons anatomiques du corps femenin* of 1543, which, according to Sawday, verifies the close connection between blazon and anatomy.[6] In this collection, each contribution celebrated a separate part of a female body, speaking 'the blazon of sweet beauty's best, / Of hand, of foot, of lip, of eye, of brow', as Shakespeare elaborates in his Sonnet 106.[7] Similarly, in the blazonic conventions of the sonnet cycles, women were pictured by means of a catalogue of interchangeable rhetoric tropes behind which the concrete body vanished almost completely. Sawday identifies 'discovery' as the determining discourse behind this trope: 'The English blazon … divided the female body to celebrate its partitioned exploration as a geographical entity. This organism could be "discovered" … and then subjected to an economy of trade, commerce and mercantile distribution.'[8] Obviously, this can only apply to a blazonic method which conceptualizes the woman to be celebrated as ultimately attainable. As I will argue in Chapter 7, the marriageable European woman provided the matrix for descriptions of the feminized New World colonies, while the economic paradigm which so strongly motivated the discourse of discovery in turn fed back into the conceptualizations of European women. In the fragmenting catalogue of body parts praised in the blazon, the body of the woman 'became arrayed as an object of consumption'.[9] This in turn constitutes the strategies of self-empowerment conveyed by these descriptions as a dynamic of male bonding and male competition. Though we should be careful not to conceptualize the audience of the sonnets in a too monolithic way,[10] the general stance behind blazonic descriptions of women was a display of their qualities and virtues in terms of an inventory of objectified items or body parts.[11] Whether the audience consisted of men or women, aristocrats, gentlemen, or merchants, the 'woman' pictured here, through the use of conventional Petrarchistic modes of aestheticization, was exhibited and rendered the aim of a desirous and commodifying gaze, while at the same time testifying to her (prospective) proprietor's wealth, as Shakespeare has aptly put it: 'I will not praise that purpose not to sell' (Sonnet 21). In the *Amoretti* this impulse becomes quite obvious in Sonnet 15, which explicitly addresses a mercantile reader- or spectatorship:

> Ye tradefull Merchants that with weary toyle
>> do seeke most pretious things to make your gaine:
>> and both the Indias of their treasures spoile,
>> what needeth you to seeke so farre in vaine?
> For loe my love doth in her selfe containe
>> all this worlds riches that may farre be found:
>> if Saphyres, loe her eies be Saphyres plaine,
>> if Rubies, loe hir lips be Rubies sound:
> If Pearles, hir teeth be pearles both pure and round;
>> if Yvorie, her forhead yvory weene;
>> if Gold, her locks are finest gold on ground;
>> if silver, her faire hands are silver sheene,
> But that which fairest is, but few behold,
>> her mind adornd with vertues manifold. (15)

Though the final couplet, as though in an afterthought, establishes the beloved woman's worth beyond the surface of her body as something which does not catch the eye, the bulk of the text dwells on the qualities of her body themselves and renders them in metaphors of commodifiable wealth. And although, admittedly, the couplet undermines the superficiality of the inventory of riches enumerated before, other sonnets establish a correspondence of outward and inward features that render the woman's virtue in terms of her beautiful body itself.[12] The sonnet cycle as a whole enacts a progression from a description of the woman in quasi-supernatural terms (as long as she declines the poet's approaches) through her gradual 'conversion' to the speaker, to the eventual confirmation of their bond in the *Epithalamion*. Interestingly, as soon as she gives up her aloof position she becomes more earthly and corporeal in the text,[13] while the bond to be established is gradually pictured in terms of captivity. While soon after the turning-point the eventual union is described with the words 'Sweet be the bands, the which true love doth tye' (65), the images that envisage this 'loss of liberty' are gradually tightened, while the lady is metamorphosed into a shy animal that is chased:

> Lyke as a huntsman after weary chace,
>> Seeing the game from him escapt away:
>> sits downe to rest him in some shady place,
>> with panting hounds beguiled of their pray,
> So after long pursuit and vaine assay,
>> when I all weary had the chace forsooke,
>> the gentle deare returnd the self-same way,
>> thinking to quench her thirst at the next brooke.
> There she beholding me with mylder looke,
>> sought not to fly, but fearelesse still did bide:
>> till I in hand her yet halfe trembling tooke,
>> and with her owne goodwill hir fyrmely tyde.
> Strange thing me seemd to see a beast so wyld,
>> so goodly wonne with her owne will beguyld. (67)

The dear/deer's initial impulse to escape here turns into a voluntary, and somehow incomprehensible, surrender, and this turning-point, via the iconography of baptism, is construed in terms of cosmic harmony, as the fulfilment of human nature in the divine nature of the universe (note that the lyrical 'I' assumes a godlike position here). The following sonnet links the imagery of spiritual renewal in baptism with the physical renewal to be expected from the projected marriage as a 'triumph over death and sin' (68), and thus temporarily cancels out the images of submission, domestication, and captivity that stand for earthly life throughout the latter part of the sequence. The effect of this submission is to aggrandize the writing subject as a 'famous warrior', and as a proprietor who has 'The happy purchase of my glorious spoile, / gotten at last with labour and long toyle' (69). This truly Protestant vision of a 'purchase' earned by long labour culminates in an image that conflates the poet's Queen, mother, and bride, and thus gives his earnest endeavour as well as its eventual outcome a social and a cosmic relevance:

> Most happy letters fram'd by skilfull trade,
>> with which that happy name was first desynd:
>> the which three times thrise happy hath me made,

> with guifts of body, fortune and of mind.
> The first my being to me gave by kind,
> > from mothers womb deriv'd by dew descent,
> > the second is my sovereigne Queene most kind,
> > that honour and large richesse to me lent.
> The third my love, my lives last ornament,
> > by whom my spirit out of dust was raysed:
> > to speake her prayse and glory excellent,
> > of all alive most worthy to be praysed.
> Ye three Elizabeths for ever live,
> > that three such graces did unto me give. (74)

Not only are women in this sonnet construed around their generative capacities, that is, their bodies, but the dialectical counterpart of this characterization is also demonstrated: the lover, son, and subject emerges as the centre of this dance of the graces, who, through his power to write 'his' women, attains eternal life: 'Where whenas death shall all the world subdew, / our love shall live, and later life renew.' (75) After the turning-point of the chased 'deer/dear's' surrender, the woman is never described as an individual but is always seen in relation to her future husband, as a future mother, or, more generally, as a valuable possession: 'Fayre when her brest lyke a rich laden barke, / with pretious merchandize she forth doth lay.' (81) Her body is even more strongly sexualized than before, and, on the basis of the conventional trope that conflates sexual and nutritional 'consumption', it is rendered as an object to be eaten. Food imagery is latent in many of the sonnets (see, for example, sonnets 35, 83, and 88), rendering the woman so described not only as an object to look at but to feast on, while her body is cast as 'the bowre of blisse (*sic*!), the paradice of pleasure, / the sacred harbour of that hevenly spright' (76), yielding good fruit already and promising more:

> Was it a dreame, or did I see it playne,
> > a goodly table of pure yvory:
> > all spred with juncats, fit to entertayne
> > the greatest Prince with pompous roialty.
> Mongst which there in a silver dish did ly
> > twoo golden apples of unvalewed price:
> > far passing those which Hercules came by,
> > or those which Atalanta did entice:
> Exceeding sweet, yet voyd of sinfull vice,

> That many sought yet none could ever taste,
> sweet fruit of pleasure brought from paradice
> By love himselfe and in his garden plaste.
> Her brest that table was, so richly spredd,
> my thoughts the guests, which would thereon have fedd. (77)

Definitely the lover-poet feels in happy control of his images; we will see how anxiety nevertheless pervades depictions of the female body as a 'bowre of blisse', and also how the reversal of the slightly cannibalistic fantasy of 'eating' the beloved('s body) creates a sense of imminent danger.

This connection between blazonic body description and cannibalism, which ultimately disrupts the Petrarchist system of signification by leading it to its literal conclusion, is staged in Book 6 of the *Faerie Queene* in the encounter of Serena with a group of cannibals. The 'salu-age nation' (6.8.35) find the errant lady sleeping in the woods and cannot decide on a course of action; with a certain voyeuristic pleasure Spenser 'documents' their decision process: 'But of her dainty flesh they did deuize / To make a common feast, and feed with gurmandize' (6.8.38). The following description of Serena's body 'raises to a new literalness the alimentary obsessions that chronically inhabit the form':[14]

Blazonic & Cannibalism

> Some with their eyes the daintest morsels chose;
> Some praise her paps, some praise her lips and nose;
> Some whet their kniues, and strip their elboes bare. (39)

At that point, Serena awakes from her innocent slumber and, to her utter horror, discovers her captors, who now proceed to disrobe her in order to reveal (to the voyeuristic gaze of the reader) 'The goodly threasures of nature ... / Which as they view with lustfull fantasyes, / Each wisheth to him selfe, and to the rest enuyes.' (41) Capturing quite precisely the central competitive dynamics of a market system, the savages' desire is channelled into a blazonic description of the – now visible – body parts:

> Her yuorie necke, her alablaster brest,
> Her paps, which like white silken pillowes were,
> For loue in soft delight thereon to rest;
> Her tender sides, her bellie white and clere,
> Which like an Altar did it selfe vprere,

To offer sacrifice diuine thereon;
Her goodly thighes, whose glorie did appeare
Like a triumphall Arch, and thereupon
The spoiles of Princes hang'd, which were in battel won.

Those daintie parts, the dearlings of delight,
Which mote not be prophan'd of common eyes,
Those villeins vew'd with loose lasciuious sight. (42–3)

We have here a description of the ultimate victimization of a woman, via the objectification of her body and its fragmentation into different objects for – literal – consumption. This ironic hyperbole stretches the image of the objectified female body to its semantic limits, and, in ascribing this misconception to a 'salvage nation', clearly denounces their alleged inability to differentiate between symbolic and literal levels of meaning. As we will see in the description of the *Faerie Queene's* other salvage nation in Book 1, this inability is also at the heart of this group's encounter with another 'errant damzell'. Both their idolatry and the cannibalism of the savages of Book 6 are inherently related to Protestant criticism of Catholic ritualistic practice.[15] The capacity to distinguish between literal and figurative meaning, a distinction upon which all signification in the representational mode is based, here emerges not only as a central differentiating criterion between right and wrong forms of religious practice but also, closely linked to that, between proper and deficient forms of humanity.

The lyrical 'I' of the *Amoretti*, in contrast, is in control of his images and their referent, the body of his beloved, which he has the duty to put to good uses. Characteristically, not even the early descriptions of her body and virtues give her an independent identity, but conceive her as instrumental in a greater social and cosmic structure. The poet–lover–husband, in contrast, emerges as a unique subject, who even manages to overcome time, from the matrix of the passive, compliant, submissive body of his bride.

The *Amoretti's* vision of the transformation of a wilful lady into a submissive bride is completed in the *Epithalamion*, which describes the wedding as a symbol of universal harmony in which all nature participates, and as instating a linear progression that even overcomes the inexorable finiteness of time. In the structural analogies between the eternity achieved in a song which erects 'for short time an endlesse moniment' (E24) and the institution of 'endlesse matrimony' (E12) helping, through the 'fruitfull progeny' (E22) which is the goal of that union, to overcome time, the subject-poet emerges as the centre of that universe. His identity is fashioned through the textualization of a (complementary) 'other' that contains all that the subject disclaims, corporeality, materiality, and 'nature', and thereby dialectically evaluates his subject position.

In the sonnets the poet is in control of his images, and his bride is rendered as contained and chaste, her store of pleasure only accessible to her lover. The matrix on which her body is textualized, however, can also be the focus of considerable anxiety, as it contains the potential, if control is released, to overthrow the carefully framed masculine identity. For Petrarchistic patterns also voice anxieties about the relationship of writing subject and described object, at court as well as in poetry, Nancy Vickers has pointed out how the figure of Actaeon that is the focus of much Petrarchist poetry constitutes a type of courtly, male anxiety. Petrarch himself employed the image in *Rime Sparse* 23, where he makes use of the stock of Ovidian metamorphoses in order to describe his inner state *vis-à-vis* his beloved Laura:

> I' seguì' tanto avanti il mio desire,
> ch'un dì, cacciando, sì com'io solea,
> mi mossi; e quella fera bella et cruda
> in una fonte ignuda
> si stava, quando 'l sol più forte ardea.
> Io, perché d'altra vista non m'appago,
> stetti a mirarla, ond'ella ebbe vergogna;
> et, per farne vendetta, o per celarse,
> l'acqua nel viso co le man mi sparse.
> Vero dirò (forse e' parrà menzogna)
> ch'i' sentì' trarmi de la propria imago,
> et in un cervo solitario et vago
> di selva in selva ratto mi trasformo;
> et anchor de' miei can' fuggo lo stormo.[16]

(I followed so far my desire that one day, hunting as I was wont, I went forth and that lovely cruel wild creature was in a spring naked when the sun burned most strongly. I, who am not appeased by any other sight, stood to gaze on her, whence she felt shame and, to take revenge or to hide herself, sprinkled water in my face with her hand. I shall speak the truth, perhaps it will appear a lie, for I felt myself drawn from my own image, and into a solitary wandering

stag from wood to wood quickly I am transformed, and still I flee the
belling of my hounds.)

Incidentally, in the *Amoretti* the Actaeon image appears in a very
prominent position: troping the turning-point in the behaviour of the
beloved towards the 'I', it marks a very precarious moment when the
whole dynamics of the poet-subjectivity is in danger of collapse.
Sonnet 75, which has been quoted in full above, evokes not only
baptism but also the myth of Diana and Actaeon in the image of the
hart and the well. Fortunately for Spenser's lyrical 'I', the bride was
willing to play the part of the hart, and yet in the identification of the
three Elizabeths, one of whom was frequently depicted as Diana, the
fear is latent that the positions of fullness and fragmentation, speech
and silence could be reversed. The rhetoric strategy of the blazon,
transforming 'a visible totality into scattered words', based on the
'dialectics between the scattered and the gathered',[17] always carries the
possibility that the relationship of subject-totality and fragmented
object be reversed; the would-be subject 'is always potentially an
Actaeon, torn apart after his vision of an unattainable Diana'.[18] In the
underlying binary relation of subject and object, the female goddess's
totality ultimately undermines the male subject's selfhood. The
Petrarchist paradigm for literary and courtly subjectivity thus negotiated a precarious subject position, one in which a unified (albeit imagined) selfhood could always collapse into fragmentation and dispersal.
Petrarch's fearful Actaeon, as a diligent reader of Ovid, is aware of the
fate ahead of him: silenced, he awaits his final dismemberment by the
overwhelming presence of the goddess. Spenser, in contrast, preserves
his integrity by assigning to his real, material bride the place of the
hart, fragmenting her in blazoning descriptions which create a sign
of the woman('s body) that is firmly controlled by the male 'I'/eye. In
The Faerie Queene the attempt to scatter the image of his Queen by
depicting her 'in mirrours more then one' (3, proem 5) testifies to a
similar endeavour.

Many of *The Faerie Queene's* female figures serve as personifications of
the dangers posed by powerful women to male subjectivity. In the
overall didactic frame of the poem, they enable the questers to
encounter and subdue the threats posed by them. Their elaborate
descriptions, however, always also convey the feeling of something
irrevocably lost through the containment of the pleasures they might
offer. By representing undifferentiated pleasure before the impact of

culture, as, for example, in the depiction of Acrasia's Bower of Bliss, the poem instates these pleasures, and with them the idea of unrestrained sexuality, as the always already-lost core of human nature, to which men hark back but which they must ultimately reject in favour of civilization. Like the bride of the *Amoretti* and *Epithalamion*, the sexualized female figures in the *Faerie Queene* serve specific functions in the poem's various quests for identity, whether personal or national. They are usually positioned as the questing subject's 'other' on a binary scale, thereby dialectically evaluating his subject-status (in the case of Redcrosse, Guyon, and Artegall) or her superior virtue (in the case of Una and Britomart). Interestingly, even the poem's most positive female figures, Una and Britomart, and by extension also their historical referent, Elizabeth, are somehow implicated in the 'female' vices of their various counterparts, Duessa, Malecasta, Acrasia, and Radegund. At least two contrasting body paradigms were available for the representation of women in Elizabethan literature. The microcosmic, humoral body with its links to the greater cosm existed in a male and female version, and no essential gender difference could thus be attributed to its physiological features. But this was gradually being superseded by a distinctly 'sexed' body formation in which anatomical difference, especially the female capacity to give birth, became the focus of attention.

Representations of Elizabeth's virginal body mostly draw on the microcosmic paradigm, rendering her, however, as the only bearer of this body form: the Queen's political body is different in kind from that of her female subjects. The advent of scientific thinking, however, further destabilized that distinction by introducing the notion of essential, biologically definable difference, a notion that applies to all female bodies. In early modern depictions of the body in 'medical' as well as literary writings, different body paradigms frequently coexist in one text. This is also the case in the *Faerie Queene*, where many instances of a virginal-microcosmic body are countered by a highly sexualized opposite. Quite obviously, the two body paradigms were no longer equivalent. Rather, the humoral, open, leaky, female body gradually emerged as the materialization of femininity on earth, while the contained, perfect, virginal body pertained to some future age of perfection, serving as a model of a teleologically conceived movement of the individual subjects towards perfection which, however, could not be accomplished on earth. In terms of medical body descriptions, it seems that the paradigm of the humoral body continued to be applied to women's bodies when it was already being superseded by ideas of contained bodies in discourses of male subjectivity. The humoral body

Gendering of humoral Body (handwritten margin note)

The Grotesque Body (handwritten margin note)

was gradually gendered, implying that it no longer constituted the norm but a deviation. In representations of women and their sexuality this paradigm, which had in earlier times been valid for all human beings, was now regarded as applying to the inferior sex only, of which the fluid, porous body became the material locus.

One of the representational forms in which, due to its economy of fluids and its porousness, the humoral body was frequently rendered, was the grotesque. The grotesque style with its features of 'exaggeration, hyperbolism, excessiveness',[19] envisaged in images of protruding or dislocated members and leaky bodies, now came to represent women's bodies. One of the prime instances of grotesque body imagery is the representation of Duessa in Book 1 of the *Faerie Queene*. The image is conveyed through the eyes of the male questers, Redcrosse and Arthur, and emerges, like the pictured woman in the sonnet cycle, as a phantasmatic construction constituted by a male gaze that projects its fascination, horror, and anxiety at the prospect of powerful women into these images. The scene of undressing Duessa thus not only discloses her true 'nature' behind a deceptive outward appearance, but also provides a means of masculine self-empowerment by stripping the woman of her usurped insignia of power:[20]

> So as she [Una] bad, that witch they disaraid,
> And robd of royall robes, and purple pall,
> And ornaments that richly were displaid;
> Ne spared they to strip her naked all. (1.8.46)

Duessa, like Acrasia, is addressed as a witch, quite in accordance with a discourse which represents powerful women who are in control of their own bodies (and their pleasures) by that seemingly natural conjunction of witchcraft, sexuality, and femininity which, in the cultural discourses of the time, is conveyed in the pictorial conventions of the grotesque. The penetrating, voyeuristic gaze of the questers insists on seeing everything; the power of the gaze here, as in the discourse of the natural sciences, emerges as the naturalizing agent that confers the status of the real on the things that are visible:

> Then when they had despoild her tire and call,
> Such as she was, their eyes might her behold,
> That her misshaped parts did them appall,
> A loathly, wrinckled hag, ill fauoured, old,
> Whose secret filth good manners biddeth not be told. (1.8.46)

The committed scientist, however, must not be deterred by questions of propriety, so our faithful chronicler of the events pertaining to the revelation of the true faith carries on:

> Her craftie head was altogether bald,
>> And as in hate of honorable eld,
>> Was ouergrowne with scurfe and filthy scald;
>> Her teeth out of her rotten gummes were feld,
>> And her sowre breath abhominably smeld;
>> Her dried dugs, like bladders lacking wind,
>> Hong downe, and filthy matter from them weld;
>> Her wrizled skin as rough, as maple rind,
> So scabby was, that would haue loathd all womankind. (1.8.47)

In contrast both with the normative frame of the microcosmic body (which was made from perfect forms) and the ideal form of the body pertaining to the 'new' subject (the contained body of Alma), this body is deteriorated, 'misshapen', and filthy. Yet it is revealing to observe which body features are devalued as being different from the normative body. Among the adjectives employed to describe this body formation are those familiar from the grotesque register, as 'filthy', 'smelly', 'ill-favoured' and 'loathly'; there are, however, others which denigrate a body formation pertaining to a certain age, that of old women: 'wrinkled', 'old', 'toothless', 'roughskinned', 'with sagging breasts'. The normative body emerging as a counter-image of this is obviously either that of a man (and men seem to age honourably), or of a young woman, with the implication that she is still useful for society, while the old one's breasts are good for nothing and discharge all kinds of unmentionable fluids. But due to their porous bodies, and the fact that they share Duessa's body form, even young women are not free from the implications of this body on their moral behaviour:

> Her neather parts, the shame of all her kind,
>> My chaster Muse for shame doth blush to write;
>> But at her rompe she growing had behind
>> A foxes taile, with dong all fowly dight;
>> And eke her feete most monstrous were in sight;
>> For one of them was like an Eagles claw,
>> With griping talaunts armd to greedy fight,
>> The other like a Beares vneuen paw:
> More vgly shape yet neuer liuing creature saw. (1.8.48)

Duessa's bodily deformity is associated with animality, constituting a monstrous, and, in the spiritual context, a polluting mixture of kinds. Yet for all her exceptional ugliness and dangerousness, Duessa's bodily attributes reappear in other descriptions of women as their 'natural', but somehow beastly, body form. Gail Paster has demonstrated how in early modern drama female bodies were construed as leaky, incontinent, and subject to involuntary bleedings and discharges;[21] the disciplining of the humoral body by means of the grotesque construed this body form as a threat to social stability while at the same time declaring it to be the 'natural' foundation of social discourses of femininity. Duessa, as we will see later, is a counter-image to the English churches' spiritual purity as troped in Una's virginal body. As such, her description draws on the iconographic conventions of early modern religious polemics: the Babylonian whore of the Romish religion, the dragon who is defeated by Redcrosse, and the monster *Errour*. But it merges these allegorical uses of the grotesque style with representations of *Madam World* and the syphilis, both of which were personified in the form of beautiful females which are rotten underneath. This representational mode not only rendered female beauty as deceptive; it also envisaged the female body, especially that of the sexually active woman, as inherently rotten and even contagious. As a result female sexuality was submitted to rigid control with the goal of intrumentalizing the female body in the service of the community. The body's pleasures were reinscribed as 'sexuality', that is, brought under the domain of procreation, while 'chastity' emerged as a body practice that kept the body's orifices closed. Nevertheless, despite all policing and despite (especially bourgeois) women's efforts to appropriate the discourse of chastity for themselves, the allegedly 'natural' junction of moral inferiority and the humoral body made it virtually impossible to escape essentialist classifications.

Grotesque body images elaborate on the female body's associations with corporeality, plenitudinousness, and excess, all of which have been purged from the well-tempered body of the ideal (and implicitly male) subject. At the same time, the female body was rendered as a part of 'nature', an object to be mastered and domesticated by the male subject, who had learned to control his 'inner' nature by exterritorializing the instances of corporeality from the contained structure of his body. In the social discourses centring on the human 'body', corporeality was ascribed to women exclusively, while the restructured male body was no 'body' any more. Increasingly the female body was envisaged as a spatial entity, while male selfhood pretended to be dislocated from the earth's materiality. The image of the (enclosed) female body as a spatial structure, a castle or a garden, has a long tradition and was employed excessively in the panegyrics of Elizabeth to trope the inviolability of the island realm in the untouched condition of the Queen's virginal body. It seems, however, that in *The Faerie Queene* the con-frontation of each of these enclosed bodies with a grotesque, leaky, or permeable one reveals this enclosure to be an artificial or utopian condition. In any case, the anxiety remained that a breach could be made in the carefully erected, ideally internalized 'wall' or armour, and that maybe the female body underneath could subvert the stability so carefully established by means of this artifical reinforcement of the skin. The representation of Britomart's counter-figure (or alter ego), Malecasta, the 'Lady of Delight', plays on the conventions of the chaste female body as a fortress and undermines them by depicting the castle as open for everybody. Malecasta's ill-guarded 'Castle Joyous' is a place of excess, 'The image of superfluous riotize, / Exceeding much the state of meane degree' (3.1.33), filled with knights and ladies 'swimming deepe in sensuall desires' (39). Its owner is 'of rare beautie' (41), though wanton and 'giuen all to fleshly lust' (48); and as her name indicates, she is a paragon of incontinence. Malecasta proves deficient and inadequate in living up to the purpose imposed by the pictorial structure (which implicitly draws on the Pauline image of the body as the temple of the spirit). Britomart, on the contrary, is on her guard and complements her enforced mobility by reinforcing her outer skin by armour which she never takes off. Nevertheless, even she is wounded in this dangerous feminized place associated with sensuality and corporeal excess: the wound is inflicted through the minimal opening that her armour permits, the vizor. Her opponent is Gardante, the first of the seven brothers personifying the stages of concupiscible desire. Evidently not even Britomart, the paragon of chastity, is free from the afflictions of lust, and, as we have seen in Guyon's adventure, it is the gaze that remains vulnerable if all other 'lower' senses have been banned from the confines of the contained body. It was Guyon's 'greedy gaze' that made him remember his 'privy bowels' on Acrasia's island, and it is Britomart's gaze that links her to Malecasta. Though Britomart is the *Faerie Queene's* model of how to contain desire in the service of the nation and civilization as a whole, there is a sense that the inherently excessive quality of pleasure associated with the female body is never to be contained completely. Stephen Greenblatt points out that '(v)irtually all of Spenser's representations of sexual fulfilment, including those he fully sanctions, seem close to excess and risk the breakdown of the carefully fashioned identity'.[22] We shall see in how far this dialectics of excess and containment structures the quester's self-fashioning in the poem's prime instance of a sexualized or spatialized female body, Acrasia's Bower of Bliss.

Acrasia's island, with the grotto-like bower at its centre, constitutes, as Patricia Parker has remarked, a 'predominantly female space – whose enclosures suggest the *hortus conclusus* of the female body'.[23] Analogous to the Lady of Delight's castle, Acrasia's depiction in an ironic reversal of the image of an enclosed space here serves the didactic purpose to alert the quester to the fact that he must never trust appearances. At the same time these figures are obviously set up as counter-figures to the 'virtuous' females that are rightfully depicted in the images. As I will argue in more detail in Chapter 5, this is a representational matrix that is so strongly determined by its usage for the Queen that the sheer fact of its appearance to textualize personifications of vice begs an explanation. In fact, the description of Acrasia draws to a large extent on the image of the female body as a paradise, offering plenty, nourishment, and rest to the weary quester. Its description is reminiscent of Ralegh's vision of Guiana, in that both seem to draw on the biblical milk-and-honey trope to render the land-body's exquisite beauty:

> There the most daintie Paradise on ground,
>   It selfe doth offer to his sober eye,
>   In which all pleasures plenteously abound,
>   And none does others happinesse enuye:
>   The painted flowres, the trees vpshooting hye,
>   The dales for shade, the hilles for breathing space,
>   The trembling groues, the Christall running by;
>   And that, which all faire workes doth most aggrace,
> The art, which all that wrought, appeared in no place. (2.12.58)

But the textualization of the feminized space of Acrasia's island based on the pictorial conventions of the *hortus conclusus* also reveals its fundamental deceptiveness: in this feminized space of her female body, corporeal superabundance pretends to be Edenic plenty, but, like that of the grotesque body, it is a plenitudinousness that verges on excess. In contrast to Guiana's natural beauty which appears 'as if ... by all the arte and labour of the world so made on purpose' (388),[24] the bower's seemingly 'natural' beauty is in fact an effect of art which is meant to hide the 'natural', grotesque condition of this artificial paradise. We

have seen before that the gesture of the 'as if' is an essential component of male strategies of self-fashioning. This does not apply to the
female body, however: her deceptive use of art to hide the natural state
of this body-island links Acrasia to Duessa, whose sumptuous apparell
and painted face also veiled her 'natural' rottenness. If the beautiful
must not of necessity be good, within a taxonomy that accords a superior truth value to visibility it is absolutely imperative to detect the
'nature' behind the appearance. Compared to the representations of
Elizabeth-as-England as an earthly Eden, Acrasia's artful paradise is cast
as a distortion or an ironic, if dangerous, reversal. And yet, while this
usage refashions the *hortus conclusus* as a locus of spiritual purity and
divine perfection that is no longer attainable on earth, the impression
of Acrasia's Bower as a paradisiacal locus of unrestrained pleasure
remains latent. Playing on different concepts of the female body, the
Bower reveals the 'new' configuration of the female body to be devoid
of paradisiacal promises and as offering a deceptive kind of rest, one
that appeals directly to the members that have been excluded from the
temperate body. The surrogate paradise of sensual pleasure as envisaged
in Acrasia's body poses the ultimate threat to a subjectivity which
emerges through the control of excess, purposeless pleasure, and
'nature'. This is why the earthly location of lust must be destroyed,
while the ideal subject channels his energy in the service of civilization: 'Soone as with fury thou doest them inspire' the poet addresses
Venus, [they] 'In *generation* seeke to quench their inward fire' (4.10.46,
emphasis added). This, however, through the elaborate representation
of the Bower as a locus of exquisite beauty, instates the pleasure Acrasia
offers as the lost core of human identity: in the structure of the contained body, there is no room for excess.

Both Malecasta's Castle Joyous and Acrasia's Bower of Bliss are feminized spatial structures serving as the matrix from which a certain form
of subjectivity can emerge. The structural features of the spatialized
body are passivity, materiality, and an extension in space bounded
by enclosures. As such, they are also present in representations of
Elizabeth-as-England in the images of the enclosed garden or the
besieged castle which will be discussed in Chapter 4. Yet while these
images, drawing on a paradox conjunction of diametrically opposed
qualities, such as virginity and fertility, rendered the person so
depicted as more than human, the spatial structures envisaged here are
dangerous because, in the logic of temperate identity formation, they
are less than human. The grotesque style as well as the implicit links of
Acrasia with Circe associate its bearers with animality, depending on an

inherent conjunction of materiality and corporeality. The restructured body belonging to the emerging form of selfhood is purged of its corporeality, casts its materiality as accidental and locates subjectivity in the mind or consciousness. This enables the subject to leave behind his domesticated 'nature' and to elevate himself into a position of godlike dominance over the material 'natural' world. What is striking in this reconceptualization of the godlikeness of humankind and the simultaneous process of refashioning of the bodies is the fact that the representations of Elizabeth and those of the 'wicked women' share the features of materiality and spatialness. Though the land–body trope as applied to Elizabeth and the association of femininity with a spatial structure for Acrasia and Malecasta are based on different body para-digms, both territorialize the female body in a way that enables the emergence of the male/masculine subject as mobile, active, and capable of political agency.

Images of the Queen as a passive, static, and otherworldly ruler origi-nated from a certain faction at court that pursued a politics depending on and in turn producing a political subject that was emphatically masculine. Though the courtier-subject emerged under subjection, the representation of the authority that is ultimately indispensable for self-fashioning was minimalized by rendering her in terms of a space that renewed energy and, in its conjunction with the idea of the 'nation', provided a focus for identity, but which had no agency of her own. However, the implicit link between these different spatialized represen-tations subtly suggests the incommensurability of femininity and political rule. This does not necessarily mean that a woman was incapacitated to rule due to her female body – the sexual differentia-tion of bodies was not yet pervasive enough to suggest this, although the representation of Duessa at least gestured toward it – but because of the detrimental effects of female power and femininity on masculine notions of selfhood. If 'femininity', defined as a seemingly 'natural' identification of women with their bodies and, causally derived from this, their subjection and inferior position in the social order, is in fact as dangerous as the pictorial conventions of the grotesque would make us believe, it is imperative that women remain under rigid social control. The policing of female bodies, voiced in disciplinary discourses of purity, chastity, and a teleology of procreation, is thus absolutely necessary to ensure social stability. The recognition of this necessity, which is closely linked to the necessity to control and discipline the subject's own inner nature, at the same time causes considerable anxi-eties as to whether this task can ever be fully achieved. For, on the one hand, femininity as identified with corporeality appeals to the subject's own 'inner nature' and endangers his own identity by resuscitating members that had been banned beyond consciousness. On the other hand, the presence of powerful women in this context is easily conflated with threats posed to a masculine identity from the site of the female body. Thus, powerful women such as Acrasia or Radegund are depicted as emasculating or castrating, with immediate repercussions for the position and representation of the Queen. For, in so far as the court of Elizabeth can be seen as a 'predominantly female space',[25] drawing on the same kind of metonymic identification of female body and enclosed space which inform representations of Elizabeth-as-England, the courtier-subject emerges as feminized by his subjection to a courtly dynamics centring around a female monarch. Some of the anxiety that materializes in images which cast female power as emasculating might thus reflect the courtier's political impotence when confronted with a female sovereign.

In the *Faerie Queene* the episode which assembles all these features of female power in order to supersede and replace them by a vision of legitimate power is the depiction of the realm of the Amazons at the core of the Book of Justice. Louis Montrose has pointed out that the Amazons constituted one of the archetypal images reserved for the reversal of dominant discourses of order for the Elizabethans.[26] Again, it is his gaze that renders the quester vulnerable to the attractions of the world: Artegall ceases to fight against the Amazon after she has revealed her beauty: 'He saw his senses straunge astonishment, / A miracle of natures goodly grace' (5.5.12). The capacity of sight to naturalize the visible as the true nature of things here interferes with vice's power to disguise itself as beautiful, and, as I have remarked before, it is one of the aims of a quest to be aware of the deceptiveness of worldly phenomena. In addition, chivalric behaviour does not permit Artegall to fight against a beautiful woman, and his knightly code of honour interferes with the necessity to eliminate vice in whatever form. In any case, it is Artegall's own fault that has made him the victim of Radegund, who as a consequence deprives him of the insignia of (masculine) power and forces him to wear women's clothing. Loss of self-control is followed by emasculation (which condition is close to death: see 5.5.26). Radegund, like Malecasta and Acrasia, is driven by her intemperate lust, and instead of steadfastly pursuing rightful government she gives in to her sexual fancies: 'the warlike Amazon, / Whose wandring fancie after lust did raunge, / Gan cast a secret liking to this captiue straunge' (5.5.26). Her intemperance, which is described as directly related to her femininity, disqualifies Radegund from lawful rule and renders her an usurper. And yet the parallels between Radegund's country as a feminized space and the female space of Elizabeth's court are only thinly disguised. Although the text never openly criticizes the Queen, any feminized space in the poem is depicted as emasculating in one way or another, and thus constitutes a threat to a subjectivity that is predicated upon masculinity. The text is quite explicit about the illegitimacy of Radegund's reign by virtue of her gender, only barely allowing for Elizabeth's reign as godly, as in an afterthought:

> Such is the crueltie of womankynd,
>> When they haue shaken off the shamefast band,
>> With which wise Nature did them strongly bynd,
>> T'obay the heasts of mans well ruling hand,
>> That then all rule and reason they withstand,
>> To purchase a licentious libertie.
>> But vertuous women wisely vnderstand,
>> That they were borne to base humilitie,
> Vnlesse the heauens them lift to lawfull soueraintie. (5.5.25)

'Nature' is here called as a witness to women's inferiority, and it is contrasted to a divinely sanctioned sovereignty. In the conflict of Radegund and Britomart the Amazon obviously represents female 'nature': corporeal, sexually voracious, deceptive, and disloyal (even to the female 'nation').

This rendition of a female space, however, not only signifies a female body but also a female realm: the Amazon nation constitutes a feminized body politic which is cast as emasculating, as allowing no room for masculine rule and government. Radegund herself claims that she would prefer to live in a relation of 'sweet loue and sure beneuolence' (33) with her male subject, but that she is too proud 'of her seruant [to] make her souerayne Lord' (27), both sentiments that could be said to apply also to Elizabeth. The Radegund episode thus insinuates that the female ruler that keeps her male subjects in a state of forced inertia and political insignificance emasculates them and condemns them to a living death.

The feminized political space has here become problematic, and even if Elizabeth is excluded from the general denigration of female rule, the vision of the English nation as identified with her female body is undermined and will ultimately be replaced by a concept of the nation as a 'band of brothers'. As it is a 'masculine' self-relation, predicated upon temperate self-control and a contained body, that makes the person fit to be a subject of the nation, femininity is more and more excluded from the national narrative. Increasingly, as we will see in the following chapters, the female body, conceived as in need of permanent control, interferes with the right to govern; and even if, by taking recourse to a different body paradigm, the Queen is rendered as a legitimate, albeit remote, sovereign, there is always the hint that her rule might be subverted by the shortcomings of her female body.

Part II
The Body of the Nation

4
Time, Space, and the Body in the Narrative of the Nation

Images of virginity and female chastity feature prominently in the cultural discourses of early modern England. Drawing on a somatic referent, their metaphorical use is dominated by ideas of purity and wholeness. However, notions of virginity changed dramatically during the sixteenth and seventeenth centuries, affecting the use of one of the central somatic metaphors of Elizabethan cultural and political discourse. From a medical viewpoint, virginity as we understand it today did not exist in the Renaissance. There is no positive evidence of the existence of a membrane that signified the closure of the untouched female body before the mid-seventeenth century, and none of the classical medical authors ever mention it.[1] Rather than implying that there was no notion of virginity in the early modern period, however, I argue that this idea was structured according to different criteria, that virginity at that time was a moral rather than a physical category. This does not mean that the notion of a physical token of virginity did not exist at all;[2] it rather seems that the physicians' denial of the hymen came in a context of denigrating female 'medical' knowledge, contrasting it with the empirical evidence provided by dissection, as can be verified in many 'gynaecological' texts of the early modern period.[3] So it is quite probable that popular belief maintained a notion of physical virginity (centring on the blood rather than the hymen), while the scientific discourse could not reconcile it with its model of one single body for men and women and with Galenic medical teaching.[4] In his *Microcosmographia* of 1615, Helkiah Crooke claimed that 'the membrane called hymen', which he analogized with the male foreskin, was not the token of virginity he had been looking for, while at the same time declaring the necessity of a visible sign of the closure of the female body. He came to the conclusion that 'we must therefore finde

81

out some other locke of Virginitie'.[5] Gradually, the way was paved for the discovery of the somatic sign of virginity by a scientific discourse which, by privileging visibility, turned the human body into a 'legible' object.

This apparent unconcern with physical virginity may come as a surprise, considering the overwhelming number of representations of the virginity of Queen Elizabeth, and also considering the emphasis given to the decidedly female virtue of chastity in the early modern period, both concepts standing in a somewhat uneasy relationship with each other.[6] The discourses of purity in which most of the anxiety about female sexual behaviour and body practice were conveyed centred on both virginity and chastity as principal virtues for a woman. As Joan Kelly has convincingly argued, the enforcement of control over women via the virtue of chastity was one of the features that distinguished late medieval from early modern times.[7] The ubiquity of the idea in the cultural discourses of the time suggests, however, that the concept of chastity was not merely concerned with individual behaviour and modern notions of sexuality, but that it reflected the changing attitudes of society as a whole. As Norbert Elias's analysis of the dialectical relationship between the development of the modern state and the modern subject has shown, both subject and community participated in and mutually enforced a growing notion of separation and isolation of political and individual bodies.[8] Discourses of 'chastity' or 'virginity' may thus have been voicing concerns of more than merely private nature; their emphasis on purity provides the link between discourses about individual and collective bodies.

Traditionally, the image of the human body was employed by the Elizabethans to symbolize the English commonwealth, most pointedly in the image of the two bodies of the Queen.[9] In the historical context of the separation of European Christendom into single states which defined themselves by their difference from and their competition with the respective others, emphasis was put on the control of individual body margins because the margins of one's own society or national territory were believed to be threatened. As the anthropologist Mary Douglas points out, 'each culture has its own special risks and problems. To which particular bodily margin its beliefs attribute power depends on what situation the body is mirroring.'[10] Diasporic communities and threatened political entities thus tend to represent their body politic as fragile and vulnerable from outside, and these anxieties reappear in the care for the integrity and purity of the physical bodies of its members. The emergence of chastity as the prime virtue for the

Renaissance woman could thus be attributed to the perceived necessity to consolidate boundaries on a social and political level. Also, as I have pointed out earlier, in times of increasingly capitalist economic structures a woman's virginity was becoming of value on the marriage market, while her chastity when married made sure that property was handed down in the male line. The appearance of 'new' sexually transmitted diseases, such as syphilis, added to the anxiety about the control of bodily orifices. Thus on a symbolic level the complete closure of female body orifices (the physical sign of which was 'discovered' not much later) stands in close relation to the closure of territorial boundaries of the newly separated states. As the paradigms of body perception were changing, from the humoral, microcosmic body towards a concept of sexually differentiated bodies, the female body's capacity to symbolize unity and wholeness came under scrutiny; it was increasingly imagined as enforced by rigid boundaries. In early modern England, I contend, it is the image of the chaste female body that provided a mirror for the reciprocal constitution of individual and collective identities, of self and nation.

In the cult of Elizabeth's virginity the image of the microcosmic, divine body, symbolizing the unity of political entities such as church and realm, was combined with a new emphasis on marginal regions and frontiers. As can be witnessed in changing social and medical practice, the constitution of new boundaries for bodies was also a result of new notions of space which especially highlighted the contrast between interior and exterior spaces. It was not only the subject but also political entities and imagined communities that were delineated by new, often strongly fortified, borders. Inner spaces were imagined as in need of defence, while outward spaces were represented as hostile and isolated. Depictions of the chaste woman reiterated these notions of space by rendering the beloved as a fortress under siege or an enclosed garden. The symbolic closure of the female body which was propagated by these images depicted it as simultaneously precious and vulnerable. The following chapters will demonstrate how the 'hybrid' form of a contained microcosmic body, retaining its links with God and its elevated position in the universe, by reworking its inner structure and reinforcing its boundaries could serve to represent the English body politic and its difference from Continental political entities. Representing an almost paradoxical conjunction of absolutist 'political theology' and national ideology, the microcosmic yet contained body of the Queen provided the matrix for imagining a decidedly Protestant English national community.

Changes in the taxonomic frame of things certainly influenced the reconceptualization of the form and contents of political iconography. Ultimately, however, the refashioning of the political body image in the service of the national narrative was effected as much by local causes and historical contingencies. Among these, the necessity for Elizabeth to ensure a stable succession and the subsequent negotiations with the (mostly Catholic) powers of Europe was paramount. While in earlier years the Queen had been pressured to marry and provide an heir at almost any cost, the political climate was changing under the weight of the anti-Protestant hostilities on the continent.[11] In the years after Elizabeth's excommunication in 1570 and the Bartholomew massacre 1572, the English establishment developed a strong sense of being set apart from and, in fact, of being threatened by the Continental political powers, and in this climate Elizabeth's marriage negotiations with her French suitor could not prosper. The Anjou courtship (1578–82), with its imminent possibility of England's losing its independent status in the European context, brought about a wave of national sentiment, especially from the Protestant side of the establishment. There seemed to be a feeling that however great the dangers of an unsettled succession might be, it was still preferable to Catholic domination of the country. This was most clearly expressed in contemporary religious discourses, but it also had immediate implications for courtly panegyrics and pageantry and, of course, for Elizabeth's politics.[12] The imagery emerging from this sentiment was one that cast the Queen as inaccessible, life-giving, and divine, all these attributes hinging on the shared signifier of her 'virginity' as an image of the vulnerability and purity of the English Protestant diasporic community. John Stubbs, in his powerful *Discoverie of a Gaping Gulf whereinto England is like to be swallowed by an other French Marriage* of 1579, for which both author and publisher were sentenced to lose their right hands, used similar imagery when he described Elizabeth as 'the royall ship of our ayde, the hyghest tovver, the strongest hold and castle in the land'.[13] His text abounds with evocations of Elizabeth as mother of her country, identifying her with the 'true' motherly Church. She is called the 'temple of the holy ghost' (A4^v), and is likened to the daughters of God in the sixth chapter of Genesis, who should not couple with the sons of men.[14] Architectural imagery is repeatedly used, rendering Elizabeth, or, to be more precise, her body, as a fortress or enclosed garden, hedged in by walls:

(T)hey of the reformed religion in both those countryes [England and France] are as a brazen doore, and an yron wall, agaynst our popish enemies. and therefore by thys match, he [Anjou] seeks to sunder them from vs and vs from them, and so by vnbarring our brazen doore and treading dovvne our vval, to lay open hys passage to vs. (B2ᵛ)

Religious and nationalistic feelings went hand in hand in representing the Catholic threat to England as an attack on the fortified walls of the body politic. The very image of the body of the English national community is used when Stubbs depicts Elizabeth as Eve (before the Fall) and Anjou as the serpent, with England as the paradisiacal setting of the scene:

(T)hey haue sent vs hither not Satan in body of a serpent, but the old serpent in shape of a man, vvhose sting is in his mouth, and vvho doth his endeuour to seduce our Eue, that shee and vve may lose this Englishe Paradise. Who because she is also our Adam & soueraigne Lord or lordly Lady of this Land, it is so much the more daunger-ous & therefore he so much the more busily bestirres him. (A2ʳ)

The over-determined imagery of this passage conveys all the anxieties an author concerned with the future of England and English Protestantism in the later years of Elizabeth's reign could possibly have; in that respect, it voices cultural anxieties while at the same time imagining a pure, Protestant, national community in the shape of the Queen's virginal body. The representation of the Catholic suitor as the subtle serpent, indicating that the Satanic dragon in the shape of the prince does his best to seduce the Queen, gives the situation a decidedly providential tone. While Elizabeth's natural body is identified with the paradise gar-den of England which promises peace and plenty as long as it remains unfallen, her political body is depicted as Adam, undergoing a change of gender in order to turn into the 'sovereign lord of the isle'. The image of the androgynous, perfect, all-containing Adam before the Fall implies that political authority can only be vested in a male, while at the same time cancelling out the possibility of providing male sovereignty by mar-riage to a European prince. Keeping the virginal body inviolate – that is, avoiding the 'sting' of the Satanic serpent – emerges as the precon-dition of the integrity of the English community, which, so the image of the androgynous Adam implies, is self-sufficient and autonomous.

As Helen Hackett has pointed out, in the course of the political events of the 1580s new iconographical conventions for the praise of the sovereign developed, images which cast the virginal body of the Queen as enclosed paradise of peace and plenty, embodying the English Church as well as the English nation, and which emphasized the inaccessibility of the virgin Queen as icon for the English body politic.[15] As an image increasingly appropriated by the narrative of the nation it embodied the integrity of the community and realm via the inviolability of the island territory, focusing at the same time on the vulnerability of what was enclosed 'inside' and the necessity to defend this precious 'body' from 'outside' dangers. The implications of spiritual purity are very pronounced in Spenser's deployment of the paradise image in the figure of Una with which the national narrative of *The Faerie Queene* begins.

Una, the personification of the true English Church, is associated with paradise by her genealogy: her parents are Adam and Eve, who have been driven out of Eden by the forces of evil (1.7.43). Being deprived of access to her home, Una is compelled to wander through the world as a type of 'errant damzell', establishing a typological link between the bride of the Song of Songs and the Woman Clothed with the Sun from Revelation and drawing on the traditional identification of the Song of Songs' bride with the Church.[16] In the complementary quest narrative of Una and the Knight of the Red Crosse, the image of the virgin female body depicts the earthly Church as extremely vulnerable, while the male believer is invested with the agency to defend his 'earthly paradise'. Redcrosse's quest obviously demands more than spiritual efforts in order to defend his 'bride' from the evils of the world, and he is rewarded in the end by being betrothed to Una, thus becoming heir to paradise.

Una, the daughter of paradise, is described with floral imagery, linking her to the May Queens of pastoral literature as well as to the *Shepheardes Calender*'s Eliza, with whom she shares the same Messianic background. Moreover, Una's light-giving capacities have precedents in the representations of the divine in Neoplatonic discourses.[17] The iconography of Una as a bride sums up all the pastoral conventions of Renaissance England, but the decidedly apocalyptic and providential nature of Redcrosse's quest, dealing with the fate of the true Church in a world of evil, adds political meaning. Not only is Una a representation of the English Church, she is also connected to the Queen via the signifier of the virgin body:

> Then on her head they set a girland greene,
> And crowned her twixt earnest and twixt game;

> Who in her selfe-resemblance well beseene,
> Did seeme such, as she was, a goodly maiden Queene. (1.12.8)

Una's appearance as Woman in the Wilderness also draws on pastoral imagery. Fleeing from Archimago, whose insatiable lust may imply a reminiscence of the figure of the Wild Man from the May game tradition, Una encounters a 'saluage nation' (1.6.11) who are so taken aback by her divine beauty that they 'worship her, as Queene, with oliue girlond cround' (1.6.13).

The identification of the pastoral version of the *hortus conclusus* motif[18] with the Queen's body gives these episodes from the *Faerie Queene* a decidedly political overtone. Protestant England as symbolized by the Queen's virginal body becomes the point of departure for the restitution of paradise (in fact, her body sometimes appears to be Eden itself), with obvious consequences for those nations that are not yet included in Una's Truth: their conversion becomes a precondition for the restoration of paradise, which will return when all 'salvage nations' have been converted. Representing the type of 'unfallen' natives as yet untouched by the evils of the world, who have not yet heard the Gospel but are willing to adopt it despite their lack of understanding of its true meaning, these savages' paradise is perfected by the appearance of Una, that is, the advent of the true faith, who effects their conquest without violence, by her mere appearance:

> During which time her gentle wit she plyes,
> To teach them truth, which worshipt her in vaine,
> And made her th'Image of Idolatryes;
> But when their bootlesse zeale she did restraine
> From her own worship, they her Asse would worship fayn. (1.6.19)

This 'salvage nation's' lack of aggressiveness makes their conversion by a woman possible, and renders them as 'good natives' which can easily be incorporated into European paradigms of civilization.[19] The fragility of the true Church among the 'wild' nations emphasizes Una's divinity even more; the savage nation's capability to recognize her as divine renders this encounter as beyond the contingencies of worldly concerns and as a manifestation of the unfolding of God's plan. The idolatrous reaction of the savages, who worship Una's donkey when being denied the worship of her person, moreover, establishes a hierarchy of religions according to their degree of adherence to the true *logos*, their capacity to comprehend abstractions and their rejection of idolatry;

Catholicism implicitly emerges as somewhere down the line towards paganism.

Like all figures represented in the image of the enclosed garden, Una has no agency of her own. Her missionary success with the savages is due to a revelation of divine 'light', but not to any concrete actions on her part. The integrity of the Church in the wilderness of the world must be protected by her believers, the prototype of which is the Redcrosse Knight. Within this textualization of the Church militant, Una provides all of Redcrosse's actions with a legitimation, but she cannot act herself: Divine revelation must be supported by human initiative in order to make it survive in the world. The symbolic closure of the female body represents the twofold aspect of the Church which, on the historical plane, is a community 'in the wilderness' endowed with paradisiacal potential which will be released when all 'salvage nations' are converted and all 'dragons' defeated. To realize this potential, the explicitly masculine agency of the quester for the true faith is necessary. Read against the background of a 'Virgin Queen' who is also the supreme governor of the English Church, Una emerges as a personification of a Protestant politics of internal consolidation; the Queen herself is textualized as an immovable centre of power who invests her male subjects with agency and legitimation, but who does not act herself. That this image conveys praise as well as criticism is evident: captured in an image of complete stasis, the Queen's 'divinity' removes her from the historical plane and defers agency to her courtiers. The autonomy and quasi-autarchy of this community imagined as English Eden depends on the militant masculinity of the subjects who defend it against violation from outside.

While Una's bodily containment is a function of her divinity, Redcrosse's integrity must be acquired in the course of a quest. In analogy with the inviolability of Una's body-realm, Redcrosse develops a body practice through which he is in absolute control of all exchange between his body and the world. In that, he is a precursor of Guyon, for whom this focus on bodily margins becomes imperative. The representation of the Knight of the Red Crosse draws heavily on the iconography of St George.[20] Displacing George's Marian associations onto Una, Spenser employed the iconographic conventions of the English saint *par excellence* and, while apparently establishing its Protestant version, appropriated it for the English Church. The characteristic typological features of the saint, who conventionally appeared as defender of virginity, fighter against the Saracens, and aid against contagious diseases, and the iconography of the red cross which since the time of Richard Lionheart had been used to mark out the defender of English territory, both establish '*George* of mery England' (1.10.61) as the ideal fighter for the community represented in Una's virgin body. The assaulting entity, be it contagion, wrong religion, or a foreign army, is represented as the dragon, thus demonized in the form of humankind's arch-enemy. The fight at the end of Redcrosse's 'painefull pilgrimage' (1.10.61) can only take place after the knight's vision of the Heavenly Jerusalem and after the eventual announcement of his 'name and nation' (1.10.67) reveal him as a decidedly English, Protestant *milites Christi*. The typological background is, of course Michael's fight against the dragon from Revelation, so that here again, eschatological allusions are evoked in order to render the continuation and full revelation of the English paradise as dependent on Redcrosse's moral and corporeal integrity. Consequently, the enemies of these two complementary principles of right religion, Una and Redcrosse, are not only represented in images of darkness (as customary in the religious polemics of the time) but also in the pictorial conventions of the grotesque, that is, with open, penetrable bodies which lack stable boundaries. Una's obvious counterpart, identifiable by her very name, is Duessa, the Janus-faced, who has the capacity to assume every possible shape and even appears to Redcrosse in the guise of Una herself, thereby undermining her (eponymous) uniqueness. As I have mentioned before, the use of body images for the representation of collective identities frequently focuses on questions of purity and pollution: Defilement must be excluded from the community and the bodily comportment of its members checked. Drawing on the sexual iconography of early modern religious discourse, this polarization is pictured as the contrast between Una's desexualized and Duessa's over-sexualized body. Sexual activity beyond the social necessity of the marriage bed is conceived of as a pollution of the collective body of the community of believers, and must be radically extirpated from it, as the Elizabethan *Sermon of Adultery*, which was read in churches all over the country, makes drastically clear:

> Christ, who is the truth, and cannot lie, saith, that evil thoughts, breaking of wedlock, whoredom, and fornication defile a man; that is to say, corrupt both the body and soul of man, and make them, of the temples of the Holy Ghost, the filthy dunghill, or dungeon of all unclean spirits; of the House of God, the dwelling place of Satan.[21]

The dragon besieging the castle of Una's parents here appears as just another guise of Duessa, for its description assembles all the iconographic conventions of the grotesque, the gaping jaws, the abysmal mouth and the infinite, unbounded body:

> His body monstrous, horrible, and vast,
>> Which to increase his wondrous greatnesse more,
>> Was swolne with wrath, and poyson, and with bloudy gore.
> (...)
>> But his most hideous head my toung to tell
>> Does tremble: for his deepe deuouring iawes
>> Wide gaped, like the griesly mouth of hell,
> Through which into his dark abisse all rauin fell. (1.11.8 and 12)

Redcrosse's fight against this dragon is staged as a contrast of the two body formations. In the dualistic framework of the fight of good against evil, the representation of evil forces in the conventions of the grotesque establishes the contained, bounded body as the ideal body of the modern subject claiming full control of his bodily margins, his spatial extension, and his exchange with the world. At the same time the containment of the female body emerges as one of the foremost instances of social control. Redcrosse's hard-won victory over the dragon establishes his body configuration as a precondition for the restitution of (the English) paradise. It contributes to the consolidation of an inward-looking, religiously defined Englishness, represented in the image of the enclosed garden of the female body whose nourishing capacities and ideological purity must be defended, if necessary, by armed fight. At the core of the national narrative of Book 1 is the idea of the self-sufficiency of a diasporic community whose spiritual purity is guaranteed by the containment and purity of every subject's body.

The image of the contained structure of the virgin body of church and political community which shields a vulnerable core against attacks from outside is at the heart of many Elizabethan representations of the Queen's body. Whereas the metaphor of the enclosed garden belonged to a religious register, drawing on biblical and contemporary religious imagery, the image of the castle under siege was traditionally employed in courtly panegyrics to picture the desirable body of a chaste and beloved lady. The castle image, combined with the architectural metaphors denoting the well-ordered bodily structure, imagines the national community as an orderly, fortified container resisting attempts at intrusion from outside. It provides a vehicle for the male subjects' desire to be part of the political structure and to master its internal dynamics as well as its ultimate referent, the female body of the Queen. In this representational matrix, the underlying oscillation between the microcosmic, transcendental body politic and the female (and sexualized) body natural of the sovereign can only barely be held in check. Its psychosocial function thus focuses as much on the anxieties the male subjects felt *vis-à-vis* the female sovereign as on their desire to refashion the political structure in a way that would assign to them a position of power. For, as Louis Montrose has claimed, courtly pageantry 'is both an offering of praise and a symbolic vehicle expressing the immediate personal and collective concerns of its promoters and participants'.[22]

The image of the fortress under siege was the thematic centre of the sumptuous courtly entertainment at the tilt-yard, *The Four Foster Children of Desire*[23] of 1581, which was probably devised, at least in part, by Philip Sidney.[24] The entertainment staged an attack on the Fortress of Perfect Beauty, the allegorical locus of the Queen, by the Foster Children of Desire, who claimed it as theirs by right. It took place not only in the presence of the Queen and court, but also of the French ambassadors negotiating Elizabeth's marriage to the son of Katharina de Medici and Henri II of France, the Duc d'Alençon, later Duc d'Anjou.[25] The Foster Children were impersonated by Philip Howard, Earl of Arundel, Frederick Windsor, Baron Windsor of Stanwell, Philip Sidney, and Fulke Greville.[26] At least one of the performers was known to be firmly opposed to the French match and had voiced his opinion in writing,[27] and three of them, Windsor, Sidney, and Greville, had been members of the train accompanying Anjou to the Netherlands a few months before the tilt. On the grounds of this constellation it seems probable that the audience expected the pageant to address the marriage question in one way or another.[28] The Protestant faction saw the match as a threat to Protestantism and, closely linked to that, to the existence of the emerging English nation. Apparently, the proposed match met with widespread disapproval throughout the establishment and probably even amongst the 'meaner sort', since Stubbs's anti-French *Gaping Gulf* pamphlet, printed two years earlier, had gained wide notoriety. Council quotes the report of the Venetian ambassador at court, claiming that '[Stubbs] has excited the feelings of many individuals, who say openly that they will not consent in Parliament to this marriage',[29] and although I do not share his view that *The Foster Children* was staged in the presence of the French in order to display to them Elizabeth's decision against the match, I propose to read it as the Protestant faction's version of things.

The Foster Children of Desire challenge the Fortress to surrender, since 'by right of inheritaunce even from ever, the Fortresse of Beautie doth belong to her [Desire's] Fostered Children' (67). The Fortresse is the location of the Queen herself: 'The Gallory or place at the end of the Tiltyard adjoining to her Majesties house at Whitehall, whereas her person should be placed, was called and not without cause, the Castle or *Fortresse of perfect beautie*' (66). In case of refusal, 'they will besiege that fatal Fortresse, vowing not to spare (if this obstinacie continue) the swoorde of faithfulnesse, and the fire of affection' (67). The 'inviolate presence' (71) of the Queen was defended by several knights, among them Sir Henry Lee, the initiator of the annual Accession day tilts, in the role of the 'Unknown Knight'. The fight for the 'never conquered walles' (72) of the Fortress was staged in the form of a tilt, interspersed with allegorical speeches by the various defendants.

The background of the setting of the Queen as 'Fortress of perfect beautie' is obviously Neoplatonic. The Queen is addressed by Desire's Foster Children as 'Earthly Venus', drawing on the well-known separation of the two Venuses which is at the core of much Elizabethan poetry in this vein. She is rendered in terms of floral and natural imagery, as a 'fortresse built by nature ... seated in this Realme' (67), which, in the logic of the Neoplatonic erotic dynamic, must yield to virtuous desire. Thus Elizabeth is admonished to 'no longer exclude vertuous Desire from perfect Beautie' and to 'yelde for so all reason requireth' (67) if she does not want to be accounted cruel. The Foster Children conceive of the Fortress in terms of natural beauty, which is Desire's by right, as desire depends on cognition and is drawn to visual beauty as a first step towards the attainment of heavenly beauty.[30] So natural beauty corresponds to the Earthly Venus, rendering the beautiful lady as an incarnation of heavenly beauty (a 'deity shrined in flesh', in Sidney's own words)[31] who incites the lover to enter the erotic dynamic. In the words of Pico della Mirandola, whose ideas had been introduced to England by Thomas More and had been adapted by Edmund Spenser among others, this can ultimately lead him to a vision of celestial beauty: 'since love is a desire for beauty, just as there are two beauties, there necessarily must be two loves, earthly and heavenly, and just as the former desires earthly or sensible beauty, so the latter desires heavenly or intelligible beauty'.[32] Representing Elizabeth as the Earthly Venus thus renders her as an appearance of the very idea of beauty in the flesh, with the underlying assumption that, although of heavenly origin, she is ultimately attainable. However, in the course of the entertainment this notion turns out to be a gross misconception.

It is corrected by the 'fortress's' defendants, who address the Queen as Heavenly Venus who is absolutely beyond the reach of any mortal. She is figured as the sun, an image which is frequently used to describe the end of the soul's yearning for the vision of God's beauty, which can only be depicted in terms of light and illumination. Linking the notion of the sun as a pale reflection of divine light to the traditional darkness–light contrast familiar from the religious polemics of the time, Sidney employs the sun image in his *Discourse* to describe Elizabeth's 'constitutional' status as the guarantor of right religion and upholder of the true faith:

> He of the Romish religion, and if he be a man, must needs have that manlike propertye to desire that all men be of his mind: you the erector & deffendour of the contrary & the onely Sunne that dazeleth their eyes. He French and desirous to make Fraunce great: your majesty English & desiring nothing lesse than that France should be great.[33]

So, in the European context, Elizabeth becomes a rival sun to the King of France, who was traditionally rendered in sun imagery. Consequently, the siege of the sun by the Foster Children is depicted by the standard Renaissance representations of *hubris*, Jason, Phaeton, the Titans, and Icarus, the classical overreacher. It is understood to be an attack on the order of nature: 'O Jove, if thou mean to resolve nature into contraries, why doe I live to see it, if into nothing, why doe I live at all, if the foote scale the head, there is no rest if Desire overshoote duetie, there is no reason, and where either of these are, there can be no rule.' (74) The invocation of Jove as a signifier of the one God, the impending reversal of the integrative power of the human body as indicated in the idea of the foot scaling the head, and sun imagery are all employed here to stress the unity and uniqueness of Elizabeth as sovereign; they also hint at her unifying qualities in an European Protestant context, for 'Who would leave the beames of so feare a Sunne for the dreadfull expectation of a devided companie of starres?'[34]

The utterer of this speech, the 'frozen knighte in the ayer' (73), invokes God to restore the order of nature. Thus an Angel is sent down to 'cause Adam and Eve to appear on the earth in that sort as they were in Paradise' (74), to exhort and correct their 'preposterous lymmes'. Two knights dressed up as Adam and Eve appear, admonishing the Foster Children to relinquish their siege and to restore the

English 'paradise': 'Sir Knights, if in besieging the sunne ye understood what you had undertaken, ye would not destroye a common blessing for a private benefite.' (75) The Queen, addressed in terms of heavenly beauty, is necessary to make the world go round and to provide her subjects with a glimpse of divine light, which cannot be monopolized by a single individual. Elizabeth, the Heavenly Venus, is depicted as the 'lighte of the worlde, the marvel of men, the mirour of nature, on which their encounter, if those favourable gleams may fall, they wil not onely thinke to have done goode herein, but to be restored againe to Paradice' (76). Drawing, like Stubbs, on the image of the enclosed garden to represent Elizabeth-cum-England as paradise, this rapturous speech culminates in a decidedly political statement: 'For whensoever the question shall be moved, No other reason shall be allowed then this: *Elizabetha dixit*.' (76) This invocation of the Queen's agency stands in stark contrast to the overall device of the fortress, which implies passivity and a need of defence, thus attributing activity to her male subjects, the 'knights' in the tilt. In addition, the sun imagery depicts her as so remote from the concerns of the world that agency on a historical plane is also transferred to the courtiers. Apparently, the absolutist statement of '*Elizabetha dixit*' refers less to actual political decisions than to the idea of Elizabethan kingship and the autonomy of England from the continental powers, as the knights argue themselves: 'For the majestie of that sunne which now pearcing our eyes hath fully subdued our hearts, that we are prest in her defence to offer the whole world defiance.' (76)

The speech of the second defendant, M. Ratcliffe, also draws on Neoplatonic notions of heavenly beauty. It tells the story of the 'mossie knight', which is a re-enactment of the Platonic parable of the cave in Book 7 of the *Republic*. Living secluded in a mossy den, 'he gave himselfe to continuall meditation, seperating his mind from his body, his thought from his hart, yea devorcing him self from himselfe' (77). Being informed by some knights about the siege on the fortress, he leaves his contemplative life to actively defend divine beauty. Approaching the Queen herself, the page delivering the speech on M. Ratcliffe's behalf explains to her that 'he is called from his solitarie Cave to your sumptuous Court, from bondage to liberty, from a living death to a never dying life, and all for the sake and service of Beawtie' (78). Leaving the dark den and entering the splendour of the court is thus analogized to the soul's leaving the cave and entering the realm of pure ideas in Plato's parable. Elizabeth emerges here as the very idea of beauty, which can never be reached by any mortal. The speech of the mossy knight being ended, the four sons of Sir Francis Knollys entered the tiltyard, disguised as 'the iiii legitimate sonnes of Despaire' (80), who has been 'banish[ed] ... as a traytor' (81) from Desire's kingdom, hinting not too subtly at Elizabeth's reaction at Knollys' daughter's marriage with her favorite Robert Dudley.[35] Their speech, conveyed by a page dressed up as Mercury, focuses strongly on fortification imagery:

> So falles it out in this attempt, Desire vaunts to conquer Beawties Forte by force, wherin the goddesse keepes continually watch and warde, so that Desire may dispaire to win one ynche of her against her will. Her stately seate is set so high, as that no levell can be laid against her walles, and sooner may men undertake to hit a starre with a stone, then to beate hir brave bulwarkes by batterie. No undermining may prevaile, for that hir forte is founded upon so firme a Rocke, as will not stirre for either fraude or force. (79)

Echoing traditional love-as-war imagery, this passage renders the 'impregnable fort' of the Queen's body as absolutely inaccessible and the mere attempt at scaling it as an attack on divine wisdom. Again, the spatial configuration that is identified with the Queen's body is represented as a locus of plenty that yields nourishment for everyone:

> And is there any hope to winne by famine such a forte as yeeldes continuall foode to all her foes, and though they feede not fat there-with, yet must they either feede thereon or fast, for Beawtie is the only baite whereon Desire bites, and love the chiefe restoritie that ladie Beawtie likes, so that she can no more be left without meat, then men can live without mindes. (79)

It is obvious, then, that a siege of that fortress is a futile and, indeed, a presumptuous enterprise. Its outcome, were it ever successful, is unthinkable. The ceasing of Desire, analogized to an eclipse of the sun (75–6), would not only signify the end of the nurturing capacity of the fortress but also the end of that erotic dynamic which moves the world:

> Of all affections that are, Desire is the most worthie to woe, but least deserves to win Beawtie, for in winning his sainct, he loseth him selfe, no soner hath desire what he desireth, but that he dieth presently: so that when Beawtie yeeldeth once to desire, then can she never vaunt to be desired againe: Wherefore of force this principle

must stand, it is convenient for Desire ever to wish, necessarie &
that he alwaies want. (79–80)

Convinced by these arguments, the Foster Children forego their siege
and, on the second day of the entertainment, confess in the presence
of a personification of Desire 'That they are not greatly companied
with hope, the common supplier to Desires army. So as nowe from
summoning this Castel to yeld, they are fallen lowly to beseech you to
vouchsafe your eyes out of that Impregnable Fortresse, to beholde what
will fal out betwixt them and your famous knights' (82). The entertainment ends with a tilt, and in the concluding speech the Foster
Children express their 'humble hearted submission, they acknowledge
this Fortresse to be reserved for the eye of the whole worlde, farre lifted
up, from the compasse of their destinie' (83). In an unmistak-
able identification of realm and fortress, they state 'That while this
Realme is thus fortified and beautified: Desire may be your chiefest
adversarie' (84).

The message of this entertainment would not be lost on the French
ambassadors: Anjou, being the obvious referent of Desire's Foster
Children, must abandon his 'siege', since nobody can monopolize
heavenly beauty. In this context, the image of the sun, as representative of divine light, carries political signification. In addition to its
use in the panegyrics of many European kings, where it stood for the
universalist claim to a pan-European monarchy, it here also implies the
divine light of the true faith. It thus emerges as the appropriate representation of a Queen who is at the same time the monarch of an
autonomous territorial entity and supreme governor of her subjects'
independent national church and who, due to her femininity, is
rendered in images that conjoin the Neoplatonic Heavenly Venus and
the Woman Clothed with the Sun. Thus in this pageant the 'fortified'
and 'impregnable' body of Elizabeth in the role of the Queen of heavenly beauty, represented in the image of a fortress yielding nourishment for all her subjects, comes to stand for the English national
territory, which is depicted as inaccessible by the French. The closure of
her body representing at the same time the closure of territorial boundaries can be understood as a negotiation of the fear of invasion, hostile
or lawful (that is, by marriage), by the continental powers. The representation of the Queen in the imagery of Neoplatonic love, however,
unequivocally depicts her 'virginity' as perpetual. There is no possibility
of marriage left in this description, which removes the historical
Elizabeth from the political sphere onto a mythological level. This shift

comes accompanied by an increasing resignation about the historical Elizabeth's power of agency, and it voices the desire that more agency be given to the courtiers who are willing to defend the English body politic. In terms of the courtiers' self-definition there seems to be a movement towards more activity or rather militancy, developing out of the desire to pursue a Protestant foreign policy and to amend the religious settlement at home. This masculinist courtier-identity as voiced in a pageant in which four courtiers, driven by desire, attack a fortress-virgin with phallic weapons, stands, of course, in stark contrast to – and has continually to be negotiated with – the fact that the sovereign, fountain of all power, is a woman.

In contrast to the courtly representations discussed here, Spenser's vision of nationhood strongly emphasizes the complementarity of active and passive virtues, represented in terms of gendered allegories which ultimately unite in a vision of divine perfection. His marriage imagery in Book 1 constitutes the Queen's body as a static paradise body and advocates the active defence of its inviolate state by its male subjects. It results in the imagination of an English Protestant community in splendid isolation from its Catholic opponents on the Continent. In the course of the poem, this vision is broadened towards a more European outlook. The double quest of Books 3 and 5 imagines a national community that reaches beyond the confines of the island realm, envisaging a British nation rather than a merely English one. Again, the bodies of the questers provide a paradigm of integrity and wholeness, for the figure of Britomart combines the implications of the contained and paradisiacal female body with the activity of a quest. In terms of body imagery, Britomart's quest for chastity appears as the female counterpart to Guyon's endeavours to control his passions and pleasures. In terms of nationhood, however, it must be complemented by Artegall's Irish quest.

Many critics have pointed out the parallels between Britomart and 'Elizabeth at Tilbury',[36] as both representations constitute their female warriors as icons of national integrity, envisaging a unity of state,[37] nation, and territory. Yet despite these obvious analogies, of all figures in *The Faerie Queene* Britomart conveys the most cutting criticism of Elizabeth. Especially in terms of the national narrative or quest for national unity, it is Britomart who provides an image of nationhood that is quite different from Elizabeth's position of static aloofness. The quest for chastity links personal bodily behaviour with the collective body as represented in terms of enclosed space, but unlike Una's static virginity, chastity is a female body practice which is closely related to the collective body of the new community. Like the narrative of the nation, the pursuit of chastity promotes the performative constitution of a contained body that can serve as an ideal to be aspired to by all its members.

But Britomart's quest has an additional dimension, that of time. Her body not only represents the inviolate island realm, but also the linear progress of British nationhood through time, from the mythological Trojan ancestry to the present day and further. In doing so it anxiously emphasizes the fact that this vision, cast in the double time-scheme that is characteristic for the nation, the future perfect, must be brought about by the Queen's and her subjects' mutual endeavours.

Britomart embarks on her quest after having fallen in love with the image of Artegall, her future spouse, which she had conjured up in her father's magic mirror. Interestingly, even before the actual onset of the quest, her mirror scene provides a coherent vision of its eventual outcome, an image which structures her future behaviour to such an extent that one could speak, with Lacan, of an identity-giving vision of perfection.[38] Reverting to Merlin for help in her love-melancholy, Britomart is given an explanation for these events that dispels their air of contingency and declares them to be the dealings of divine providence:

> It was not, *Britomart*, thy wandring eye,
>   Glauncing vnwares in charmed looking glas,
>   But the streight course of heauenly destiny,
>   Led with eternall prouidence, that has
>   Guided thy glaunce, to bring his will to pas:
> (...)
>   Therefore submit thy wayes vnto his will,
> And do by all dew meanes thy destiny fulfill. (3.3.24)

Displacing the frivolity of the 'wandring eye' onto the fulfilment of providence, this explanation instrumentalizes Britomart's erotic energy in the service of the nation. Having established Britomart's erotically motivated quest as preordained by providence, Merlin provides her with a vision of the dynasty she is to instigate. As Helgerson has argued, chronicles constituted the prime forms in which national identity was articulated in Tudor times.[39] Structuring events according to a linear time-scale, Merlin's chronicle endows the Elizabethan 'nation' with a continuous history that inevitably culminates in the Queen.

By representing Britomart's present as the mythical past of Elizabethan times, this narrative of national history renders Elizabeth herself as the climax of the chronicle. At the same time, the representation of Britomart as a personification of an aspect of the Queen makes them contemporaries: both are manifestations of the *dignitas* of English kingship, that is, in Kantorowicz's terms, the political fiction of a diachronic one-man corporation in which the present monarch is considered to exist, in his or her body politic, in a metonymic unity with all former monarchs.[40] So if, as this legal fiction suggests, Britomart and Elizabeth are one and the same person, we might conclude that Britomart carries in her person, indeed in her womb, the complete time span of the English nation. Elizabethan politics, or, to be more precise, the political programme of the Protestant faction at court, emerge in Merlin's chronicle as emanations of divine providence and thus as universal truth, while Elizabeth herself appears as the returning virgin who indicates the dawning of the Golden Age:

> Thenceforth eternall vnion shall be made
>   Betweene the nations different afore,
>   And sacred Peace shall louingly perswade
>   The warlike minds, to learne her goodly lore,
>   And ciuile armes to exercise no more:
>   Then shall a royall virgin raine, which shall
>   Stretch her white rod ouer the *Belgicke* shore,
>   And the great Castle smite so sore with all,
> That it shall make him shake, and shortly learne to fall.
>
>   But yet the end is not. (3.3.49–50)

It is the final sentence of this chronicle which must structure our understanding of this prophecy in relation to English nationhood. Providence alone cannot bring these visions to pass; on the contrary, human agency is demanded:

> ... Indeed the fates are firme,
> And may not shrinck, though all the world do shake:
> Yet ought mens good endeuours them confirme,
> And guide the heauenly causes to their constant terme. (3.3.25)

Nationhood as envisaged in Merlin's prophecy must be performed continually, and only if both Queen and subjects structure their endeavours according to the ideals provided in turn in the mirror image,

Merlin's chronicles, and, indeed, *The Faerie Queene* as a whole, can this vision become reality. As I have mentioned, the poem's narrative of the nation operates within a double time-scheme which is characteristic for the genre of Golden Age literature, and which Bhabha has analysed as being a specific feature of writing the nation.[41] It represents the English national community, identified with the ruling dynasty, as emerging 'from the myths of time',[42] and at the same time, in the image of the paradisiacal and inviolable body of the Queen defended by her male courtiers, it provides an ideal of nationhood yet to be achieved. There is, however, a deep discrepancy between Elizabeth's actual politics and her courtly writers' visions of the nation, and Spenser in particular is highly critical of her achievements. The Queen as an image of stasis at the end of history is, in his view of things, contrasted with Britomart actively pursuing her quest. Like so much of late Elizabethan panegyrics, this image voices anxiety about England's future and about the Queen's way of dealing with her national 'quest'. The chronicle of the Tudor dynasty ends with Elizabeth declaring the dynasty synonymous with English history. In the logic of Elizabethan panegyrics she must be the obvious culmination of history, because English national history has reached its *telos* and now enters a state of fulfilment. On a historical level, however, despite the usual *fin-de-siècle* anxieties, it will have been obvious that time would go on after the Queen's death, so that this representation of the end of Tudor history-cum-dynasty also hints, not too subtly, at Elizabeth's unsettled succession which disrupts the continuity that is so important for the national community.

Britomart, in contrast, deals with her task differently. Since she instrumentalizes her very body in the service of the nation by giving birth to a whole dynasty, her fertility aspect is not merely metaphorical: it is Britomart's womb from which the Tudor Rose Tree springs, as Merlin's prophecy makes plain:

> For so must all things excellent begin,
> And eke enrooted deepe must be that Tree,
> Whose big embodied braunches shall not lin,
> Till they to heauens hight forth stretched bee.
> For from thy wombe a famous Progenie
> Shall spring, out of the auncient *Troian* blood. (3.3.22)

In the tree-image, the juridical fiction of *translatio imperii* is linked with the myth of the Arthurian ancestry of the Tudors, so that this prophecy casts Britomart as uniting the Trojan civilization and the Tudor empire that is yet to come in her person. It tropes Britomart's prospective fertility in an emblem of dynastic continuity while her very body is the ground out of which the 'tree' grows. So clearly, Britomart's female body is at the core of the national enterprise, providing the material basis for both the synchronic and the diachronic aspect of the nation. In its fertility connotation it denotes the paradisiacal qualities of the English 'garden' as well as the progress of the English national community through time. Yet as the female body is conventionally regarded as in need of defence rather than being capable of self-determined action, Britomart's physical comportment is absolutely crucial to the completion of her task. This is even more precarious as all Spenser's knights must learn how to acquire their respective virtues, with the danger of failure and regression always imminent. Since part of the overall design to 'fashion a Gentleman' is, as we have seen, the containment of the pleasures, many of the *Faerie Queene's* quests include 'narrative(s) of the advance and control of sexuality',[43] and the quest for chastity is certainly paramount among those. Read as such, Britomart's quest is charged with many anxieties: while the national quest is threatened by the difficulties of policing the female warrior's potentially uncontained body, it also voices scepticism about the Queen's willingness to follow Britomart's example: whereas Britomart, like Guyon before her, undergoes this internal 'process of civilization' in order to emerge as a political subject, Elizabeth, by dint of her static virginity, remains remote and thus unfit for action on the historical plane.

The central parameters of chastity as a disciplinary discourse are established during Britomart's encounter with Malecasta, the Lady of Delight, who, by the mere etymology of her name, is introduced as the embodiment of unchastity. Her 'wanton eyes' (3.1.41) are contrasted sharply with Britomart's controlled gaze, and yet their 'wandering eyes' (3.3.24) link Britomart and Malecasta, as the gaze is Britomart's most vulnerable spot. For, characteristically enough, her internal 'wound' (3.2.36) has itself been constituted by an erotic gaze which, in the Neoplatonic context of the quest, has been internalized and transformed into a vision of perfection by Artegall's absence and the impossibility of immediate gratification: 'Tho gan she to renew her former smart,/And thinke of that faire visage, written in her hart' (3.2.29). Although Britomart shares Malecasta's knowledge about erotic desire, she manages to contain her erotic energy in order to fuel her quest. In contrast to Malecasta, who, by satisfying her lust immediately, never even acquires an 'inside', Britomart's body practice is determined by the necessity to control what is 'inside' and to close it off against the 'outside'. So, while her body is a distinct entity, the porous bodies of her adversaries lack this particular distinction. This clear separation of body and world is promoted by Britomart's assumption of a male habitus, for the wearing of armour helps her to control her affective impulses and to shield her vulnerable body surface. Starting as an artificial reinforcement of the outer skin, this containment will ideally be internalized in a mechanism that controls intrusion from 'outside' as well as affective eruptions from 'within'. It thus constitutes her body as having an inside kernel and a protective shell. Yet while Britomart's corporeal containment and the Neoplatonic subtext of the quest clearly show her capable of subjectivity, this potential is not pursued in the poem. Ultimately, the two interior spaces of her body, heart and womb, must merge into one, instrumentalizing erotic desire for a national quest that is concerned with (dynastic and national) continuity. In the service of the nation, the chaste woman's interiority (a precondition for modern subjectivity) is reduced to the material interiority of her womb which is absolutely devoid of transcendental implications. Unburdened by this *gravitas*, the male subject, induced by exactly the same erotic 'wound', can embark on his ascent towards divine perfection.

Like all other knights in *The Faerie Queene*, Britomart is granted a vision of the completion of her quest before the final combat. In the Isis Church episode in Book 5, Canto 7, she has a dream which emphasizes again the complementarity of her quest and Artegall's Irish enterprise. It also voices the anxieties and difficulties besetting the beginnings of British nationhood. In her dream, Britomart is first a priestess of the goddess and is then transformed, to her utter delight, into a queen, a change in appearance and status that may be a vision of the completion of her quest. During this metamorphosis, however, another alteration happens which threatens her royal position:

> And in the midst of her felicity,
>> An hideous tempest seemed from below,
>> To rise through all the Temple sodainely,
>> That from the Altar all about did blow
>> The holy fire, and all the embers strow
>> Vppon the ground, which kindled priuily,
>> Into outragious flames vnwares did grow,
>> That all the Temple put in ieopardy
> Of flaming, and her selfe in great perplexity. (5.7.14)

In terms of body topography, this tempest from 'below' represents Britomart's erotic desire, which had 'kindled priuily' before being attributed providential significance by Merlin. Dispersed sexual energy which must be channelled and put to civilized use is only one manifestation of erotic desire that imperils Britomart's integrity, for as the dream continues a crocodile threatens to swallow her and must be controlled by Isis herself. When Britomart allows the crocodile to approach her,

> ... he so neare her drew,
> That of his game she soone enwombed grew,
> And forth did bring a Lion of great might;
> That shortly did all other beasts subdew. (5.7.16)

The crocodile obviously represents Artegall, but in a very ambiguous way. Drawing on the iconographic conventions of the grotesque and on the emblematic representation of fraud and guile,[44] Britomart's designed lover appears as a creature in whose description untempered aggression and civilization hold a delicate balance, as his somewhat violent courtship of Britomart and the subsequent initiation of a Lion-dynasty seem to indicate. So the second part to the national quest, which broadens the cosy English 'interiority' introduced by Redcrosse towards a preoccupation with the margins, seems to be freighted with ambiguities resulting not only from the difficulties besetting the quest from 'outside', but also from the nature of the quester himself. The prevailing marriage imagery suggests that only the combination of the two national questers can fulfil the visions proclaimed by Merlin and the Isis Church dream, as the dream's translation into a narrative of national destiny by a priest of Isis indicates:

> For that same Crocodile doth represent
> The righteous Knight, that is thy faithfull louer,
> Like to *Osyris* in all iust endeuer.
> For that same Crocodile *Osyris* is,
> That vnder *Isis* feete doth sleepe for euer:
> To shew that clemece oft in things amis,
> Restraines those sterne behests, and cruell doomes of his. (5.7.22)

The dream foreshadows the ambiguities of the Irish quest, and thus complicates the national quest narrative in a way that makes easy polarizations impossible. Erotic desire is necessary, the image implies, but it needs to be stored in the proper place and controlled. Likewise, sternness and even violence might be unavoidable during Artegall's quest, but must be tempered by 'clemence'. Britomart's and Artegall's cross-dressing also contributes to these destabilizing ambiguities. The dream-narrative at Isis Church couples both parts of the British quest by staging both questers' processes of civilization in one and the same vision.

After this vision, Britomart moves on to free Artegall from his enslavement to Radegund, the Amazonian queen, so that he can complete his quest. Radegund is Britomart's counterpart in terms of body practice and also her *alter ego*, as Mihoko Suzuki has demonstrated.[45] The fight of the two woman warriors establishes the limits of female self-determination accompanying a male appearance; yet, as I have pointed out, while the sexually voracious and effeminizing Radegund is a projection of Elizabethan anxieties about female government,[46] Britomart makes use of her divinely sanctioned male appearance within the bounds of a patriarchal order. Whereas Radegund forces Artegall to wear 'womans weedes' (5.5.20) and breaks his sword, Britomart, after having killed Radegund, reinvests him with the insignia of male domination:

> … when as she him anew had clad,
> She was reuiu'd, and ioyd much in his semblance glad.

> So there a while they afterwards remained,
> Him to refresh, and her late wounds to heale:
> During which space she there as Princess rained,
> And changing all that forme of common weale,
> The liberty of women did repeale,
> Which they had long vsurpt; and them restoring
> To mens subiection, did true Iustice deale. (5.7.41–2)

Nevertheless, Britomart is not free of the implications of female insubordination, for, as Suzuki points out, 'the scapegoating of Radigund works ultimately to destroy Britomart as well'.[47] After having restored patriarchy, she leaves Artegall to his task and disappears from the poem. The prospective marriage which will initiate the Tudor dynasty is projected into the apocalyptic future. As with all quests in *The Faerie Queene*, there is no closure to this narrative of the nation, for, as the prophecy runs, 'yet the end is not'. Providing a visionary image of the shape of the ideal national community and its ideal ruler is only the first step, this implies, which must be followed by performative reiteration of the national narrative and continual efforts to put it into practice. In that respect Spenser's visions seem highly disillusioned, for Elizabeth neither lived up to the expectations envisaged in the various images of a quest for chastity and, by implication, national integrity, nor was she willing to identify with the models set up for her. Oscillating between praise and criticism, Elizabethan courtly writers' narratives of the contained body of the Queen as much voice disappointment with the present state of affairs as desire to amend it in the future.

5
Internal Imperialism: Domestic Loyalties

Representations which draw on the inviolability of the Queen's body to symbolize the integrity of the island realm and the exceptional status of the national community form a major part of late Elizabethan courtly panegyrics. Another substantial part is covered by images of the Queen as 'unphysical' goddesses. Many of the classical figures employed to depict Elizabeth are distinctly bodiless, two well-known examples being the chaste moon goddess Cynthia, and the goddess of justice, Astraea. Both are virginal figures with decidedly imperialist implications.

Although both representational matrices can be found throughout the whole of Elizabeth's reign, we can nevertheless witness a gradual shift towards representations of the Queen as an unphysical goddess: cult images of the Queen became more unphysical and esoteric towards the end of the reign. Whereas earlier representations had oscillated between her virginal body, the national community, and the macrocosm, and had merged all three into an image of divine order, the identity-giving concept was later envisaged as a mere idea in the form of a non-physical goddess, while the Queen's actual body was dismissed completely. Detecting a crisis of somatic symbolism in the late sixteenth century, Claire McEachern argues that the image of a centralized body politic, in containing the possibility of a horizontal social community not controlled by the royal will, 'possesses an inherent instability ... also phrased in terms of an excessive corporeality'.[1] Consequently, the control of this levelling potential was voiced in terms of the regulation of corporeality on the part of the multitude as well as on that of the sovereign:

> soueraignes [who] through their natural frailties, are subject as well to the imbecillitie of iudgment, as also to sensuall and irrationall

mocions, rising out of the infectious mudd of flesh and bloud, ... do at the making of Statutes ... drawing supplies out of their politicall bodie ... make good what wanteth in their naturall.[2]

Apparently, as the sixteenth century drew to a close the sovereign's body, like those of her subjects, came to be thought of in terms of physicality and particularity. Presumably this change in perception was coextensive with 'scientific' discoveries and the subsequent restructuring of the taxonomy of medical discourses. It clearly indicates that the belief in analogies between microcosm and macrocosm was on the wane. These new ways of conceptualizing the human body, which were mirrored in new notions of subjectivity as well as in the shift from the notion of one body in two versions to a fundamental sexual dimorphism, ruled out the possibility of convincingly representing a commonwealth in the image of the human body of its ruler. Since the body turned into a signifier of particularity when subjectivity was not conceived in terms of somatic wholeness any more, the human frame could no longer stand for perfection and completeness. In addition, corporeality was increasingly ascribed to the female body while male subjectivity was rendered in terms of transcendence. On the basis of this taxonomy, the female body could no longer embody Edenic completeness, fertility, and inviolability, and stronger symbols were required in order to formulate the universalist claims of the body politic and the nation. They were provided by Neoplatonic 'love' discourses and the idea of empire, both drawing on images which rendered the Queen as disembodied 'first mover', but beyond worldly concerns. The body endowed with an aura of divine order did not, however, immediately cease to exist. In the representations of the Queen in the later years of her reign, both kinds of images were being employed and coexisted more or less unproblematically, voicing different versions of the national community. While the territorialized body image stressed the development of the national community into a 'deep horizontal comradeship',[3] representations of disembodied goddesses focussed on the monarch's unifying role.

Discussing the 'imperial' idea and its representations does not necessarily imply that the doctrine of 'imperial' monarchy as voiced in England from the 1580s on did have political implications, or that it led directly to imperialist action. As William Sherman has recently claimed, 'As long as Elizabeth reigned – and for some time after – the British Empire remained a textual affair.'[4] Rather, the notion of 'imperial' monarchy could be comprehended as a mode of expressing the claims of the monarch to sovereignty within her realm (which was soon to become the national territory), and, subsequently and still closely tied to her person, the universalist claims of the ideology of 'nationhood' for all members of the community. In this context, the 'imperial' idea represented the absolutist claims of the Queen against internal divisions along the lines of the ancient feudal loyalties. Thus it was also an instrument in the struggle of a centralized state power against the particularized power of the landed aristocracy.[5] It seems that the articulation of 'imperialist' aspirations, even if they were later instrumentalized for the legitimation of colonialist ventures, voiced domestic anxieties about the subjects' loyalty to the Queen and the 'nation' rather than the desire for territorial expansion. Frances Yates has pointed out in her magisterial study of the imperial idea in the sixteenth century, that

> the extravagant language used of Elizabeth need not necessarily imply that Elizabethan hopes went so far as to expect a world empire for the queen. (...) The lengths to which the cult of Elizabeth went are a measure of the sense of isolation which had at all costs to find a symbol strong enough to provide a feeling of spiritual security in the face of the break with the rest of Christendom.[6]

The ideology of 'imperial monarchy' casts Elizabeth as the 'empress' who is responsible for the entry of the right faith into the world, who will reform a scattered Europe and reunite it under the auspices of universal peace, justice, and a unified belief.[7] The notion of the translation of empire from Troy via Rome to London emphasized the point that, having descended from one root, Europe should be brought back to unity in a new Augustan age. As Yates has argued, the 'feudalization' of the imperial idea accompanying the representation of northern emperors since Charlemagne had also provided it with a decidedly political tone.[8]

In courtly panegyrics, the idea of imperial monarchy was activated in moments of domestic crisis. The tradition of 'imperial' ideology, with all its facets of religious reform, teleological derivation of rulership, and the translation of empire from Troy to England, provided the framework for a set of non-physical representations of the Queen which formulated royal claims to the undivided loyalty of her subjects. The image in particular of Cynthia, goddess of the seas and the moon, set the standards for negotiations of the relationship of male courtier and female 'goddess' under the auspices of 'imperialist' aspirations. The Cynthia image, which is very ambiguous in its balance of praise and criticism, linked the notion of the 'chaste beloved' of Petrarchan discourse with the imperial idea, endowing it with a political dimension. As Helen Hackett has pointed out, the moon aspect of Cynthia and Diana images could be employed to voice disillusionment with the Queen's reign while on the surface upholding the impression of praising her as a goddess: 'For one thing, the moon as a source of light was dependent upon and secondary to the sun; it was therefore often used as an image of female inferiority. It was also associated with the troubling changeability of the female body (...) The moon as symbol was therefore an effective vehicle for challenging the Queen as icon.'[9]

For the male courtier, the rhetoric of courtly love addressed to the Queen-as-beloved thus constituted a means to voice concerns about his personal relationship with the centre of power and his position at court, as well as his standing within the community as a whole. The Queen was represented as a goddess to be adored, as a divine person different in kind, not merely in degree. Rather than dealing with actual romantic attachments, the courtly love rhetoric was 'a highly codified system, a series of signs aimed at reassuring the prince or mistress of the suitor's unquestioning and dutiful service'.[10] Drawing on the ambiguities inherent in the fact that ' "being at court" and "wooing a lady" share a semantic field',[11] the courtier fashioned himself as a (Petrarchan) lover, offering his loyalty in exchange for patronage. In a very elementary sense, the courtier-subject thus 'originates as one who is under domination',[12] as a creature of his Queen. At the same time, the 'Queen' was a creature of his: imagining her as Cynthia, Astraea, or Gloriana likewise enabled the courtier to 'write his Queen anew'.[13] Mastering courtly discourse was thus not only instrumental in fashioning a male courtier subject in relation to the Queen, but was also a means of fashioning the Queen and the political entity she represented. As Louis Montrose puts it, 'the Petrarchan lover worships a deity of his own making and under his own control'.[14]

I have claimed before that the courtier-subject developed interdependently with the imagined community he was part of, endeavouring to imagine both in a way that assigned to him a position of power. Consequently, any representation of the Queen was also a statement about state power and the emerging national community. Starting out from Sidney's sonnet cycle *Astrophil and Stella*, Andrew Hadfield analogizes the courtly lady and the nation as both authorizing the lyrical 'I', while at the same time both 'Stella' and the nation 'depend upon the prior articulation of the male voice'.[15] Within this decidedly gendered framework, writing Stella (or, as it were, Cynthia), fashioning the (male) self, and imagining the nation emerge as complementary articulations of the same process, or as Richard Helgerson puts it, 'text, self, and nation are "true images" of one another'.[16] In Helgerson's description of the Elizabethan younger generation's efforts to write a nation whose literary spokesmen they could then become, the same impetus at mastering a discourse that would then evaluate the author's self is at work, as in the sonnet writer's attempt to fashion himself by writing his beloved. Applying to the lyrical 'I' of Sidney as well as to any effort to fashion a self by imagining the desired 'other', Hadfield concludes that the Petrarchan 'lover' 'may not know the addressee who does not appear, but he does come to know himself through writing it (...). She becomes the vanishing point of a discourse of national identity which is never explicitly stated but depends upon the identity of the poet speaking.'[17]

Once again, the national community is envisaged as female. Though this version of the imagined community is different from the visions drawing directly on the contained body of the Queen, they both provide the kind of otherness necessary to fashion a male subject, but they do so on the basis of different taxonomies. Whereas articulations of England as earthly paradise drew on the notion of a unified, 'microcosmic' body containing, as a possibility, both genders, articulations of the body politic as disembodied, transcendental entity operated on the basis of a fundamental difference between male and female bodies. They offered subjectivity to the male courtier while casting the female body as mere matter, unable to transcend its earthly limitations.

Articulations of the Queen, the nation, and the lyrical 'I' of the poet hold a precarious balance in representations addressing Elizabeth in terms of Petrarchan love discourse. What happens when the divine addressee proves to be unwilling to correspond to the poet's imaginings is enacted in Walter Ralegh's poem *The 21st: and last booke of the Ocean to Scinthia*. This text, ostensibly a fragment of a longer poem written during the 1580s, the time of Ralegh's rise to power, presents the lover as one whose ambition has been thwarted by the unexpected behaviour of his beloved. The poem and its use of the Cynthia image may be read as a re-enactment of Ralegh's misdeed (he had married one of Elizabeth's maids of honour), and thus as the attempt to write his transgression out of the narrative, presenting him as ever faithful and loyal. Drawing heavily on the moon aspect of the image, it provides him with the vehicle to voice his disillusionment while allegedly assuring the Queen of his loyalty. Written in the Tower in 1592 during

Ralegh's imprisonment for his clandestine marriage to Elizabeth Throckmorton, this way of self-fashioning draws on the love paradigm in a conscious distortion of actual events: within the Petrarchan love pattern, the lady's withdrawal of favour is by definition not the lover's fault. Instead of admitting his trespass and showing contrition, the lyrical 'I' here presents his error as a trifle while blaming Cynthia for her cruelty and arbitrariness. Striving to prove his loyalty, that is, assuring Cynthia of his everlasting love, he puts the blame for the failure of their relationship on her: she has withdrawn her light from him, thus runs the dominant image, and so condemned him to a living death:

> Sufficeth it to yow my joyes interred,
> in simpell wordes that I my woes cumplayne,
> Yow that then died when first my fancy erred,
> joyes under dust that never live agayne. (1–4)[18]

Cynthia is the central light in his universe, endowed with the power to give and withhold life. She is fickle Fortuna, governing the fates of men, and at the same time is the ruler of nature who is not subject to time or change. The lyrical 'I', on the other hand, presents himself as having followed her every command, even against his own personal interest:

> The honor of her love, love still devisinge
> woundinge my mind with contrary consayte
> transferde it sealf sumetyme to her aspiringe
> sumetyme the trumpett of her thoughts retrayt
> To seeke new worlds, for golde, for prayse, for glory,
> to try desire, to try love severed farr
> when I was gonn shee sent her memory
> more stronge then weare tenthowsand shipps of warr
> to call mee back, to leve great honors thought
> to leve my frinds, my fortune, my attempte
> to leve the purpose I so longe had sought
> and holde both cares and cumforts in contempt. (57–68)

Yet instead of rewarding him for his loyalty and compensating him for what he has lost by obeying her command, Cynthia has forsaken him, leaving him lifeless, 'as a boddy violently slayne / [that] retayneath warmth although the spirrit be gonn' (73–4) and 'Alone, forsaken, frindless onn the shore' (89).

Re-enacting the scene of his transgression, the lyrical 'I' draws on the well-known Neoplatonic distinction between heavenly and earthly love, and sets a difference in kind between Elizabeth-as-Cynthia and Elizabeth Throckmorton: Cynthia is the unphysical mover of the universe, while his wife is cast in terms of earthly matter that is only a poor copy of a divine reality. Being addressed as 'form (...) externall', she is not even mentioned as a person:

> And though strong reason holde before myne eyes
> the Images, and formes of worlds past
> teachinge the cause why all thos flames that rize
> from formes externall, cann no longer last,
> then that thos seeminge bewties hold in pryme,
> loves ground, his essence, and his emperye,
> all slaves to age, and vassalls unto tyme
> of which repentance writes the tragedye. (174–81)

This split represents Cynthia as the idea of love while reinscribing earthly love as corporeality, thus synecdochically identifying women, the deficient materialization of the divine idea, with their bodies. The distinction between the Earthly and Heavenly Venus here serves to promote and establish new concepts of love and gender difference. Although being already slightly anachronistic and gradually replaced by Protestant ideas about married love (which contain female corporeality in the service of the community), the Neoplatonic paradigm is here employed to envisage an essential difference between the Queen's and ordinary women's bodies on the basis of a polarization between corporeality and transcendence. Love of the Heavenly Venus enables the male subject to leave behind his physical confinements, a transcendence that, due to the gendered positions in this discourse, is not available to women. Intertwining his former imaginings of his beloved with his present condition, the lover proves unable to fashion himself without her. Whereas his situation has changed dramatically, Cynthia is still the focus necessary for his self-fashioning. The dominant feeling that regulates the lover's self-relation as well as his relation to the centre of power by providing a site for introspection is still dealt with by the pen. By writing his Queen, even if only 'in the dust' (91), he still writes himself, except that now sorrow or woe have replaced love as the central emotion. The erotic paradigm, constituting the 'I' by writing an absence, is still valid.

And yet the poem is pervaded by an overwhelming sense of fragmentation as an effect of Cynthia's withdrawing of light and life. His relationship to Cynthia determines the lover's image of himself and is crucial to the development of his subjectivity. As his mistress has proved reluctant to correspond to her written image, the lover's 'object, and invention' (37), his self-image is likewise shattered: the lyrical 'I' speaks about the 'broken monuments of my great desires' (14) and casts the instigator of his 'fall' in terms of tempestuous nature:

> Yet as the eayre in deip caves under ground
> is strongly drawne when violent heat hath rent
> great clefts therin, till moysture do abound
> and then the same imprisoned, and uppent,
> breakes out in yearthquakes teringe all asunder,
> So in the Center of my cloven hart,
> my hart, to whom her bewties wear such wounder
> lyes the sharpe poysoned head of that loves dart
> which till all breake and all desolve to dust
> thence drawne it cannot bee. (450–9)

Taking the erotic matrix of courtly rhetoric literally, in his frustration the lover sometimes conflates the two Elizabeths, representing Cynthia, in accordance with the moon paradigm, as a fickle female, who 'will (...) be a wooman for a fashion' (203). We should remember here that this is exactly what the author has been ousted from court for: having taken the materialization for the idea of love, he has disrupted the signifying economy of the court. Struggling to retain control over his narrative, Ralegh's lyrical persona now casts his representation of the Queen as a kind of Machiavellian Fortuna (which he is unable to constrain), and describes her in terms of unbounded water which is traditionally associated with 'uncontained' female corporeality:[19]

> And as a streame by strong hand bounded in
> from natures course wher it did sumetyme runn
> by sume small rent or loose part douth beginn
> to finde escape, till it a way hath woone
> douth then all unawares in sunder teare
> the forsed bounds and raginge, runn att large
> in th'auncient channells as the wounted weare
> such is of weemens love the carefull charge
> helde, and mayntaynde with multetude of woes

> of longe arections such the suddayne fall
> onn houre deverts, onn instant overthrowes
> for which our lives, for which our fortunes thrale. (221–32)[20]

The Fortuna image, which is latent throughout the poem and ties in neatly with the moon imagery, renders Cynthia's behaviour as completely arbitrary while clearing the lover from any charges of misconduct. And yet the mastery he hopes to gain over his 'lady' by reinscribing her as cruel and arbitrary goddess collapses when he fails to distinguish clearly between his earthly and his heavenly 'mistress'.

As a consequence of his fall from favour, the lover's perception of the court changes. Whereas it was seen as another Arcadia while Cynthia's light was still shining on him, he now perceives it as a kind of Hobbesian wasteland where whoever is cast out of the sovereign's favour is doomed to death:

> So of affection which our youth presented
> when shee that from the soonn reves poure and light
> did but decline her beames as discontented
> convertinge sweetest dayes to saddest night
> all droopes, all dyes, all troden under dust
> the person, place, and passages forgotten
> the hardest steele eaten with softest ruste
> the firme and sollide tree both rent and rotten,
> thos thoughts so full of pleasure and content
> that in our absence weare affections foode
> ar rased out and from the fancy rent
> in highest grace and harts deere care that stood
> ar cast for pray to hatred, and to scorne
> our deerest treasors and our harts trew joyes
> the tokens hunge onn brest, and kyndly worne
> ar now elcewhere disposde, or helde for toyes
> and thos which then our Jelosye removed
> and others for our sakes then valued deere
> the on forgot the rest are deere beloved
> when all of ours douth strange or vilde apeere. (249–68)

His description captures beautifully the essential mechanisms of the courtly dynamics and behaviour, the wearing of tokens, the preferment of the favourite's friends, the insistence that those be removed who are disliked by him. Yet all of a sudden Fortuna has turned the tables on him;

thus the lover's self-presentation subtly elides the fact that his fall from favour was his own fault. While he is cast out, others assume his place; while his identity is shattered, theirs is framed. Striving to put the pieces together, the lover turns again to Cynthia, or, to be precise, to himself via the goddess. Sorrow as the central topic of the complaint now gives him another identity in that, by thematizing a structuring loss, it provides a site for introspection which enables him to rewrite himself by rewriting the Queen. The poem concludes, however, not with a reconciliation of the lover and his goddess, but by his turning, like his literary forebear Petrarch at the end of the *Canzoniere*, to the grace of a greater God:

> as it was herrs, so lett his mercies bee,
> of my last cumforts, the essentiall meane.
>> But be it so, or not, th'effects, ar past,
>> her love hath end, my woe must ever last. (519–22)

Even this last move towards transcendence is overshadowed by the lover's sorrow, so that, as Stephen Greenblatt remarks, 'The Twenty-First Book ends not on a note of divine consolation, but with an expression of private grief.'[21]

Ralegh's use of the Cynthia image in order to prove his loyalty and to reinscribe himself as a faithful subject is unique in its gloomy mood and its enactment of failure. Other subjects were obviously more successful in their use of the image. The Earl of Hertford's entertainment for the Queen at Elvetham in 1591 likewise functions on the base of a conjunction of courtly love rhetoric and the idea of imperial monarchy. It casts the Queen as Cynthia, empress of the sea, who transforms the world and performs miracles by her mere presence (which rules out, as the editor Jean Wilson dryly remarks, the possibility of disruption of the performance by the Queen).[22] This exquisitely lavish entertainment – the host had completely remodelled his estate, creating a crescent-shaped lake of about a hundred yards across at its widest point with three islands in order to stage an Italian-style water-pageant – presents the Queen in various guises, all of them sharing features of disembodiment and imperial connotations.[23] She is Astraea, the Fairy Queen, and, most prominently, Phoebe or Cynthia. She is the sun and likewise the moon; she

> like the Sunne for shew, to Gods for vertue,
> Fills all with Majesty, and holy feare.

> More learned then ourselves, shee ruleth us:
> More rich than Seas, shee doth commaund the Seas:
> More fair then Nimphs, she governs all the Nimphs:
> More worthy then the Gods, she wins the Gods. (104)

The symbolic centre of the visit is the second day's entertainment, which stages a water pageant, the participants being Nereus, the Prophet of the Sea, the gods Neptune, Oceanus, Phorcus, and Glaucus, several ships carrying Neaera, the supposed beloved of the wood-god Sylvanus, and other nymphs being beleaguered by Tritons. The setting of the scene is the crescent-shaped lake with a fully armed fort on one island and a 'Snayl Mount' on the other, and the Queen's location is in a canopy at the lake's head.

Nereus' oration assembles all the features of the imperial idea as manifest in Elizabethan renderings of the Cynthia figure. Addressing the Queen as 'Faire Cinthia the wide Ocean's Empresse', he represents the sea gods as

> impatient, that this worthles earth
> Should beare your Highnes weight, and we Sea-gods,
> (Whose jealous waves have swallowd up your foes,
> And to your Realme are walles impregnable),
> With such large favour seldome time are grac't. (109)

Attributing the Armada victory to the active intervention of natural powers, he renders England's geopolitical isolation not in terms of the Queen's virginity but as effected by the geographical location of the island realm, whose surrounding waters are shown to be serviceable to the Queen-goddess. The Spanish, threatening the integrity of the island realm of Cynthia, which is represented as a fort raised by Neptune for the Queen's defence (110) and thus also testifies to the underlying dissociation of her body from the national territory, are transformed by her mere look and revealed for what they are:

> Yon ugly monster creeping from the South
> To spoyle these blessed fields of Albion,
> By selfe same beams is chang'd into a snaile. (109–10)

The power of the Spanish is here ridiculed as of 'not of force to hurt' (110) and diminished by the beams of the Queen's gaze: 'For what cannot your gracious looks effect?' (109)

The Queen's gaze, figured in the conventional images of divine light and the beams of the sun, seems to be the sole agent in this pageant. It is not the physical presence of the Queen but the gaze of the divinely hypostasized Elizabeth-as-Cynthia that works miracles in this entertainment and that refines and quasi-sublimates (in the alchemical sense of the word, which is not too far from the modern psychoanalytical usage) the natural world into some higher order of being. When Sylvanus, the wood god, is confronted with 'Cynthia's' beams he claims that, almost like a magnet, they draw everybody's eyes to them: 'those faire beames that shoote from Majesty, … drew our eyes to wonder at thy worth' (111). Thus, the beams of 'faire Cinthia' also have the power to civilize the savage wood-god, a passage that in a way echoes Una's encounter with the 'salvage' nation in *The Faerie Queene* I, 6.[24] The possible usefulness of this image of Elizabeth-as-Cynthia who civilizes the wild men of the earth in a colonial context is obvious, although colonialist activity is not (yet) the dominant context of the image. However, the subject of sea venture and discovery is hinted at in Neaera's speech, which concludes the second day's entertainment. Elizabeth is here presented with a ship by Neptune and asked to name it, her appearance being prophesied before by Nereus:

> Thine eyes (Neaera) shall in time behold
> A sea-borne Quene, worthy to governe Kings:
> On her depends the fortune of thy boate,
> If shee but name it with a blisfull word,
> And view it with her life-inspiring beames.
> Her beames yeeld gentle influence, like fayre starres. (112)

Elizabeth duly names the ship 'The Bonadventure', thus subtly linking her political impact ('worthy to governe Kings') with the economical implications of the sea-venture in the image of the ship, a gift of Neptune, incidentally, just like the island fort which is to shield Elizabeth from her 'southern' enemies. The ship image here intricately links the island realm, a territorialized version of the 'ship of state', the Queen, and the economic possibilities of overseas ventures. We should, however, discern economic from political 'imperialism': authorizing overseas ventures does not automatically imply sanctioning territorial conquest.

I have argued before that the imperial idea as voiced in the image of Cynthia might be closely linked to questions of domestic loyalty and courtly self-fashioning. When regarding the actual audience of the Elvetham spectacle and their relations to the Queen and state power, it becomes clear that loyalty to Elizabeth was indeed the central issue here. The fact that Cynthia was chosen as an appropriate representation of the Queen in this context sheds some light on the psychosocial function of the image. The host of the Elvetham entertainment was Edward Seymour, who was Earl of Hertford, nephew of Jane Seymour, third wife of Henry VIII, and son to the Lord Protector Somerset. A family connection to the Queen, Seymour had in 1561 clandestinely married Lady Catherine Grey, a sister of Lady Jane Grey, who had been set on the throne in 1553 by Somerset's successor Norfolk and then executed, and a cousin to the Queen from the (Protestant) Suffolk line. Both Seymour and his wife were thus closely related to the Queen and had claims to the throne. Had Elizabeth died before 1567, Lady Catherine would have been next of blood in the Protestant line; Mary Stuart had a similar claim, but was a Catholic.[25] Both Catherine Grey and Edward Seymour were therefore eyed with suspicion by the Queen as possible malcontents. Catherine Grey, however, died in 1567, and by the time the pageant took place the Earl of Hertford was married to Frances Howard (not to be confused with the notorious Countess of Somerset of the same name). It is obvious, however, that Seymour, who was being honoured with a royal visit for the first time in his life, felt the necessity to stage his loyalty. And it seems from the evidence of other instances in which it was brought up that the 'Cynthia' image was deemed appropriate when one's loyalty was called in question. Interestingly, clandestine marriages – that is, matches not sanctioned by the Queen – were frequently regarded as a disloyalty towards the sovereign, and Elizabeth's obsession with controlling her subjects' marriages is well-known. Yet rather than interpreting it as the manifestation of jealousy or simply the spleen of the unmarried Queen, her marriage policy may be seen as a necessary measure to prevent agglomerations of power outside the court. As David Lindley's brilliant study on the fate and representations of Frances Howard, Countess of Somerset, has shown, marriage in the early modern period was still very much concerned with the strengthening of kinship ties and the building-up of power connections.[26] The control of these alternative power centres and the confirmation of their loyalty to the sovereign must therefore be a central concern of any 'absolutist' monarch.

In representing his Queen as Cynthia who rules the wild men of the woods as well as the inhabitants of the sea, Seymour casts her as holding complete sway over the minds of men, and as ruling all the world by her gaze. Gaze and vision, however, presuppose presence, and possibly Seymour, by staging the life-giving and civilizing power of the Queen's gaze, subtly acknowledges the purpose of the Queen's visit by hinting at the necessity of royal ubiquity as a precondition that ensures her subjects' loyalties.

The Cynthia image was used in a similar context in John Lyly's court play *Endimion* of 1586.[27] One of the most striking features of this play is the complete reversal of the roles of courtier and monarch, Endimion and Cynthia, in Lyly's allegory of courtly life. It has been said before that it was in the interests of the Leicester–Walsingham faction to represent the Queen as more or less static 'prime mover', and thus ascribe agency to the male courtier, who then chose the role of forester or wild man rather than shepherd, as Leicester did in the Woodstock entertainment of 1575. The emphasis on the active rather than the contemplative way of life was consistent, of course, with a political focus on militant Protestantism and active intervention. Lyly however, being a protégé of Lord Burghley's son-in-law Edward de Vere, earl of Oxford,[28] presents us with a vision of the courtier as favouring a contemplative life. His version of the Endymion myth casts Cynthia as the divine centre of the courtly 'universe', who not only authorizes all actions but who is active herself (if only by 'influence'), while Endymion is doomed to complete passivity. Though Elizabeth might have applauded this turn in her courtly representations, she will certainly not have liked the criticism of her person and politics implied in the moon image which is predominant in the play. We shall see how far Lyly's play, though ostensibly endowing her with more agency, nevertheless voices criticism of Elizabeth's role in the courtly dynamics.

The Greek source of the myth relates how the shepherd Endymion is found sleeping by the moon goddess Selene and, upon her kiss, falls into some deeper sleep which preserves his youth and beauty (in some versions the moon is said to have fifty daughters by Endymion).[29] Lyly attributes the enchantment to the jealousy of another female character, Tellus, who is in love with Endymion, who in turn has forsaken her for his hopeless passion for Cynthia. With the help of the witch Dipsas, Tellus enchants him into a perpetual sleep, during which he ages dramatically. His friend Eumenides finds out that the spell can be broken by Cynthia's kiss. The goddess, in a reversal of the classical Briar Rose situation, awakes Endymion with a kiss and, upon reaffirmation of his courtly service to her, restores his youth.

Interestingly, the central dyad of the myth is here widened into a triad: Tellus, Cynthia, and Endymion are the key personages of the play, and it is Tellus who actually instigates the main plot. As a counter-figure to the moon goddess, Tellus (whose name signifies 'earth') is a projection of all that Cynthia is not. Although both are addressed as female, it is Tellus who embodies female corporeality and who is the subject of many 'sexist' allusions in this rather misogynistic play. In terms of Neoplatonic love, Tellus and Cynthia impersonate the Earthly and Heavenly Venus and are thus foci of different kinds of desire. Both are beautiful but in fact incomparable as being different in kind, as Tellus' confidante Floscula points out in the very beginning of the play:

> Madame, if you woulde compare the state of *Cynthia* with your owne, and the height of *Endimion* his thoughts, with the meanenesse of your fortune, you would rather yeeld then contende, being betweene you and her no comparison. (I.2.13–16)

In dealing with her beauty and the desire it attracts, Tellus is represented as endowed with all the negative attributes traditionally ascribed to women. Her body, by her mere name associated with the earth, has an actual sensual presence, and is described in images of plenty and fertility:

> (I)s not my beauty diuine, whose body is decked with faire flowers, and vaines are Vines, yeelding sweet liquor to the dullest spirits, whose eares are Corne, to bring strength, and whose heares are grasse, to bring abundance? Doth not Frankinsence & Myrrhe breath out of my nostrils, and all the sacrifice of the Gods breede in my bowels? Infinite are my creatures, without which neyther thou, nor *Endimion*, nor any could loue, or liue. (I.2.19–26)

In contrast to the representations of Elizabeth's body as virginal locus of peace and plenty, these associations of abundance are now being discredited as grotesque and anarchic. Tellus' 'earthy' beauty is no longer divine (and maybe the question form hints at the ambiguities of the image), while Cynthia's incorporeal beauty instigates the contemplation of divine beauty: 'O Fayre *Cynthia*! O vnfortunate *Endimion*! Why was not thy byrth as high as thy thoughts, or her beautie lesse then heauenlie? or why are not thyne honors as rare as her beautie?' (II.1.1–4). In fact, it is the contemplation of the beloved lady and the desire to catch a glimpse of divine majesty through the vision of the lady's beauty that is advocated as the ideal courtly behaviour in this play. As Endymion puts it in the very beginning:

> O *Cynthia*, if thou shouldest alwaies continue at thy fulnes, both Gods and men woulde conspire to rauish thee. But thou to abate the pride of our affections, dost detract from thy perfections, thinking it sufficient, if once in a month we enioy a glymse of thy maiestie. (I.1.58–62)

This very ambiguous passage, which could be read as criticism and praise alike, hints at the dual nature of the moon, endeavouring to give her mutability a positive turn. In any case, this variation of the *constans in levitate* topos makes clear that Cynthia has no palpable physicality, no body which could be possessed by any lover. Endymion's wish 'eyther to die, or possesse the Moone herselfe' (I.1.14–15) is consequently termed madness by his friend Eumenides: 'Without doubt *Endimion* is bewitched, otherwise in a man of such rare vertues there could not harbor a minde of such extreame madnes.' (I.1.76–8) Ideally, the lover's relationship to this 'Heavenly Venus' should be one of contemplation, leading to his elevation to some higher sphere of being. But a necessary precondition for this transcendence is the realization that physical gratification is impossible and that, refraining from worldly pleasures, he will be led to pleasures of a higher order:

> I am that *Endimion* (sweet *Cynthia*) that haue carryed my thoughts in equall ballance with my actions, being alwaies as free from imagining ill, as enterprysing; that *Endimion*, whose eyes neuer esteemed anie thing faire but thy face, whose tongue termed nothing rare but thy vertues, and whose hart imagined nothing miraculous but thy gouernment. Yea, that *Endimion*, who diuorsing himselfe from the amiablenes of all Ladies, the brauerie of all Courts, the companie of al men, hath chosen in a solitarie Cell to liue, onely by feeding on thy fauour, accounting in the worlde (but thy selfe) nothing excellent, nothing immortal; thus maist thou see euerie vaine, sinew, muscle, and artery of my loue, in which there is no flatterie, nor deceipt, error, nor arte. (II.1.33–45)

Endymion, staging himself as contemplative lover vowing the integrity of his love, is revealed in the course of the play to be a master of courtly self-fashioning and the rhetoric of courtship: the above-quoted speech ends with an aside that uncovers the full degree of his courtly dissembling: 'But soft, here commeth *Tellus*, I must turne my other face to her like *Ianus*, least she be as suspicious as *Juno*.' (II.1.45–6) There is no doubt about the propriety of the ideal of contemplative love; however, there seems to be some doubt about whether the court is the right place to enact it. The play is full of allusions to dissembling and deception as the main survival techniques at court,[30] and Endymion's plight is to a large degree caused by his deceptiveness towards Tellus. It is Tellus, however, who is represented as the master and, due to her gender, the quasi-embodiment of court intrigue. In the encounter following Endymion's impersonation of the contemplative lover, he Janus-facedly vows his love to Tellus: 'You know (fayre *Tellus*) that the sweet remembrance of your loue, is the onely companion of my life, and thy presence, my paradise.' Upon Tellus' suspicious question, 'Is it not possible for you *Endimion*, to dissemble?' the answer is: 'Not, *Tellus*, vnlesse I could make me a woman.' (II.1.53–60) The gendering of the discourse of courtly deception supposedly clears Endymion of the negative implications of deceptiveness: as a courtier he moves in a medium in which social ambition is reinscribed as desire, and both are voiced in a discourse of love.[31] This way of self-fashioning naturally presupposes a high degree of self-reflexivity and thus almost necessarily leads to highly strategic versions of the 'self'. Deceptiveness as an essential part of courtly rhetoric is what is expected of the courtier in order to master this highly codified ritual. The fact that a female monarch is the central figure of this courtly world provides a whole set of references and paradigms of behaviour for her male courtiers and regulates their comportment by a complex web of codes and rituals. The rigidly gendered nature of this discourse, however, makes it impossible for women to approach the Queen in the same way. Rather, there is a strong sense of competition in other women's relations to Cynthia in Lyly's play, and the code of approved behaviour for them differs completely from that for men. Thus, deception is coded as an inherently female vice, while for men it is an essential part of their self-fashioning. In Tellus' case, deception is linked to her 'earthy' femininity, in which Cynthia does not participate. Tying in with that, Tellus is also associated with the witch Dipsas, whose wickedness is manifest in her grotesque body, rendering the ideal of female beauty as deceptive in itself: Tellus and Dipsas here emerge as a kind of Madam World-allegory, the beauty of the young woman being inextricably linked to the foulness of the crone. In a comic sub-plot mocking the ideals of love and beauty of the main plot, Sir Tophas describes the qualities of his beloved Dipsas:

> O what a fine thin hayre hath *Dipsas*! What a prettie low forehead! What a tall & statelie nose! What little hollowe eyes! What great and goodly lypes! Howe harmlesse shee is beeing toothlesse! her fingers fatte and short, adorned with long nayles like a Bytter! In howe sweete a proportion her cheekes hange downe to her brests like dugges, and her pappes to her waste like bagges! What a lowe stature shee is, and yet what a great foote shee carryeth! Howe thrifty must she be in whom there is no waste! Howe vertuous is shee like to be, ouer whom no man can be ielous! (III.3.52–60)

His vision is contradicted by one of the pages, who sums up the dominant judgement on old women: 'That vglie creature? Why shee is a foole, a scold, fat, without fashion, and quite without fauour.' (III.3.88–9) In a discourse in which so much depends upon vision while at the same time eyesight may be deceptive, it is of course imperative that the distinction between Cynthia and Tellus be made clear. While the body of Tellus is thus marked out as the site of sensuality and immanence, her counterpart Cynthia, the Heavenly Venus, is no such thing. She possesses the kind of esoteric beauty that moves her lovers to the contemplation of divine perfection, but is not physically alluring. The contemplative life, quite in accordance with Neoplatonic philosophy, is here valued more highly than the active life, with direct implications on the representation of the relationship of Queen and courtier.[32]

As it is the vision of divine beauty that triggers the ascent towards divine perfection by way of contemplative living, it is of course only consistent of Tellus to bereave Endymion of the capacity to see and contemplate Cynthia's beauty. Having proved to be as deceptive as Tellus herself, Endymion turns to earth, as Corsites remarks (with a wonderful pun on 'lying' as a synonym for 'deception'): 'turnd, I thinke, to earth, with lying so long on the earth' (IV.3.11–12). The symbolic representation of Endymion as having almost merged into Tellus/the earth might also hint at possible misconduct in terms of sexual behaviour. If Endymion can indeed be read as an allegorical figure for the Earl of Leicester, as Bond and other nineteenth-century editors of the play read him, this might be an allusion to his clandestine marriage to Lettice Knollys in 1578. Being caught in a kind of suspension between life and death for having given in to the Earthly Venus while professing to chastely adore the Heavenly one, Endymion becomes estranged from court, lacking the means to ingratiate himself again with the centre of power. His friend Eumenides thus takes the role of intercessor. In the desert, contemplating his friend's fate and his own unrequited love to Semele, he finds the remedy for Endymion's plight in a magic well. Again it is the power of vision that grants access to divine truth: only the true lover can read the message of the well:

> *When shee whose figure of all is the perfectest, and neuer to bee measured – alwaies one, yet neuer the same – still inconstant, yet neuer wauering – shall come and kisse Endimion in his sleepe, hee shall then rise; els neuer.* (III.4.155–9)

Cynthia's power thus reinscribed as divine truth actually restores Endymion to life: with a climactic kiss (which only the nineteenth-century editor, not the text itself, describes as a remedy 'coyly applied'),[33] the only instance of touch on the part of Cynthia, Endymion is restored to life. Cynthia's kiss is the first acknowledgement of her favour for Endymion, and a very exceptional one at that, as she herself claims:

> (A)lthough my mouth hath beene heere tofore as vntouched as my thoughts, yet now to recouer thy life … I will do that to *Endimion* which yet neuer mortall man coulde bost of heretofore, nor shall euer hope for heereafter. (V.1.20–3)

Besides the air of sexual innuendo accompanying this representation of the Queen and her favourite, Cynthia is also rendered as being completely unaware of Endymion's share of guilt in his situation. His self-presentation as her lover and as victim of Tellus' sorceries is so convincing that it is believed as truth, while Tellus and the witch Dipsas are cast as vile enchantresses. Endymion, vowing courtly love again, is rejuvenated by Cynthia, which sets him on a level with the goddess who is not subject to time, while all the others have aged by forty years. Unable to see the full degree of his deceptiveness, she determines the hegemonic versions of events by virtue of her power, just as, quite arbitrarily, she determines the position of each courtier. As a comment on the relationship of Elizabeth and her court and on the influence of Leicester on the Queen, this is of course highly revealing.

Court life is a constant struggle for the attention of the Queen – so much is obvious from Lyly's play – and intrigue and dissembling are

the vehicles through which status is gained. After waking up, Endymion
relates a rather ghastly dream vision of courtly life:

> I behelde many wolues barking at thee *Cynthia*, who hauing ground
> their teeth to bite, did with striuing bleede themselues to death.
> There might I see ingratitude with an hundred eyes, gazing for ben-
> efites, and with a thousand teeth, gnawing on the bowelles wherein
> shee was bred. Trecherie stoode all cloathed in white, with a smyling
> countenance, but both her handes bathed in blood. Enuye with a
> pale and megar face...stood shooting at starres, whose dartes fell
> downe againe on her owne face. There might I beholde Drones, or
> Beetles...creeping vnder the winges of a princely Eagle, who being
> carried into her neast, sought there to sucke that veine, that woulde
> haue killed the Eagle. (V.1.120–32)

It is the 'outside', the hermit's place, that is represented as the locus of
truth in the play.[34] In this confrontation of court and hermitage
Cynthia does not really take sides. She rules both, as she does all the
world, not by active participation but by 'influence', that is, without
actually being part of the political world: 'Is it not impossible to measure her, who still worketh by her influence, neuer standing at one
stay'. (III.4.171–2) Yet she governs 'court' and 'country' in different
ways, and the spaces are gendered: the 'wilderness' outside court is a
male space where Cynthia governs the hearts of her hermit-lovers.
The court, however, the locus of falseness and dissembling, is a
female space, and here she is obsessed by governing female tongues.
The tongue, besides being conceived as an instrument of domination
equivalent to the penis,[35] seems to be the somatic token of court
intrigue: 'I will tame your tongues, and your thoughts, and make
your speeches answerable to your dueties, and your conceits fitte for
my dignitie, els will I banish you both my person and the worlde.'
(III.1.16–20) Thus speaks Cynthia to her lady-in-waiting Semele, the
beloved of Eumenides, who offers to ransom his tongue for the
tongue she is doomed to lose as a consequence of having spoken
when she was sentenced to silence. The tongue as synecdoche of the
courtly figure of false semblant,[36] so essential to courtly life, must
be ruled by Cynthia. The gendered framework of this discourse,
however, prevents the goddess from seeing that in fact Endymion
is the great enchanter in the play, as, by dint of his treacherous
tongue, he can make her believe in his version of things (comple-
menting, in a way, his historical referent's going astray by means of

the tongue's symbolic equivalent: eloquence restores the favour lost through sexual incontinence).

Lyly's vision of courtly life enacts another crisis of loyalty and its solution, which in his version is not effected by truth but by the sovereign's will. Again the image chosen for the Queen in that situation is Cynthia, the unphysical personification of the imperial idea and focus of courtly love rhetoric. The play reveals, however, that power relations and strategic considerations govern the relationships of Queen and courtiers, and that whoever is master of courtly discourse (which is here completely dissociated from any claim to truthfulness) will dominate at court.

On the whole it appears that the Cynthia image dissociates the symbiotic unity of the Queen's body and her kingdom; it casts the Queen as divine 'prime mover' ruling over 'court' and 'country' while at the same time introducing the idea of universal peace and justice as emerging from the 'empress'. There is no implication, however, that these notions extend to more than Elizabeth's realm. Asserting the loyalty of the courtiers towards the Queen, the rhetoric of Neoplatonic love voices the conviction that Elizabeth alone is the centre of the (English) universe, and that she alone can command the 'love' and loyalty of her subjects. It is obvious that this is a semantic context in which the human body cannot stand for the integrity of the realm and the functioning of political relationships. Here it has instead become the focus of everything that hinders the courtier's ascent to his 'goddess'; it is associated with femininity, and denigrated as mere matter. We shall see how these representational parameters of the imperial idea in Elizabethan England, the 'disembodiment' of the Queen, the love-and-loyalty paradigm, and the denigration of femininity and corporeality will intersect with and reinforce each other when the imperial idea leaves the domestic context.

6
Astraea's Substitute: Ireland and the Quest for National Unity

One of the most familiar representations of the imperial idea is of course Astraea. In her famous study on this 'imperial' goddess, Frances Yates has repeatedly pointed to the fact that the virginal figure of Astraea, embodying the central tenets of the imperial idea, that is, universal peace, justice, and a unified faith, offered itself for representations of the unmarried Queen.[1] In the classical versions by Ovid and Virgil, Astraea is the last of divine lineage to leave the earth after the decline of morals and Arcadian harmony among men.[2] She will return when the wheel of history has come full term to announce the dawning of the Golden Age: 'iam redit et virgo, redeunt Saturnia regna'.[3] One of the key functions of the image was the representation of an ideal of political and religious unity, which would replace the present state of decline and disintegration. In the image of Astraea-Elizabeth, the central tenets of the imperial idea, just rule, unity, peace, and right religion emerged as incorporated in the concept of the English or rather, seen in relation to Ireland, the British 'nation'. In that respect the poem provides a perfect example of Protestant panegyric, delineating an ideal to be aspired to rather than praising its actual fulfilment.

When reflecting it in terms of body imagery, the Elizabethan Astraea image turns out to negotiate two different body paradigms linked with a twofold time structure. On a political plane – that is, in the fallen, Iron Age world – the equation between Elizabeth and Astraea is inconsistent with the temporal logic of the image, since the virgin will only return when historical struggle is over. In Elizabethan panegyrics, however, the image was explicitly used to represent the Queen's reign as that very same return of the Golden Age, so that Elizabeth appears as Astraea herself.[4] Naturally, the question of whether Astraea is embodied on earth or whether she is a sign of the zodiac has direct implications on the status of the body image in her representations. Having no physical body, the elevated virgin is a constellation in the heavenly spheres, that is, a body of a different kind. The idea of Astraea returned, in contrast, ties in neatly with images of the virginal body as paradise or the Golden Age *locus amoenus*. By linking the double time-structure of *The Faerie Queene* with Astraea-Elizabeth's twofold time, Spenser 'doubles' Astraea by giving her a substitute to act in the historical world while at the same time projecting Elizabeth's own time as the future in which the virgin will have returned. Like Britomart, Astraea is thus not only a typological precursor of the Queen, but also the image of fulfilment at the end of a teleological course of history. The proem to Book 5, the Book of Justice, elaborates on this time structure, which, as previously noted, is characteristic for narratives of nationhood. Complementary to genealogical projections of Elizabeth's ancestry which show the English nation, in its identification with the ruling dynasty, as emerging from a mythical past, the text here even more anxiously insists on what must yet be done to achieve a state of perpetual peace and justice, conceived in terms of political, religious, legal, and linguistic conformity. Thus, for the 'imagined community' of Englishmen and -women existing in 'double-time', the mythological (or, in Bhabha's diction, 'pedagogical'[5]) and the performative, separated by the Fall in Spenser's version, do not necessarily function according to the same logic: while mythological time is predetermined by providence, the performative aspect depends on the initiative of man and may be subject to historically contingent factors. The split time-structure will, however, be reunified when historical strife is over. The issue of how to achieve this 'alliance between a plenitudinous present and the eternal visibility of a past'[6] is further complicated by the conflicting body paradigms behind the Astraea image. Here the full extent of Spenser's disillusionment becomes obvious, for as the fullness of the microcosmic body is almost irretrievably lost, so is the cosmic harmony the image is to convey. The body form pertaining to the Iron Age is necessarily fragmented, and unity and closure can only be achieved by force. Since, as the proem complains, the world is 'runne quite out of square' (5 proem 1), the bodies of the human inhabitants of the fallen world must also be incomplete and fragmentary. This in a way also includes the Queen's natural body, which, for all its exceptionality, is mortal and gendered. Despite drawing on established panegyrical conventions, merging Astraea and Elizabeth in the proem thus voices anxiety about Elizabeth's power to fulfil the promise inherent in the picture of Astraea by her politics. The body politic, being displaced into the heavenly spheres, lacks immediate power to act in the world; its unifying capacities can only be upheld by the martial prowess of her male substitute:

> Dread Souerayne Goddesse, that doest highest sit
> In seate of iudgement, in th'Almighties stead,
> And with magnificke might and wondrous wit
> Doest to thy people righteous doome aread,
> That furthest Nations filles with awfull dread,
> Pardon the boldnesse of thy basest thrall,
> That dare discourse of so diuine a read,
> As thy great iustice praysed ouer all:
> The instrument whereof loe here thy *Artegall*. (5 proem 11)

As in the figure of Britomart, who embodied the complementary time aspect, Elizabeth is here alluded to as taking part in both historical and mythological time, and so does the nation she 'incorporates'. Astraea as reincarnated in Elizabeth thus identifies the virginal body of the Queen with the Arcadian setting of the Golden Age, while Astraea as elevated to the heavenly spheres is figured as the unphysical *idea* of justice. Oscillating between these two positions, Spenser's Book of Justice tries to establish imperial justice and peace as the aims of national endeavour, but with a clear option for a British unity under Elizabeth's rule. Interestingly enough, the divine perfection of the 'microcosmic' body is in the process displaced beyond the poem into some apocalyptic future while, at the same time, it serves as the paradigm structuring the quest's struggle for wholeness.[7] The body configuration which in fact makes the quest possible, that is, Artegall's, is one pertaining to the Iron Age: like that of Guyon before him, it is a fragment of the perfect divine body, and is emphatically gendered, yet gesturing at androgynous perfection through the envisaged reunion with the poem's other quester for nationhood, Britomart. Clearly, the completion of the Irish quest is crucial for the establishment and exis-tence of the English nation, for it is the champion of justice whom Britomart, the representation of the English national communities' genealogy and territory, has seen as her designed spouse in the magic mirror. Artegall is figured in the poem as complementary to Astraea as well as Britomart (two very different representations of Elizabeth's body politic), and is thus of vital importance for the dealings of the English national community. For he is predestined not only to implement justice and political unity on the historical level, but also, on the mythological plane, to sire the Tudor dynasty. As a representation of a policy of action and military intervention, and at the same time a mythological precursor of contemporary advocates of such a policy, he likewise participates in the double time-structure of the poem. In *The Faerie Queene's* poetic vision of the national community, Artegall triggers and fulfils English national destiny.

As I have argued before, imperial peace and justice depend on unity. Domestic unrest and rebellion, on the other hand, denote fragmentation. As the issue of imperial monarchy in England in the 1590s was always closely linked with questions of loyalty, Ireland was of course a major problem. Unsurprisingly, then, the solution of the 'Irish problem' is the focus of Spenser's quest for justice. It is aestheticized as the oppression by the monstrous tyrant Grantorto of the princess Irena, who applies to the Fairy Queen for redress. Cast in the traditional romance structure, the quest emerges as the effort to implement justice in terms of a chivalric enterprise carried out by the divinely appointed champion of justice, rendering a contingent political problem as the unfolding of a providential plan. Consequently, the righteousness of the agent of justice, Artegall, is undebated from the very start, his capability to perform his task being established by a narrative of his upbringing as Astraea's foster child:

> For *Artegall* in iustice was vpbrought
> Euen from the cradle of his infancie,
> And all the depth of rightfull doome was taught
> By faire *Astraea*, with great industrie,
> Whilest here on earth she liued mortallie. (5.1.5)

Characteristically, prowess with the sword and 'manly' rigour are the main features of the 'discipline of justice' (5.1.6) in *The Faerie Queene*, and the magic sword 'Chrysaor' that is given to Artegall at the end of his training has more than merely emblematic character. In addition, Astraea bequeathes her groom Talus to her substitute when leaving the earth. Equipped with an 'yron man' (5.1.12) and a golden sword, the champion is sent to mete out justice to an Iron Age.

The gendering of the positions in this representation of England's relation to Ireland is revealing. Diasporic communities like Belgae, Una, and Irena are troped in the well-known pattern of the Lady-in-distress, as passive, fragile, and incapable of self-defence. Their defenders are knightly, virtuous, yet frequently over-masculine. Displaced beyond mundane concerns is the goddess Astraea, who has instigated the quest for justice and whose female body bears the paradisiacal promise of perfection at the end of historical strife. Her other embodiment on earth, Britomart, is capable of manly action, yet it is her female body which is crucial to the completion of the quest for national unity. Of all body forms in Book 5, it is only the body of Astraea which is modelled on the microcosmic paradigm that also served to represent the Queen; and this one, unfortunately, is absent, and must be complemented by Artegall's militant corporeality. Like Spenser's other poetic representation of the Irish body politic – the goddess Diana, who has left Arlo Hill[8] – Astraea's departure has left the world in chaos. Yet contrary to the sulking Diana, who departed after an Irish Faunus saw her naked and went unchallenged (a clear subversion of the fate of Actaeon), Astraea is still powerful, if remote. The wolves that have taken over in Arlo Hill after Diana's departure, like the thieves that followed them, must be driven out, and the original sweetness of the place must be restored, a task reserved for the champion of justice. Like Astraea, who needs her masculine substitute to bring the divine will to pass, Elizabeth should rely on masculine (that is, military) aid, so Spenser insinuates, to complete her 'quest for justice' in the service of national unity.

Artegall's quest to liberate Irena is one of Spenser's versions of how to unify the realm and bring Ireland under English dominion. A slightly different one is to be found in his prose treatise *A View of the Present State of Ireland* of 1596.[9] The *View*, being a proposition for reform of that 'ragged common-weale' (5.12.26), differs from *The Faerie Queene* in that it presents itself as a non-fictional text objectively describing Irish matters from the viewpoint of an English settler. Although this generic difference has frequently been taken as a difference in kind, I agree with Anne Fogarty that 'for Spenser, as for any other Elizabethan writer, there is no easy line of demarcation between the rhetoric of politics and the rhetoric of fiction'.[10] The tropes and metaphors drawn on in both the *View* and *The Faerie Queene* Book 5 are similar, if conventional, and have a certain location in sixteenth-century political discourse,[11] so that, though operating with different degrees of aestheticization, both texts can be read as cultural artefacts determined by the paradigms and patterns valid at their specific time in history. Written in the form of a dialogue between an English humanist, *Eudoxus*, and an English settler with first-hand experience of Ireland, *Irenius*, the *View* makes use of the Renaissance tradition of instructive dialogue in order to convey its arguments.

The *View*'s idea of nationhood draws on an inextricable link between nation and civilization, both being conceived in similar terms as continual endeavours to establish justice, peace and national unity. Spenser's concern for a British nation focuses especially on the fusion of the two people: '(S)ince Irelande is full of her owne nacion that maye not be roted out and somwhat stored with Englishe allreadye and more to be, I thinke it best by an vnion of manners and Conformitye of mindes to bring them to be *one people*' (4767–70, emphasis added). There seems to be little doubt that this unity can ultimately be established; the strategies, however, are manifold and disputable.

Consistent with this vision of a unification of the British Isles, problems with Ireland are treated as issues of domestic loyalty throughout the *View*. Ireland is conceived as a part of the British commonwealth, yet England's right to dominion and her cultural superiority are never disputed. Although modern critics speak of English 'colonialist measures' in Ireland,[12] justifiably so in regard of English aims and strategies and the fact that the Irish were not given a voice in any decisions, legally the phrase is incorrect. Since 1541, when Henry VIII was declared King of Ireland, the country was under direct control of the English crown – in theory, that is. In fact, from the deposition of the Kildare Ascendancy and the 'Silken' Thomas Rebellion in 1534 onward, which caused a withdrawal of English settlers' loyalties from the crown, English policy in Ireland had to rely on military support. An effectual plantation policy was only started in the second half of the century, leading to even stronger confrontations between settlers whose ancestors had come to the country in the first wave of conquest in the twelfth century ('Old English') and newcomers from England ('New English').[13] Both groups differed strongly in their respective self-definitions in relation to the English government and nation. Due to their religious convictions, they also had completely different views on the ordering of the relationship between England and Ireland. The 'Old English' had remained Catholic and had lived in the country for generations, so their loyalties were divided. As proponents of Erasmian-humanist ideas, they advocated a politics of persuasion and gradual reform, and demanded restraint in dealing with Ireland, while at the same time claiming superiority over the native Irish. In contrast, many of the 'New English', being adherents of a stout Protestantism, called for stern measures of reform including military conquest. As Nicholas Canny has demonstrated, relations between the two groups, which had always been characterized by tension, completely collapsed in the wake of the second Desmond rebellion in 1579 and its apparent backing by the pope and Catholic forces on the continent.[14] More strongly than ever, the loyalty of the 'Old English' was in question, and the new settlers seized the opportunity to push into the power vacuum left by the deposition of the old élites. Spenser, who was a member of the latter group, strongly polemicized against the 'Old English' as having 'gone native' and, in submitting to the corrupting influence of the country, having given up their position of cultural superiority. The polarization between 'Old' and 'New' English was thus at the centre of his proposals for reform in Ireland. His goal of national unity, however, included not only the Old and New English but also the native Irish population.

Andrew Murphy has recently commented on the use of the colonial paradigm when discussing English–Irish relations in the early modern period.[15] Drawing on postcolonial theory, he points out that the settlers' attempts to conceptualize Ireland in terms of binary oppositions of civilized and barbarous, reason and corporeality, self and other resulted, in the case of Ireland, in a fundamental instability of the central categories of discourse. Although the means and measures of English domination in Ireland were clearly colonialist, the geographical, historical, and cultural proximity between the two islands undercuts any attempt to classify the Irish in the same way as, for example, the inhabitants of the New World. It therefore generated considerable conceptual anxieties to which the text of the *View* testifies as well. The structural impossibility of fixing meaning is mirrored in its rhetoric and imagery; particularly the use of the body metaphor with its complex negotiations of different body paradigms destabilizes any attempt at defining the categories of inclusion and exclusion. In its capacity to signify a unity of diverse elements, the traditional, organic body image appeared as an apt representation of a unified British body of the nation. In this paradigm, gender difference would be conceived as a positioning on a sliding scale of perfection, and femininity would mean inferiority, but not essential difference. This is constantly undermined, however, by genderings which draw on a fundamental incompatibility of male and female bodies, as envisaged, for example, in the metaphorical feminization of Ireland and the Irish population, which is complemented by the militant masculinity of the questers for unity.

In the semantic context of medicine and body lore, the role of the English government in Ireland is repeatedly likened to the duty of the physician. When discussing the 'reasonable waie to settle a sounde and perfecte rule of gouernement by shvnninge the former euills and followinge the offered good', Eudoxus proposes to model it on the method of the 'wise Phisicions, which firste require that the maladye

be knowne thoroughlie and discouered, afterwardes doe teache to cure
and redresse the same, And Lastelie do prescribe a diet with streighte
rules and orders to be daylie observed for feare of relapse into the former disease or fallinge into some more daungerous then it' (56–63).
The simile once established, the representation of the English as
physicians and the law as redress for the body politic's ailments evokes
sentiments of benign superiority, and tacitly naturalizes the claim of
the English to bring Ireland under dominion on their own terms:

> (A)ll Lawes are ordayned for the good of the Common weale and for
> repressinge of licenciousnes and vice, but it falleth out in Lawes no
> otherwise then it dothe in Phisike, which was at firste devised and is
> yeat dailye mente and mynistred for the healthe of the patiente, but
> neuerthelesse we often see that either thoroughe Ignoraunce of the
> disease or vnseasonablenes of the time or other accidentes com-
> minge betwene, in steade of good it worketh hurte and out of one
> evill throweth the patient into manye miseries. (79–86)

The unity of the body politic, according to the *View*, can only be
established by imposing English law, religion, language, and customs
on Ireland. Lingering in an Iron Age state of fragmentation and disintegration, the body politic can be turned into a (British) *locus amoenus* by
the redress of these evils, that is, by establishing unity through imperial justice and a unified faith. It appears, then, that the ideological aims
of the 'Irish quests' in the *Faerie Queene* and the *View* are very similar.
The high degree of aestheticization of the poetic text, however, facili-
tates its task of providing a coherent narrative of the quest for right
rule and national unity, even if it is never properly completed. The
claim to objectivity and the political status of the prose text, on the
other hand, both render it a much more unstable medium to convey
these ideas, since they have to be tested against political realities and
moral precepts.

Once again, the image of the human body is employed to represent
the goal of political unity while English activity in Ireland is figured as
necessary for the health and wholeness of the body politic. The redress
for the 'Irish evils', however, is often rendered in more sinister terms.
On the basis of an overlap of the semantic fields of medicine and
warfare as advocated in Edward Forset's witty variation of Ovid, 'Militat
omnis Medicus',[16] the 'physician' can now operate with the soldier's
instruments in the best interests of the patient – an unwilling one, to

say the least:

> And as it is but the peeuishnes and queasinesse of the diseased that
> will abide no Phisike, so it is the wilfulnesse and malecontencie of
> the wicked, that will not come vnder lawes. But the Phisicions do
> not therefore giue ouer their patient because hee is vnruly, but
> rather handleth him more roughly: So Magistrats must not desist
> from the duties of their offices for the waywardnesse and vnaptnesse
> of the people, but the more stir vp their spirits & forces against
> them with all austeritie.[17]

As we know from the iconography of Astraea's substitute Artegall, the
emblem of imperial justice is the sword. Symbolically and literally, the
sword is advocated as the instrument of imperial reform in Ireland, and
in different semantic contexts the use of the sword or its derivatives,
the pruning knife and the surgeon's scalpel, are suggested to set matters right. When discussing the degree of 'contagion' (that is, rebellion)
in the Irish part of the body politic, Eudoxus and Irenius cannot agree
on the appropriate remedy. Even Irenius claims that it would be 'evill
surgerye to Cutt of everye vnsounde or sicke parte of the bodye which
beinge by other dewe meanes recured mighte afterwardes doe verye
good service vnto the bodie againe and happelye helpe to saue the
wholle' (2522–5). Yet the idea of amputating the infested part is latent,
drawing on the well-known biblical instruction[18] which is also alluded
to by Forset when putting forward his ideas on necessary political measures.[19] Elsewhere in the text, Irenius is not so reticent about the use of
the sword, pointing out that

> all those evills must firste be Cutt awaie by a stronge hande before
> anie good Cane be planted, like as the Corrupte braunches and
> vnholsome boughes are firste to be pruned and the foule mosse
> clensed and scraped awaye before the tree cane bringe forthe anye
> good fruite. (2956–60)

By metamorphosing into a pruning knife, the sword turns into a cutting instrument of a different kind. It now evokes the image of the
goodly husbandman weeding his garden in order to make it fertile
according to the divine commandment, a trope well-known from colonial discourse. Linking the image of the physician with the gardener by
drawing on the same kind of well-intentioned superiority, the activity
of cutting off what is threatening to ruin the whole is naturalized, and

the implications of violence disappear. Yet Eudoxus is not fooled so easily by Irenius' rhetoric, asking 'Is not the sworde the moste violent redresse that maye be vsed for anie evill?' (2963/4) In his answer, Irenius explains that he used the signifier 'sword' metaphorically, denoting the power of the sovereign:

> (F)for by the sworde which I named I doe not meane The Cuttinge of all that nacion with the sworde, which farr be it from me that euer I shoulde thinke soe desperatlye or wishe soe vncharatablie: but by the sworde I meante the Royall power of the Prince which oughte to stretche it selfe forthe in her Chiefe strengthe to the redressinge and Cuttinge of all those evills which I before blamed, and not of the people which are evill: for evill people by good ordinaunces and government maye be made good but the evill that is of it selfe evill will never become good. (2973–81)

The question remains, however, as to what way the emblem is to materialize in order to reform the 'evil people'. Upon Eudoxus' question to that effect, Irenius responds:

> The firste thinge muste be to sende ouer into the realme suche a strong power of men as that shoulde perforce bringe in all that Rebellious route of loose people which either doe now stande out in open armes, or in wanderinge Companies doe kepe the woodes spoilinge and infestinge the good subiecte. (2985–9)

Thus the wheel comes full circle, and the sword reassumes its literal sense. Although the ideological aims of the text are clear, there is a fundamental insecurity on the issue of how to effect reform and the unification of the English and the Irish into one people under the imperial reign of Elizabeth. The instability of the signifier 'sword' in this passage is symptomatic for the instability of meaning throughout the whole text. As Eamon Grennan has pointed out, in the *View* 'metaphor functions implicitly as argument, drawing one unobtrusively between areas that are not in point of fact related'.[20] Yet the impossibility of keeping metaphors stable throughout the argument also points to a structural impossibility to fix meaning in the national narrative, 'to determine exactly what forms of difference a nation will be prepared to include and what will have to be castigated as the alien "other" against which such a body will seek to define itself'.[21]

Implementing justice 'by the sworde' appears as one precondition for the establishment and return of the Golden Age of English national greatness. The other one is, of course, religion. Difference in religion is an issue that hinders the unification of the English and Irish into one people, for in the cultural logic of Elizabethan England a unified nation can only be established on the grounds of a unified faith. As I have pointed out before, Protestantism was a major factor in the fashioning of the English national community. Represented in the image of a virginal body, drawing on the biblical image of the enclosed garden or earthly paradise, the true faith is cast as pristine, if vulnerable. Its counterpart, false religion or Catholicism, is rendered as the whore of Babylon, that is, in terms of defilement, (female) corporeality, and grotesque bodies.[22] Contrasting Irish intemperance with English containment and purity, the *View* employs these gendered images to render the difference between English Protestantism and Irish Catholicism: 'Therefore what other Coulde they learne then suche trashe as was taughte them And drinke of that Cupp of fornicacion with which the purple Harlott had then made all nacions drunken.' (2639–41) Rather than marking off Ireland as alien, England is here cast as different from all other (Catholic) nations. Yet Britain's return to paradisiacal conditions is prevented by Ireland embracing the wrong religion. To wrest her out of the hands of the Babylonian whore, that is, to cleanse and purify that part of the body politic, necessitates harsh measures which are again rendered in terms of medical treatment. Drawing on traditional medical lore, purgation is here advocated as the proper therapy for cleansing the body of evil influences; the contagion, conceived as the effect of poisoned drink, is to be flushed out in a kind of material exorcism:

> (S)ince they drunke not from the pure springe of life but onelye tasted of suche trobled waters as weare broughte vnto them the druggs theareof haue bred greate Contagion in theire Soules the which dailye encreasinge And beinge still Augmented with theire owne lewde lives and filthie Conuersacion hathe now bred in them this generall disease that Cannot but onelye with verye strong purgacions be Clensed and Carryed awaie. (2651–7)

As the purity of the community depends on the containment of the individual as well as the political body, temperance leading to bodily containment emerges as the first step to lead the degenerate and 'barbarous' Irish to embrace the true faith. When cataloguing the 'errors' of the Irish religious establishment, the text names '*Symony*: gredye Covetousnes, fleshlye incontinence, Carelesse slouthe, and generallye all disordered liffe in the Comon Clergie men' (2707–9). Personal intemperance, so the text implies, leads to degeneration. In terms of the proposed therapy this calls for strict control of body boundaries and behaviour: the Irish, feminized, 'humoral' body must turn into a part of the contained body of Britain. Again, individual and collective body are linked by a discourse of purity which calls for a regimen of temperance in order to keep the body inviolate. Astonishingly, there is no doubt here about the possibility of bringing Ireland into religious conformity with England, yet again there is the inevitable question of how to effect reform: 'instruccion in religion nedethe quiett times', Irenius points out, and 'it is ill time to preache amongest swordes' (2674/6). Legal and religious reform emerge, in the context of the prevailing body imagery, as care for the body and soul of that part of the commonwealth, yet still the proper order of proceedings is disputed. While Eudoxus argues that 'Care of the soule shoulde haue bene preferred before the Care of the bodie' (2684–5), Irenius advocates political and legal prior to religious reform. His stern measures emerge as necessary operations which will eventually solve all problems at one stroke:

> (M)oste trewe *Eudox* the Care of the soule and soule matters is to be preferred before the care of the bodye in Consideracion of the worthines of bothe: but not in the time of reformacion for if youe should knowe a wicked persone daungerouslye sicke havinge now bothe soule and bodye sore diseased, yeat bothe recouerable, woulde ye not thinke it ill advizement to bringe the preacher before the phisicion? for if his bodie weare neclected it is like that his Languishinge soule beinge Disquieted by his diseasfull bodye woulde vtterlye refuse and lothe all spirituall Comforte, But if his bodye weare firste recured and broughte to good frame shoulde theare not then be founde best time to Recure his soule allso: so it is in the state of a realme. Therefore as I saide it is expediente firste to settle suche a Course of gouernment theare as thearby bothe Civile disorders and allsoe ecclesiasticall abuses maie be reformed and amended whearto nedethe not anie suche great distance of times as ye suppose, I require, but one ioynte resolucion for bothe that eche mighte seconde and Confirme the other. (2686–701)

Spiritual and physical 'purity' of the Irish part of the commonwealth are to be effected, once again, by the sword. In the context of a programme of imperial reform leading to a unified British nation incorporating Ireland, coercion by military intervention is presented as the appropriate means of establishing imperial peace and justice.

Despite this confidence that a British union can be established, the *View* is a text divided against itself on the issue of how to conceptualize the Irish. There is no clear opinion on the problem of whether the difference between the English and the Irish – or rather, between 'New English' on the one and 'Old English' and 'mere' Irish on the other hand – is one of degree or in kind. Andrew Hadfield has suggested that one reason for the inherent instability in writings about Ireland might be a 'lack of a coherent ideology of national identity in the sixteenth century',[23] which in a way corresponds to the inability to establish clear polarities between civilization and barbarism, self and other. Nevertheless, the discourse of Irish 'barbarism' plays a crucial part in discourses of British nationhood which draw on a 'natural' link between nation and civilization. The nation here emerges as the 'location of culture' (Bhabha), that is, the form in which civilization materializes. Its proper representation is the contained body purged of its material corporeality.

As we know from the writings of Hayden White and Homi Bhabha,[24] tropes such as 'barbarism' or 'wildness' are frequently made use of to designate the negative 'other' against which the respective entity establishes itself. According to White, one of the primary functions of the 'Wild Man' trope is to distinguish between the members of a community and alleged outsiders.[25] It is thus instrumental in fashioning an imagined national community, in that it provides patterns of approved behaviour by marking off the opposite as 'other'. One function of the trope (which was well-established in Renaissance cultural discourse from classical literature on foreign cultures) in Elizabethan writing on Ireland was certainly the evaluation of English identity as a civilized nation in contradistinction to Irish 'barbarism'. Yet, as I have mentioned, easy identifications between classical representations of savagery and the Irish are undermined by the fact that, in Spenser's opinion, it is the 'Old English' part of the population which hinders reform. Being less interested in marking off the native Irish as 'barbarous' than in proving the degeneration of the 'Old English', and thus denigrating that part of the population which was most influential with the Queen, Spenser asserts that 'the Chiefest abuses which are now in that realme are growen from the Englishe and the Englishe that weare are now muche more Lawles and Licentious than the verie wilde Irishe' (1951–4). The 'Old English' emerge as the main impediment for the unity of the realm, for, having grown 'out of frame' (2001) and 'forgo[ne] their owne nacion' (1485), they pose the principal threat to a unified and civilized British nation. In the context of his project of proper nationhood, the parameters of which Spenser endeavours to represent as divinely sanctioned, the 'Old English' demonstrate the contingency of English cultural categories. According to the *View*, their subversive power must be eliminated if the English nation is to prosper. It must be clear from this context, however, that 'barbarism' here does not designate the insuperably alien. Rather, it denotes a position on a sliding 'scale of social development'[26] on which the 'Old English' have gradually moved downward through the corruptive influence of the country, and on which the native Irish occupy an even lower position. Consequently, Spenser's approach towards their 'barbarism' focuses on the reforms which, in the logic of national self-fashioning, are absolutely necessary to perfect the English commonwealth and reintroduce a paradisiacal state in Britain. The representational matrix of this state is the contained microcosmic body in its capacity to symbolize divine order and universal harmony.

At the same time, Spenser's propositions concerning the proposed reform of the Irish reflect anxieties about English 'barbarism' that must be overcome in order to accomplish proper nationhood, and which are dealt with, in the first place, by establishing a difference between English and Irish that makes the English look comparatively civilized:[27]

> (F)for the Inglishe weare at firste as stoute and warlike a people as ever weare the Irishe And yeat yee see are now broughte vnto that Civilytie that no nacion in the worlde excelleth them in all goodlye Conuersacion and all the studies of knowledge and humanitye. (342–6)

The hallmarks of English 'civilization' as opposed to Irish 'barbarism' are English law and religion, so both have to be implemented in Ireland to effect uniformity. We should not forget, however, that this also applied to England, where issues of loyalty were a frequent cause of concern. Apparently, the discourse of Irish 'degeneracy' both threatened and confirmed the hard-won containment of the English body politic. Unsurprisingly, the text of Spenser's *View* also displays considerable insecurity on the issue of what the term 'barbarism' actually signifies. As many critics have remarked, in the latter half of the sixteenth century, arguments which assumed a difference in kind[28] coexisted with arguments which proposed a difference merely in degree between English and Irish, and which thus believed in the possibility of gradually improving Irish manners. It seems that throughout the process of defining

English 'civilization' by marking off Ireland as its 'other', the signifier 'barbarism' remains unstable, depending on the urgency with which the issue of Irish loyalty was perceived in different political circumstances. In terms of body discourses, this instability of the somatic referent in medical, social, and cultural texts reflects the gradual emergence of notions of the fundamental difference of male and female bodies: forms of sexual and racial differentiation emerged coextensively.

While predominantly proposing reform based on the possibility of improvement of the Irish and their subsequent incorporation into the English nation, some of Irenius' proposals and descriptions of the Irish population seem to assume an essential difference which precludes any possibility of assimilation. One instance of such absolute otherness in the *View* is the use of the trope of cannibalism which, in colonialist discourses, functions as the hallmark of the absolutely 'other'.[29] Drawing on patterns and images from classical writers, the Irish are here cast as *anthropophagi*, as drinkers of blood (1935–42) and eaters of men's flesh (if only in cases of absolute extremity):

> Out of euerie Corner of the woods and glinnes they Came Crepinge forthe vppon theire handes for their Leggs Coulde not beare them, they loked like Anotomies of deathe, they spake like ghostes Cryinge out of theire graues, they did eate the dead Carrions, happie wheare they Coulde finde them, Yea and one another sone after, in so muche as the verye carkasses they spared not to scrape out of theire graues. (3259–64)

In the logic of the body politic image, cannibalism denotes an attack on the integrity of the human body which stands as a symbol for the imagined community. In that respect, the use of the cannibalism trope is incompatible with propositions for reform of the 'less civilized' parts of the commonwealth, for whoever is marked off as a cannibal can never be assimilated into the community but must be rigidly excluded. Though also drawing on the image of the body politic, allegations of Irish cannibalism establish an essential difference between the English and their savage other. The attack on the boundaries of the body politic, here figured not in terms of penetration but of consumption, emerges, in the image of the cannibal, as the 'traumatic' projection which consolidates identity *ex negativo* by thematizing the ultimate threat that can never be assimilated into the culture. Cynically, Irish savagery and English measures of domination converge in the image, for it is the reduction of Irish bodies through starvation which produces their savagery in the first place. Again, the attempt to fix meaning on a binary scale has failed, the oscillation between absolute other and *alter ego* destabilizing its intended signification.

The *View*'s fundamental insecurity over how to conceptualize Ireland and the Irish reflects an inability to draft a non-controversial, coherent concept of British nationhood. Not only the *View* but also the poetic version of the 'Irish quest' in the *Faerie Queene* is characterized by a plurality of possible models and a host of problems that cannot be solved without contradictions. The fragmentation of the Iron Age world makes an overview nearly impossible, and although Artegall is convinced of his righteousness, his task is almost overwhelming. In his endeavours to divide the world into neat patterns of right and wrong, good and evil (and it is no coincidence that equity is not part of his task but conceived as an effect of divine grace), he frequently takes recourse to violence: to his colonialist mind, things either fit his pattern or are eliminated.

In their capacity to restore and keep order, justice and right religion are the main forces of 'civilization' and right rule as envisaged in *The Faerie Queene*. The completion of the 'Irish quest' thus depends on the performance of many different deeds concerning their installation, with the fight against the tyrant oppressing Irena as the culmination of the whole enterprise. Again, the central tenets of the imperial idea are linked as crucial issues in a quest concerned with British national identity in a European context. In Book 5 the Protestant diasporic communities of Europe are represented as the virgins Una, Belgae, and Irena, who depend on male aid for their survival. The fights against their idolatrous and grotesque oppressors Geryoneo and the Souldan are placed in an apocalyptic setting, and thus again render political contingencies in terms of a providential plan. As thinly veiled allegories of a proposed military intervention in the Netherlands oppressed by the Duke of Alva (Geryoneo) and the fight against Philip II (Souldan) and his Armada, these episodes emphasize active intervention for the Protestant cause in Europe as the only possible measure to reduce Europe to imperial peace and unity under British leadership. Consequently, the final combat with the oppressor of the Irish Irena, Grantorto, is staged in terms of the eschatological fight of good and evil:

> Of stature huge and hideous he was,
>   Like to a Giant for his monstrous hight,
>   And did in strength most sorts of men surpas,

Ne euer any found his match in might;
Thereto he had great skill in single fight:
His face was vgly, and his countenance sterne,
That could haue frayd one with the very sight,
And gaped like a gulfe, when he did gerne,
That whether man or monster one could scarse discerne. (5.12.15)

The monstrous giant, whose representation combines stock images of anti-Catholic propaganda with elements from traditional descriptions of 'barbarism', and who wears the armour and weapons of the Irish foot-soldier,[30] is contrasted with Artegall's shining armour and strategic warfare, the signs of his superior civilization. Characteristically, the text introduces a differentiation between the foreign oppressor and the inhabitants of the 'saluage Iland' (5.11.39) and subjects of Irena, so that, again, no direct identification is possible. While Grantorto is cast as insuperably alien, the population of the island seem to welcome their liberation by the champion of justice and to embrace the civilized way of life his victory heralds.

The conditions of the Iron Age demand personal initiative to the point of violence to restore (or even simply maintain) order, without which a restitution of the Golden Age cannot take place. Activity, coded as masculine, is necessary in order to defend and sustain political entities which are here represented as – passive – female bodies, and to restore the contained Edenic body of Astraea. As in the *View*, justice here not only means equal dealing, but is conceived in a wider framework of right rule as opposed to tyranny, the one objective law as against many, fragmented, subjective laws. The return of the fallen world to divinely ordained right rule which the champion of justice is to bring about as a precondition for the return of the virgin is, however, fraught with problems. Having fallen from a state of grace into one characterized by self-interest, the denizens of the Iron Age are reluctant to submit to Artegall's concept of justice, and thus reform in the Book of Justice is likewise implemented 'by the sworde':

Who so vpon him selfe will take the skill
True Iustice vnto people to diuide,
Had neede haue mightie hands, for to fulfill
That, which he doth with righteous doome decide,
And for to maister wrong and puissant pride.
For vaine it is to deeme of things aright,

> And makes wrong doers iustice to deride,
> Vnlesse it be perform'd with dreadlesse might.
> For powre is the right hand of Iustice truely hight. (5.4.1)

Justice without power is futile, and reform has to be carried out sword in hand: that is, in chivalric terms, by combat. Artegall's opponents in the quest, being offenders against true justice, are consequently either killed in fight or punished in pageants of 'sacramental' violence which demonstrate the victory of divine justice. He swims in blood (5.4.41) while 'reforming' his opponents 'with all his force', but it is his groom Talus who carries out the ultimate acts of atrocity. Reform by persuasion and education seems to be impossible in the episodes of the quest for justice, where offenders are rigidly excluded from the community Artegall is sent out to create. Matching the punishment to the offence, the transgressors against divine justice, who have brought fragmentation to the body of the community, are punished by having their bodies torn to pieces, as in the case of the Sarazen's greedy daughter Munera:

> But he her suppliant hands, those hands of gold,
> And eke her feete, those feete of siluer trye,
> Which sought vnrighteousnesse, and iustice sold,
> Chopt off, and nayld on high, that all might them behold. (5.2.26)

Justice has to be backed by power, and it has to be made visible, whether by putting the offender's head on a pike (5.2.19) or chopping off the guilty body parts. These measures, proposed in the *View* as well as in the *Faerie Queene*, reveal the implementation of right rule to be a bloody business, and one which depends on masculine endeavour.

In its attempt to make order visible the quest for justice is very concerned about gender roles. The analogous structures of the books of Temperance and Justice[31] point to the complementary character of both virtues: without self-control and bodily containment Artegall's active intervention for the cause of divine justice would be doomed to failure, and without Britomart's intervention for the sake of just rule Artegall would not even have begun his final adventure. Temperance, like the militancy necessary for reformation, is a masculine virtue, and, as we have seen in Guyon's destruction of the Bower of Bliss, it does not imply pity or restraint of violence. Indeed, pity might be detrimental to the proceedings of the quest, as Artegall learns during his fight with the queen of Amazons, Radegund. Instead of killing her, as the rules of single combat demand, he is stunned by her beauty, takes pity, and casts away his sword: 'At sight thereof his cruell minded hart/ Empierced was with pittifull regard, / That his sharpe sword he threw from him apart' (5.5.13). Although the regime of women is termed 'tyranny' and conceived as a severe threat to right rule, Artegall is unable to perform his task of eliminating it because of his opponent's beauty. Temperance in his case would have meant self-control even in the face of female attractiveness, for, as the poem insists throughout, female beauty can be treacherous. As a result of his 'unmanly' behaviour, Artegall is submitted to a reversal of gender roles: 'she made him to be dight / In womans weedes, that is to manhood shame.' (5.5.20) In addition, he is forced to relinquish his sword, the emblem and agent of imperial justice and power (5.5.21). Having forfeited the attributes of his manhood, Artegall depends on a complementary role reversal for his liberation: Britomart, a woman acting like a man, sets matters right by mercilessly killing Radegund. She completes Artegall's task by implementing just rule, that is, by abolishing the female usurpation of power.

Quite obviously, for Spenser, 'right rule is ordered, self-controlled, Protestant and masculine. Wrong rule is disorderly, uncontrolled, Catholic, and feminine.'[32] The reversal of gender roles is cast as a reversal of the 'natural' order of things, gesturing also towards the reversal of order in Ireland. As the quest for justice is concerned with naturalizing a specific form of political order as divinely appointed, the text here insists on Britomart's exceptional status. She descends on Radegund as an agent of imperial justice and reveals the necessity of divine intervention in order to keep worldly order stable. 'Human' powers might accomplish much, so the text insinuates, but in order to complete a divinely sanctioned task the quester depends on grace. Thus, the divinity of masculine rule as well as of the social order as a whole is demonstrated and confirmed:

> He maketh Kings to sit in souerainty;
> He maketh subiects to their powre obay;
> He pulleth downe, he setteth vp on hy;
> He giues to this, from that he takes away.
> For all we haue is his: what he list doe, he may. (5.2.41)

Gender difference, however, is not conceived in terms of essential otherness; anatomy in Fairyland is certainly not, as Sheila Cavanagh has claimed, destiny.[33] Britomart acts in a 'manly' way and is perceived as a male knight by her opponents, for apparel and demeanour make the man. Artegall, on the other hand, behaves 'unmanly' and is consequently dressed in women's clothes. 'Masculinity' and 'femininity' here range on a vertical scale of perfection, on which upward and downward movements are possible independent of physiological features. Rather, it is social behaviour which determines one's place on this sliding scale, on which the ultimate poles are activity at the 'top' and passivity at the 'bottom'. In this framework the rule of women must not necessarily transgress social order. Female rule, when sanctioned by divine appointment, is godly, because rule does not depend on gender and anatomy. Rather, female activity and self-determination are conceived as transgressive; it is Radegund's determination to rule according to her own law that is regarded as a severe threat to social order. Given the dependence of 'masculinity' on apparel, diet, and martial behaviour, female militancy blurs gender boundaries, and the usurpation by women of the 'phallic' sword must remain an exception.

As in the case of the concepts of racial otherness, the text has no univocal position on the question of how to conceptualize gender difference and its social consequences, and one might add here that in Book 3 a more positive view of female rule is offered, perhaps testifying to Spenser's growing disillusionment with the Queen's reign in the course of the 1590s:

> But by record of antique times I find,
>   That women wont in warres to beare most sway,
>   And to all great exploits them selues inclind:
>   Of which they still the girlond bore away,
>   Till enuious Men fearing their rules decay,
>   Gan coyne streight lawes to curb their liberty;
>   Yet sith they warlike armes haue layd away,
>   They haue exceld in artes and pollicy,
> That now we foolish men that prayse gin eke t'enuy. (3.2.2)

Negotiating ideas about essential and cultural difference, the *Faerie Queene* keeps both in an uneasy balance by attributing the necessity of female submission to the conditions of the Iron Age while proposing equality for the world to come. In any case, femininity is rendered as an issue that problematizes the question of right rule; even on the 'mythical' plane the goddess's absent body is not strong enough to maintain order, and must be supported by worldly, if 'fragmentary', bodies which materialize only one aspect of the divine body. Yet if even Astraea's substitutes are prevented, like Artegall and his historical referent, Lord Grey, from completing their tasks, right rule will never be implemented and the Golden Age never return. In Irena's realm unity is prevented, and though she is free now, the corrupting and fragmenting influences have not been completely rooted out, so that the return of the virgin is once more displaced. It is monarchic presence that is demanded here, first in the form of her male agents who restore order, peace, and unity, and subsequently in the form of the Queen-goddess herself, who, like Diana, seems to have turned her back to 'Arlo Hill'. The structural pattern of the Astraea myth, while representing the expectation of the virgin's return as the *conditio humana* of the Iron Age, reveals divine harmony to be a condition of the future.

Apparently, the ideology of imperial monarchy is the dominant force behind Spenser's arguments in the *View* as well as the narrative of Artegall's Irish quest in the *Faerie Queene*. The *View of the Present State of Ireland* and *The Faerie Queene* Book 5 thus emerge as two different variations on the imperial theme in Elizabethan England. Negotiating a precarious balance between different types of 'otherness', but in principle still clinging to the symbolism of the *one* unified body politic as embodied in images of Astraea, these texts stand at the threshold of a new taxonomy, in which essential otherness becomes a main factor of differentiating between social and ethnic groups as well as between sexually demarcated bodies and their social functions. Difference in the new taxonomy is written on the body, which becomes an instance of particularity and can no longer provide a model for universal order and unity. We shall see how far the idea of anatomically defined gender difference affects the cultural meaning of the signifier 'virginity' and the conceptualization of female bodies, including the Queen's, in a colonial context. The disruption of the unity envisaged in the Edenic virginal body of the Queen threatens the balance of royal sovereignty and subjective identity and ultimately destabilizes the loyalty which the image of the imperial virgin was originally meant to envisage.

7
Female Territories: Textualizing the Body of the Other

The image of the virgin body and the meaning of the signifier 'virginity' underwent remarkable changes towards the end of the sixteenth century, changes which emerged simultaneously with alterations in social and economic discourses and practices and which in turn reflected and shaped the production of knowledge about both newly discovered countries and European notions of gender difference. In close conjunction with configurations of the body politic and emergent concepts of subjectivity, the central tenets of the imperial idea assumed different meanings when applied to non-European countries. The gradual shift towards a new taxonomy was only just beginning in the 1590s, and many texts from this and the following decade contain and negotiate both traditional and novel ways of attributing meaning to cultural phenomena. Read in the context of emerging notions of anatomical gender difference, the extension of the imperial idea to as yet 'virginal', but emphatically feminized, countries demonstrates how new 'knowledge' about the body was produced by, and in turn produced, new cultural and political tropes and discourses.

By turning from the relationship of the imperial idea with national and subjective identity in a domestic context to applications of these ideas in non-English, even non-European contexts, I want to demonstrate how the 'imperial' idea gradually became 'imperialist' politics. As discussed in Chapter 6, the transfer of the concept to different political and social circumstances, that is, to Ireland, necessitated alterations in the notion of the loyal subject, investing him with a greater share of agency. The subject was then conceived as the active, militant, emphatically masculine substitute of a remote, virginal goddess who nevertheless authorized all his actions as manifestations of a universal order. In this last chapter we will see how even this overarching system of meaning was gradually destabilized, so that imperialist action was no longer motivated by divine will, but by the more secular considerations of material gain and subjective reason. Walter Ralegh's *Discoverie of the large, rich and beautifull Empire of Guiana* of 1596 is a text that offers itself for such a reading, since, written during Elizabeth's lifetime, it draws on the imagery of the divine, perfect, virginal body politic while simultaneously negotiating emergent discourses of 'othering' and commodifying the newly discovered country on the matrix of sexual otherness. Although this text might be considered exceptional in its density, its negotiation of different subject positions and different approaches to the female body can be taken as representative for late Elizabethan cultural discourses.

At first glance, the *Discoverie*'s use of the image of the female body for the newly discovered land seems quite conventional. Drawing on a well-established tradition in Western thought, the gendering of Guiana relies on the pattern of a paradisiacal promise represented in the image of the virginal body. The text itself, however, gives a very ambiguous account of what this 'virginity' of the land actually signifies. Written at a time in which the virginity of the monarch was at the core of many courtly representations, any mention of the concept would immediately be understood in the light of that cult, that is, as somehow referring to the Queen. At the same time, the text carries decided hints for a different conceptualization of the notion of 'virginity', marking out the virginal body as the focus of a desire which is not to be perpetually deferred but which aims at its eventual appropriation by the male subject.

Descriptions of Guiana in the biblical image of a land flowing with milk and honey are frequent throughout Ralegh's text, implying that the country remains in a quasi-prelapsarian state:

> On both sides of this river, we passed the most beautifull countrey that ever mine eyes beheld: and whereas all that we had seene before was nothing but woods, prickles, bushes, and thornes, here we beheld plaines of twenty miles in length, the grasse short and greene, and in divers parts groves of trees by themselves, as if they had beene by all the arte and labour in the world so made of purpose: and still as we rowed, the deere came downe feeding by the waters side, as if they had beene used to a keepers call. (387/8)[1]

Included in this vision of abundance and internalized order are the 'innocent' inhabitants of the place, offering whatever they have to the strangers 'in great plentie, as venison, porke, hennes, chickens, foule, fish, with divers sorts of excellent fruites and rootes' (399). Guiana is envisaged as an unspoilt paradise, and the image of the 'countrey that hath yet her maydenhead' (428) is latent throughout these descriptions. The untouched condition of the country and the virgin body of the Queen are analogized by the use of the conventional land–body trope and its Elizabethan deployment, to signify the integrity of the island realm through the aura and the symbolic power of the Queen's inviolate body.

Descriptions of native women, however, provide a different view of the female body. Indeed, the treatment of native women by the indigenous men, by the Spanish and the English, is the text's prime vehicle of differentiating between the three groups. Quite frequently, these women are described as objects in economic transactions:

> Among many other trades, those Spaniards used canoas to passe to the rivers of Barema, Pawroma, & Dissebeque, ... and there buy women and children from the Canibals, which are of that barbarous nature, as they will for three or foure hatchets sell the sonnes and daughters of their owne brethren and sisters, and for somewhat more, even their owne daughters. Hereof the Spaniards make great profit: for buying a maid of twelve or thirteene yeres for three or foure hatchets, they sell them againe at Margarita in the West Indies for fifty and an hundred pezos, which is so many crownes. (376)

Ralegh's reaction to this practice is divided: while the natives are associated with cannibals and are thus disqualified as 'barbarous' there seems to be some grudging admiration for the Spaniards' sense of trade. On another level, however, the distinction between the 'Canibals' and the Spaniards is obscured here due to the Spaniards' unscrupulous participation in the natives' 'barbarous' practices.

Many colonialist texts of the period provide descriptions of the native populations as 'man-eaters' or 'cannibals'. The existence of *anthropophagi* at the margins of the known world had been described by Herodotus and other travel writers of antiquity, and it was assumed that they lived on the newly discovered continent. Though they had never actually been watched by anyone, the existence of ferocious tribes feeding on human flesh had been taken for granted ever since Columbus assumed this to be the meaning of explanations given to him about a tribe of Caribs in a language he did not understand. Columbus' account disseminated rapidly, and the word 'cannibal', with its multiple meanings of barbarous, man-eating, New World inhabitant, entered many European languages during the sixteenth century. Peter Hulme has shown that the concept of the cannibal as a particularly ferocious eater of human flesh serves the ideological function of 'mark[ing] out the boundaries between one community and its others'[2] by representing the cannibal as the hallmark of the absolutely alien. Cannibalism not only attacks the human body as a symbol of universal order; by separating the body into its component parts it also isolates them as objects for consumption. As Sigrid Brauner has pointed out, this idea already featured in Vespucci's descriptions of the New World: 'Vespucci uses the imagery of human flesh as commodity for consumption to stress another "uncivilized" characteristic of the natives. They are unable to use commodities commercially in order to accumulate wealth.'[3] Thus the cannibals in Ralegh's text prove their 'barbarous nature' not by devouring human flesh, but by putting it on the market without capitalizing on the exchange. The image of trade in women quasi-extends the notion of 'human flesh' to bodies that are still alive, and the economic transaction which the natives cannot perform, that is, exchange for profit, is completed here by the Spaniards. However, the idea of distinguishing Europeans and natives by referring to the exchange of women as a 'barbarous' practice is in fact not very convincing when taking into consideration the practice of arranging marriages in Renaissance Europe.[4] In both cases the exchange of women, conceptualized as commodified objects, was contracted between men in order to profit them politically or commercially. In terms of gender difference, the positions in this transaction were not reversible: male bodies could not be commodified in the same way. In European transactions of this kind, the 'virginity' of the object of exchange was of vital importance: it constituted a value on the 'marriage market' and was one of the factors determining the eventual 'price'.[5] Voiced in discourses of purity and honour, virginity and commodification became inseparable when talking about marriage in the early modern period in Europe, and girls were constantly admonished to preserve their virginity in order to keep their value high. It is obvious that in a context of emergent capitalism, price and value constituted categories that could be expressed in terms of money, and virginity ceased to denote an exceptional condition of perfection endowed with a quasi-divine aura. The gradual transformation of the signifier 'virginity' mirrors changes in the constitution of human bodies as well as socio-economic changes within European societies. The commodified female body, sealed by its 'virginity', is only conceivable on the basis of a sexual dimorphism.

The physical token of virginity that was discovered soon afterwards marked gender difference and commodifiability on the female body, its appearance reflecting the need of a culture that was increasingly drawn to scientific and imperial discovery to find new modes of classification to differentiate between male and female, white and non-white bodies. In the process 'virginity' emerged as the ideal condition of an object to be appropriated by one male exclusively. John Donne's well-known elegy *Going to Bed* is a fine example of this conjunction:

> Licence my roaving hands, and let them go,
> Before, behind, between, above, below.
> O my America! my new-found-land,
> My kingdome, safeliest when with one man man'd,
> My Myne of precious stones, My Emperie,
> How blest am I in this discovering thee!
> To enter in these bonds, is to be free;
> Then where my hand is set, my seal shall be.[6]

Donne's transfer of the image of the American colony to the commodified female body evokes the image of the virgin soil, to be possessed and exploited by the European colonizer. Thus, the virginity or 'maidenhead' of the country assumes a different or, in Ralegh's case, an additional meaning. What marriageable women in England, native women as objects of trade, and Donne's mistress have in common is that they are neither able to decide matters for themselves, nor are even given a voice in the discourses conceptualizing them. Ralegh's native women are victims of male actions, either by native American or Spanish men. He takes care, however, to establish the English men as different in their handling of women, for it is their behaviour in dealing with the female population which differentiates the English from the Spanish, as the English prove to be 'gentlemen' in the encounter with indigenous women:

> (T)hey beganne to conceive the deceit and purpose of the Spaniards, who indeed (as they confessed) tooke from them both their wives and daughters dayly, and used them for the satisfying of their owne lusts, especially such as they tooke in this maner by strength. But I protest before the Majestie of the living God, that I neither know nor beleeve, that any of our company one or other, by violence or otherwise, ever knew any of their women, and yet we saw many hundreds, and had many in our power, and of those very yong, and

excellently favoured, which came among us without deceit, starke naked. (390/1)

This usage of the native women not only distinguishes the English and the Spanish on the basis of a discourse of temperance, by disqualifying the Spanish as tyrants unfit to rule on a moral basis; it also links the untouched native women and the untouched soil of Guiana with the inviolate state of the Queen's body, who authorizes Ralegh's command:

> Nothing got us more love amongst them then this usage: for I suffered not any man to take from any of the nations so much as a Pina, or a Potato roote, without giving them contentment, nor any man so much as to offer to touch any of their wives or daughters: which course so contrary to the Spaniards (who tyrannize over them in all things) drewe them to admire her Majestie, whose commaundement I tolde them it was, and also wonderfully to honour our nation. (391)

He thus proves a good subject of his virgin Queen by restraining male desire from the female population and the country. In the process he also proves to be a master of duplicity and dissembling. As Louis Montrose in his brilliant essay on the *Discoverie* points out, 'The circuitous movement of Ralegh's discourse at once admires the Indians for their innocent trust and displaces onto the Spaniards the implicit betrayal of that trust which is at the heart of the English enterprise.'[7] Female bodies and feminized country both emerge as the focus of desire of the European male subject; what Ralegh negotiates here is the moral right to possession, or, as Gesa Mackenthun put it, 'how to translate desire into just title'.[8]

Characteristically, the only women Ralegh encounters are victimized and passive; but the Arawacan women are by no means the only female inhabitants of the New World. At the confines of European domains of influence there are women who are quite different from the native women encountered by Ralegh: the Amazons. Like the cannibals, this ancient tribe of female warriors is said by classical as well as early modern travel writers to dwell just beyond the pale of civilization. Ralegh is thus not in the least astonished to be informed about the existence of a tribe of female warriors on the new continent, but is quite eager to find out about them. Astonishing in Ralegh's relation is the exact geographical location he provides for the realm of the Amazons, which is at odds with the highly mythological nature of the rest of his tale. His narrative obviously consists of a mixture of referential and symbolic discourses, one feeding back into and thereby authenticating the other:

> The nations of these women are on the South side of the river in the provinces of Topago, and their chiefest strengths and retracts are in the Islands situate on the South side of the entrance some 60 leagues within the mouth of the sayd river. The memories of the like women are very ancient aswell in Africa as in Asia ... in many histories they are verified to have bene, and in divers ages and provinces: but they which are not far from Guiana doe accompany with men but once in a yere, and for the time of one moneth, which I gather by their relation, to be in April: and that time all kings of the borders assemble, and queenes of the Amazones; and after the queenes have chosen, the rest cast lots for their Valentines. ... If they conceive, and be delivered of a sonne, they returne him to the father; if of a daughter they nourish it, and reteine it: and as many as have daughters send unto the begetters a present; all being desirous to increase their owne sex and kind: but that they cut off the right dug of the brest, I doe not find to be true. (367)

The contrast with the victimized, and in Ralegh's eyes somehow 'civilized', Arawacan women could not be more pronounced: this is a tribe of female warriors, a whole 'nation' of active, independent women who determine their own lives, actions, and political and sexual relations, and who are able to defend the integrity of their own bodies. Their ordered, almost ritual form of cohabitation only just tempers the fact that these women, quite randomly and without any social obligation attached to it, choose their sexual partners. The spectre of civil disorder raised by the image of independent women who, in another stark contrast to European practice, are only interested in the births of daughters, is enforced by this display of their self-determined sexuality. Anxieties about voracious female sexuality feature prominently in European discourses about social order in the early modern period, linking the threat of female insubordination to fears about male sexual inadequacy. Although the organization of sexual intercourse between the Amazons and the men of neighbouring tribes does not seem particularly voracious, the fact that these women own their own bodies renders them threatening to European concepts of civilization. In England a woman's body was regarded as the possession of her husband,[9] and a man's dominion over his wife was conceived as the divinely ordained, 'natural' order of things. The elements chosen for reversal in this negative projection of social order seem to be symptomatic of the anxieties besetting Elizabethan England and to serve a certain psychosocial function for this society.[10] Little wonder, then, that projections that usually occupied the mental space reserved for the reversal of European order now populated the newly discovered land that was about to metamorphose from *Terra Incognita* into the 'New World'.

The Amazons, however, are not the only representations of sexually active New World women in the colonial texts of the time. Amerigo Vespucci in his writings on the newly discovered continent also describes native American sexual practices:

> They have another custom, very shameful and beyond all human belief. For their women, being very lustful, cause the private parts of their husbands to swell up to such a huge size that they appear deformed and disgusting; and this is accomplished by a certain device of theirs, the biting of certain poisonous animals. And in consequence of this many lose their organs ... and they remain eunuchs.[11]

Giving in to the excessive lust of their women, native American men emerge as emasculated. As Sander Gilman has pointed out concerning early modern depictions of non-Christian male bodies in Western culture, any alteration of the male genitals was conceived as effemination.[12] Thus only the uncircumcized and untampered-with male body was regarded as an image of Christ's body, implying an emphatic gendering of the divine body of king and Christ. Although for obvious reasons this might not have applied to England until after Elizabeth's reign, the idea that only the white European male has the right to govern is latent in Ralegh's text. The right to rule unquestionably hinges on a certain kind of masculinity that is construed in contradistinction to the passive femininity of the land-body, and is based on the ability to take a 'maidenhead'. The underlying representational matrix here distinguishes clearly between two different body forms that are mutually exclusive. Another significant feature of this masculine form of subjectivity is temperance, and especially sexual continence, which women and indigenous men lack. Unable to contain their intemperate wives, they also prove unfit to rule their own land. Though Ralegh is generally not concerned with indigenous agricultural practices (as he obviously does not propose settlement in Guiana, but exploitation of natural resources), the notion that the natives do not work the land according to divine commandment surfaces in statements such as '(t)hey never eat of any thing that is set or sowen: and as at home they use neither planting nor other manurance, so when they come abroad, they refuse to feed of ought, but of that which nature without labour bringeth forth' (383). As the idea of husbandry is closely tied to the masculinist image of penetrating the female land in order to 'inseminate' it with European culture and civilization, the representation of the native population as unable to till the soil inherently signifies their incapability to rule the land in their own right. Thus the European right to govern the New World is constructed by a transfer of European gender hierarchies, conceived as the 'natural order' of things, to the relationship of male colonizers and effeminate population.[13] In the course of this transformation the natives merge into the 'female' land and disappear from the surface of the text, so that the land can be re-conceptualized as empty.

Though Ralegh does not depict sexually voracious women and emasculated men, his efforts to establish English legitimation to conquer the New World and enact English concepts of right rule draw strongly on the idea of sexual continence. For obvious reasons, however, he displaces intemperate behaviour from the native population onto the Spaniards, the more immediate competitors for dominion of the new continent. Right rule and temperance are inseparable in this discourse, just like tyranny and sexual licence. Consequently, his report of the country of the Amazons concludes with a description of their aggressive distemper when the integrity of their body politic is under threat:

> It was farther tolde me, that if in these warres they tooke any prisoners that they used to accompany with those also at what time soever, but in the end for certeine they put them to death: for they are sayd to be very cruell and bloodthirsty, especially to such as offer to invade their territories. These Amazons have likewise great store of these plates of golde. (367)

As in the case of Vespucci's native women, we find a conjunction of lust and violence, rendering these women as voracious consumers of male 'flesh', in analogy to the 'cannibals' and in a negative projection of European cultural practice. Interestingly, both projections of 'barbarous' disorder are, in Ralegh's version, possessed of the gold the Europeans so ardently desire.

Much of what has been said about the Amazons likewise applies to Elizabeth, and yet Ralegh is at pains to distinguish between them. His anxiety on this issue appears to be symptomatic of the fact that the female monarch in the consciousness of the Elizabethan courtier occupies some of the space reserved for projections of the reversal of order, which is here displaced onto the Amazons. Thus the text, in representing female rule as an inversion of European concepts of order, negotiates the paradox situation of the male subject confronted with a female ruler in a patriarchal society. The highly territorialized notion of the Amazon nation ties in neatly with representations of Elizabeth in a metonymic identification with the inviolate island realm, which is also, incidentally, threatened by Spaniards. Ralegh's attempts to displace anxieties about the reversal of order onto an allegedly 'uncivilized' Amazonian society, however, do not function as unproblematically as he could wish, and so the *Discoverie* oscillates between projecting the Queen as a compliant woman like the Arawacan girls, depending on male aid for defence and sustenance, and imagining her as an Amazon, who is able to defend her own territory but does not provide a place for male agency. And yet, despite all his efforts to dissociate his Queen from the Amazons, Ralegh in the end presents Elizabeth as an example to this warlike, well-guarded tribe:

> And where the South border of Guiana reacheth to the Dominion and Empire of the Amazones, those women shall hereby heare the name of a virgin, which is not only able to defend her owne territories and her neighbours, but also to invade and conquer so great Empires and so farre removed. (431)

Ralegh's textualization of the female inhabitants of the New World prompts the conclusion that the conceptual separation of compliant and cannibalistic natives which is at the heart of so many colonial narratives is reiterated here in the contrast between the passive and victimized Arawacan women and the aggressive, sexually licentious Amazons. In both cases the latter, rather than actually inhabiting the New World, are European projections of the dangers lurking beyond the pale of civilization. Such projections – so much is obvious – are directly related to the anxieties of the white, male European colonizer confronted with the need to legitimize his presence and claim to possession of the New World. Concluding from the notion of 'femininity' and 'virginity' advocated in these representations, both are depicted on the basis of an emergent essential difference between male and female bodies, conceptualizing the female body as an object and as a signifier of particularity, while the male (Christian) body emerges as universal, Christlike, and endowed with the capacity to rule. These presuppositions, of course, also qualify what was said at the beginning about the trope of the virgin land as an image of paradisiacal plenty. It seems that, from the evidence of Ralegh's text, the desire to appropriate and possess is now gradually inscribed in the image. Representations of Guiana as a land flowing with milk and honey are, more often than not, concluded by a catalogue of commodities:

> It hath so many plaines, cleere rivers, abundance of Phesants, Partridges, Quailes, Railes, Cranes, Herons, and all other fowle ... both for health, good ayre, pleasure and riches I am resolved it cannot be equalled by any region either in the East or West. (...) Where there is store of gold, it is in effect needlesse to remember other commodities for trade: but it hath towards the South part of the river, great quantities of Brasil-wood, and diverse berries that die a most perfect crimson and carnation ... All places yeeld abundance of cotton, of silke, of balsamum, and of those kindes most excellent, and never knowen in Europe, of all sortes of gummes, of Indian pepper. (426/7)

And the inhabitants too, even though rendered as in quasi-prelapsarian condition, are regarded with a view to their incorporation in this vision of economic plenty. Whether by cultural misunderstanding or by deliberately taking advantage of their innocent trust, the natives are included into the bargain Ralegh is contemplating (or rather, the theft he represents as a commercial transaction): 'I gave among them manie more peeces of gold, then I received, of the new money of 20 shillings with her Majesties picture to weare, with promise that they would become her servants thencefoorth.' (415) Their innocent acceptance of Ralegh's gift of English coins 'betokens their uncomprehending entry into the circulations of England's nascent imperial economy – an economy to be fueled, in the future, by their own gold'.[14] Thus their fall from the 'state of nature' is accomplished without their even recognizing it, but with fatal consequences for their future lives. As parts of a feminized country whose depths are as yet unprobed, the natives are also objectified on the matrix of sexual difference, their entry into 'civilization' being completed by their disappearance from the surface of the 'body' of the New World. Thus Ralegh's concluding remarks on the country reveal an understanding of 'virginity' which is very different from Elizabethan courtly discourse:

> To conclude, Guiana is a countrey that hath yet her maydenhead, never sackt, turned, nor wrought, the face of the earth hath not

bene torne, nor the vertue and salt of the soyle spent by manurance, the graves have not bene opened for golde, the mines not broken with sledges, nor their Images puld downe out of their temples. It hath never bene entered by any armie of strength, and never conquered or possessed by any christian Prince. (428)

This commercialized vision of a country, figured as a female body, is constituted by and in turn constitutes new concepts of gender difference and body perception. Penetration here emerges as a central signifier for appropriation, rendering the prospective proprietor as invariably masculine: women lack the means to take maidenheads. And again Donne's poem comes to mind: Guiana too is 'safeliest when with one man man'd':

> Guiana hath but one entrance by the sea ... for any vessels of burden: so as whosoever shall first possesse it, it shall be found unaccessible for any enemie. (...) Besides by keeping one good Fort, or building one towne of strength, the whole Empire is guarded. (428/9)

The image of the female body waiting for appropriation by the male colonizer is at the core of many colonialist representations, in the New World as well as in Europe.[15] The notion of 'colonial romance' inherent in these views of eroticized 'female' landscapes[16] penetrated by a male gaze naturalizes the emergent subject–object split along the lines of sexual difference and gives it an ideological frame in which the 'feminine' part is rendered as even desiring appropriation. Not only countries but many other objects to be investigated by the male subject are also conceptualized as female. This is what Francis Bacon's notorious dictum on the fruitful marriage of nature and the mind suggests, admonishing the 'masculine' partner in the enterprise to penetrate 'into nature's inner chambers'.[17] But I am not arguing that it was female bodies alone which came to be perceived as objects in the course of these developments. Rather, it is the human body *per se* that was conceived as different from and, eventually, was seen as the 'other' of human subjectivity.[18]

As many critics have pointed out, representations of America as a female nude become very conspicuous in the writings about the New World from the 1570s on,[19] representing the European colonizer as the exotic female's prospective lover. Unfortunately, the conqueror's position in the 'romance' was not available to Walter Ralegh: upon his arrival, he 'discovers America in the arms of a Spaniard', as Montrose wittily extends the image.[20] Though Ralegh makes no secret of the fact that he treads in the Spaniards' footsteps everywhere, he claims that they have not yet been in Guiana and that, in fact, the country is reserved for England: 'It seemeth to mee that this empire is reserved for her Majesty and the English nation, by reason of the hard successe which all these and other Spanyards found in attempting the same.' (362) On the background of Anglo–Spanish hostilities in Europe as well as the Caribbean, these 'Spanish difficulties' also analogize England and Guiana, in that both resist Spanish invasion. The Spaniards might have inscribed themselves on the blank page of other parts of the New World and may have left their traces in other places, but Guiana, like England, is still untouched. This similarity is construed as an inherent affinity and a sign that Guiana is awaiting English conquest.

As I have mentioned before, the establishment of a difference between English and Spaniards is crucial to the English colonial venture, since it is the precondition for conquest and colonization. In the terms of Ralegh's patent, he is entitled to

> discover, search, finde out, and view such remote, heathen and barbarous lands, countreis, and territories, *not actually possessed of any Christian prince, nor inhabited by Christian people*, as to him, his heires and assignes shall seeme good, and the same to have, hold, occupy & enjoy to him, his heires and assignes for ever, with all prerogatives, commodities, jurisdictions, royalties, priviledges, franchises and preeminences.[21]

As the Spaniards are fellow Europeans and undisputably Christian (albeit of the wrong 'brand'), their fundamental right to rule must be discursively discredited. In the *Discoverie*, it is disputed (ironically enough, considering Ralegh's situation) on the grounds of sexual incontinence. As I have argued before, the subject's temperance was a central criterion for his suitability as a political subject and as a moral legitimation to govern those who are unable to govern themselves.[22] Self-mastery was first and foremost established in relation to the subject's inner nature and, by extension, in relation to his domestic surroundings.[23] Testifying to an underlying mind–body split which situates subjectivity beyond the body, the subject who is able to govern his 'private' realm, that is, his wife and household, is also entitled to rule in the public sphere. Thus, the construction of Spanish 'failure' to govern their concupiscible appetites disqualifies them from the rule of the colony. As noted before, Ralegh claims that the Spaniards 'tooke from them both their wives and daughters dayly, and used them for the satisfying of their owne lusts' (391), while the English contained themselves, or were forced to do so by their betters:

> But I confesse it was a very impatient worke to keepe the meaner sort from spoyle and stealing, when wee came to their houses: which because in all I coulde not prevent, I caused my Indian inter-preter at every place when wee departed, to knowe of the losse or wrong done, and if ought were stolen or taken by violence, either the same was restored, and the partie punished in their sight, or else was payed for to their uttermost demand. (391)

Moral considerations here intersect with class concerns, and the male white European subject that is textualized in the process also proves to be aristocratic.[24] The English colonial venture is thus legitimized by the self-restraint of the Englishmen, who are construed as morally entitled to govern the country because they are capable of self-control. Whereas, as Montrose observes, for the Spaniards in Ralegh's text, the rape of the land and the rape of native women go hand in hand, 'masculine sexual aggression against the bodies of the native women has been wholly dis-placed into the exploitation of the feminized new found land'[25] in the case of the English.

As a consequence of their intemperate behaviour the Spaniards are cast as tyrants. In the logic of the imperial idea, tyranny is the counter-part of right rule that is divinely legitimized; according to Aristotle's *Politics* (1252b, 1295a) it is also the organizational pattern of 'bar-barous' communities. Thus, the Spaniards' cruelty towards the native population morally disqualifies them from government.

In accordance with the ideology of imperial monarchy, Ralegh's tem-perance is a function of his loyalty to the Queen, and the text conveys the impression that, without her, he would be very much like the Spaniards. Whenever Ralegh reports about his measures to restrain his men from similar cruelties, from assaulting native women or from exploiting the country, he refers his actions to the command of his Queen:

> (B)y my Indian interpreter, which I caried out of England, I made them understand that I was the servant of a Queene, who was the great Casique of the North, and a virgine, and had more Casiqui under her then there were trees in that yland: that shee was an

enemie to the Castellani in respect of their tyrannie and oppression, and that she delivered all such nations about her, as were by them oppressed, and having freed all the coast of the Northren world from their servitude, had sent mee to free them also, and withall to defend the countrey of Guiana from their invasion and conquest. I shewed them her Majesties picture which they so admired and honoured, as it had bene easie to have brought them idolatrous thereof. (353/4)

The virgin body of the Queen as well as the vulnerable bodies of the native women thus serve as matrices distinguishing the English from the Spanish, the distinction being based on the withholding of desire from more or less commodified female bodies. (Perhaps the idolatrous impulse implied in worshipping the Queen's picture is, in its fetishizing impetus, itself a kind of commodification.) The desire itself, however, unites English and Spanish in their approach to the New World. In terms of the underlying pattern of gender difference, English and Spanish are both male, different merely in their respective degree of self-restraint, while the difference between Europeans and natives, conceived in terms of the sexual dimorphism of subject and object, is one in kind. Subjectivity is here reserved for the European aristocratic male, desiring to appropriate the feminized country and her hidden wealth. The desire for gold is an especially strong discursive force in Ralegh's text, and the main difference between the English and the Spanish in that respect is that the Spanish – like, incidentally, the cannibals and Amazons – are 'accomplished with what the English lack':

(W)e finde that by the abundant treasure of that countrey [Peru] the Spanish king vexeth all the princes of Europe, and is become, in a few yeeres, from a poore king of Castile, the greatest monarch of this part of the world, and likely every day to increase, if other princes forslow the good occasions offered, and suffer him to adde this empire to the rest, which by farre exceedeth all the rest: if his golde now indanger us, hee will then be unresistable. (358)

The exploitation of the New World is thus conceived as a major competition between the two 'nations' which constitute themselves precisely by that competition. The difference between European self and American other which is textualized by the conception of the newly discovered continent as a female body containing hidden wealth is apparently criss-crossed by the necessity for national self-affirmation among the contesting Europeans. Withholding of desire from the commodities the New World so freely offers emerges as one means to establish the English as a nation different from the Spanish. Making a virtue of necessity, Ralegh here renders his failure to provide any evidence of the gold that ostensibly awaits the English in Guiana as a deliberate strategic move. In analogy to Spenser's knight of Temperance, he turns down the corrupting gold Mammon offers to him.[26] The associative chain that connects those in possession of gold links the Spanish with the Amazons and the cannibals, and thus with the insuperably alien: in conjunction with earlier reports about Spanish cruelties, their conquest is represented as 'barbarous' and their rule as tyranny. This difference is the preliminary step to claiming the right to rule as inheritors of imperial monarchy, now translated to the New World. The indigenous population, however, must also be convinced of the difference between the two groups of European invaders. Thus Ralegh presents himself to the Indians as being the servant of a goddess-like sovereign who will relieve the world from Spanish oppression:

> I made him [the Arawac king] knowe the cause of my comming thither, whose servant I was, and that the Queenes pleasure was, I should undertake the voyage for their defence, and to deliver them from the tyrannie of the Spaniards, dilating at large...her Majesties greatnesse, her justice, her charitie to all oppressed nations, with as many of the rest of her beauties and vertues, as either I could expresse, or they conceive. (399)

Carefully balancing his own agency, manifested in his capacity to dissemble, and his dependence on the Queen (thus endeavouring to make his readers believe that what he says about his Queen is true, though the alleged purpose of his voyage is not), Ralegh justifies English presence in the Caribbean by recourse to ideas of imperial justice and right rule. Ralegh's captain on the second voyage, Laurence Keymis, gives an impression of the effect of Ralegh's speech and behaviour on the natives in his report on the second Guiana voyage in 1596, and elaborates on the moral obligation to bring civilization to the natives who, as yet, linger in a Hobbesian state of war:

> It may be pertinent (as surely it is a thing worth the noting) to consider howe this president of your moderation and good order, which to us seemeth a matter but of small and ordinarie respect, hath both alienated their heartes altogether from the Spaniard, and stirred up

in them true love and admiration thereof. For as governement is the onely bond of common societie: so to men lawlesse, that each one to other are, Omnes hoc jure molesti, quo fortes: To men, I say, that live in dayly tumultes, feares, doubtes, suspitions, barbarous cruelties, never sleeping secure, but alwayes either drunke, or practising one anothers death: to such men as these bee, who wanting discipline, justice and good order to confirme them in a quiet and peacable course of living, knowing not where to finde it: the sence and sweetenesse thereof is as the dewe of Hermon: it is as the Harmony of a well tuned Instrument: to bee briefe, it carieth in it selfe not onely a due and worthy commendation; but is avayleable without stroke striking to gaine a kingdome.[27]

Keymis establishes a difference between English and Spanish as well as between English and Native Americans. In his relation, the natives, though remaining in a state of lawlessness and disorder, are willing to embrace English civilization. Thus the whole country could be brought under English dominion without bloodshed, by the mere force of imperial order and justice. The real obstacle to this venture are the Spaniards, who in this account emerge as more barbarous than the indigenous population. Consequently, the English narrative must be continually supported by action; the English must continuously enact their difference from the Spanish. For Ralegh, temperance and restraint prove the means to project the violence of intrusion and exploitation onto the Spaniards, thus marking them out as the common enemy of English and native Americans:

For mine own part (...) I thought it were evill counsell to have attempted it [war against the Inga] at that time, although the desire of gold will answere many objections: but it would have bin in mine opinion an utter overthrow to the enterprize, if the same should be hereafter by her Majesty attempted: for then (whereas now they have heard we were enemies to the Spaniards & were sent by her Majesty to relieve them) they would as good cheap have joyned with the Spaniards at our returne, as to have yeelded unto us, when they had proved that we came both for one errant, and that both sought but to sacke & spoile them, but as yet our desire of gold, or our purpose of invasion is not known to them. (413–14)

The carefully drafted difference between the English and the Spanish is here temporarily destabilized in Ralegh's attempt to prove himself a master of strategic dissembling. Having revealed the purpose of the Guiana voyage and the fundamental similarity in the approach of English and Spanish to the new continent, he again hastens to point at the English nation's superior claim on the basis of ideas about divine justice and right rule. Plotting strategic restraint against intemperate greed, Ralegh in his role as 'polytropic man'[28] here demonstrates his capability to dissemble for the sake of England's glory:

> (I)t is likely that if her Majestie undertake the enterprize, they will rather submit themselves to her obedience then to the Spaniards, of whose cruelty both themselves and the borderers have already tasted: and therefore till I had knowen her Majesties pleasure, I would rather have lost the sacke of one or two townes (although they might have beene very profitable) then to have defaced or indangered the future hope of so many millions, & the great good, & rich trade which England may be possessed of thereby. I am assured nowe that they will all die even to the last man against the Spaniards in hope of our succour and returne. (414)

The idea of imperial monarchy, which hinges on the universal validity of its precepts and their sanction by divine authority, is here countered by a taxonomy in which the main aim is subjective gain, for the individual as well as for political entities. The gradual loss of objectively verifiable ideals is reflected, on the level of individual subjectivity, in the development of concepts of 'subjective reason' (Horkheimer), prompting individuals as well as communities to organize their existence according to the laws of self-interest and mercantile demands. In this context, the ideology of imperial monarchy is gradually instrumentalized in the service of imperialist politics which motivate the conquest of the New World through the dynamics of competition instigated by the presence of the Spanish.

And yet the *Discoverie* is a text divided against itself on the issue of imperial monarchy and individual autonomy. As in *Oceans Love to Scinthia*, Ralegh here represents the withholding of his desires even to his own disadvantage as a token of loyalty to his Queen and nation. His textualization of himself as a masculinist colonizer is subverted by the fact that he is subject to the Queen, that is, positioned in a web of political dependencies at an absolutist court. The whole of Ralegh's text, and, indeed, the voyage as an event, testifies to this fact. According to Ralegh's own allegations he has undertaken this 'painfull pilgrimage' in order to prove his worth as a subject after having been released from the Tower where he was imprisoned for his disastrous match with Elizabeth Throckmorton. In his dedicatory letter to Robert Cecil and Charles Howard, he claims that:

> I did therefore even in the winter of my life, undertake these travels, fitter for bodies lesse blasted with mis-fortunes, for men of greater abilitie, and for mindes of better incouragement, that thereby, if it were possible, I might recover but the moderation of excesse, & the least tast of the greatest plenty formerly possessed. If I had known other way to win, if I had imagined how greater adventures might have regained, if I could conceive what farther meanes I might yet use, but even to appease so powreful displeasure, I would not doubt but for one yeere more to hold fast my soule in my teeth, till it were performed. (339)

Modelled on the quest for Temperance in Book 2 of *The Faerie Queene*, the voyage, or rather its description, serves the goal of proving Ralegh's loyalty. By writing the virgin country, Ralegh-as-Guyon fashions himself as a master of courtly discourse as well as a paragon of continence. Like Amerigo Vespucci, who marked the 'unknown' territory with the feminized form of his own name, Ralegh here textualizes Guiana as a 'blank space' inscribed with the feminized name of his own role model, Guyon. This feminization again establishes the passive, virginal, plenitudinous country as the appropriate counterpart of the masculine, self-contained quester for selfhood, for whom she functions, at the same time, as his 'other' and *alter ego*. In this re-enactment of the scene of his transgression, in Mary Fuller's interpretation of the *Discoverie* Ralegh strives to cancel out his previous incontinence, which constituted not only a betrayal of the Queen in its displacement of desire onto another woman, but amounted to 'a crude or naive disruption of the economy of symbols and desires in and by which Elizabeth ruled'.[29] Consequently, the demonstration of his capability to withhold desire is one of Ralegh's main aims when composing the *Discoverie*, and the text is very carefully construed around that issue.

Within this framework of 'imperial' loyalty material gain is only a secondary consideration. In fact, the text of the *Discoverie* construes 'profit' as directly antithetical to loyalty, and Ralegh endeavours to fashion himself as one who is not after present gain: 'From my selfe I have deserved no thankes, for I am returned a beggar, and withered, but that I might have bettred my poore estate, it shall appeare by the following discourse, if I had not onely respected her Majesties future Honour, and riches.' (340) Since both the source of commercial wealth and the source of honour are represented as female allegories, he must be careful to distinguish between the two. Re-enacting on the textual level a withholding of male desire in which the author himself had failed, the *Discoverie*, like *Oceans Love to Scinthia*, sets the Queen's body apart from worldly women's (commodifiable) bodies. His Guiana-text thus necessarily negotiates both concepts of 'virginity', drawing on the image of the inviolate, paradisiacal virgin 'body' of Queen and realm when assuring the Queen of his loyalty while squinting desirously at the as-yet unprobed depths of the 'virginal' Guiana. This delicate balance, however, tips over at the end when he exhorts Elizabeth to take possession of the country, realizing quite clearly that she lacks the means. In a rather aggressive assertion of his own masculinity, which puts him at an advantage in the context of the image, he disrupts the courtly system of signification, claiming autonomy from the restraints imposed upon him by a system of political dependencies:

> I trust in God... that he which is King of all Kings and Lord of Lords, will put it in her heart which is Ladie of Ladies to possesse it, if not, I will judge those men worthy to be kings thereof, that by her grace and leave will undertake it of themselves. (431)

What can be witnessed here is an emphatically masculine concept of subjectivity contending with the Queen's claim to absolute superiority. As in the case of Ireland, militant activity is necessary in 'uncultivated', hostile surroundings. Unsurprisingly, the conflict is displaced onto foreign territory; but it is of course latent in many late Elizabethan representations of the relationship between Queen and courtiers. The gradual emergence of notions of sexual dimorphism and the introduction of a mercantile economy both instigate renegotiations of gender difference that make it difficult to reconcile a female monarch's exalted position with emergent ideas about female essential inferiority. The masculine 'I' that is erected when writing the New World is, in the *Discoverie*, subverted (but not shattered, as in the case of *Oceans Love to Scinthia*) by the mention of the patronage system and the requirements of an absolutist court which, ironically, appear in the text whenever Ralegh is very close to discovering the riches of the country. Indeed, it seems that the appearance of this other voice makes the gold flee from Ralegh's text. His 'fugitive gold' (to use Fuller's phrase) and the conspicuous absence of profit guarantees his loyalty in the logic of the text, where he frequently claims that desire for gold destabilizes loyalties which should have priority over everything else: the loyalties to sovereign and nation. When in his dedicatory letter to two of the most influential men at the late Elizabethan court Ralegh strives to acquit himself of charges of having made the voyage merely for gain, or of not having embarked on it at all, he accusingly claims that '(t)hey have grosly belied me, that forejudged, that I would rather become a servant to the Spanish king, then returne, and the rest were much mistaken, who would have perswaded, that I was too easefull and sensuall to undertake a journey of so great travell.' (339) Echoing Spenser's Knight of Temperance,[30] he acknowledges the destabilizing effect of gold in order to render his merit even greater: '(I)t is his [the Spanish king's] Indian gold that indangereth and disturbeth all the nations of Europe, it purchaseth intelligence, creepeth into counsels, and setteth bound loyaltie at libertie, in the greatest Monarchies of Europe.' (347) Later in the text (373/4) he discredits the Spanish by claiming that they betray each other for gain instead of prioritizing the national community before personal considerations (like himself). Ralegh, in contrast, has undertaken this voyage not as a privateer but as a loyal subject desirous of increasing English power and dignity. Though still drawing on ideas of imperial monarchy, the concept of the English 'nation' emerging from this text reveals it to be strongly defined by its competition with the Spanish, and also strongly interested in establishing a mercantile economy. The political conflict between the English and the Spaniards is transferred to the New World, with the effect that the English turn even more anxious about their cultural and economic belatedness. In justifying his project of collecting the voyages made by members of his 'nation', Richard Hakluyt is clearly driven by this fear when he inquires why the English have not yet embarked on maritime ventures, being ostensibly predisposed to do so by their geographical location. In fact, it seems that it is this very geographical isolation, formerly construed as precondition and symbol of England's inviolability, which now causes its cultural and economic backwardness by providing a feeling of safety from invasion:

I both heard in speech, and read in books other nations miraculously extolled for their discoveries and notable enterprises by sea, but the English of all others for their sluggish security, and continuall neglect of the like attempts especially in so long and happy a time of peace, either ignominiously reported, or exceedingly condemned.[31]

Hakluyt's vision of the English nation is clearly propagating expansion, focusing on 'outward' enterprises instead of concentrating 'inward' on the country's own boundaries. If Ralegh shares this vision, he is also strongly aware of the problem of persuading those in power of its propriety and practicability. Besides proving his loyalty, the other aim of the *Discoverie* is to persuade Elizabeth to embark on this venture for the sake of England's power and glory. The Queen was probably right in being cautious about the conquest of Guiana: a careful reading of Ralegh's *Discoverie … of Guiana* reveals that, in fact, the country remains as yet undiscovered.[32] The only proof for the existence of Guiana and its wealth, as well as for Ralegh's loyalty, is the textual event of the *Discoverie*, which might be one reason why the author constantly claims that this so carefully constructed and rhetorically refined text is in fact merely an artless relation of what actually happened. As an essay in self-fashioning, the *Discoverie* testifies to the inextricable link between imperial expansion and Ralegh's version of male subjectivity, which is clearly modelled on Spenser's version as embodied in the knights of Temperance and Justice, Guyon and Artegall. This masculinist notion of the individual cannot be integrated with a version of the nation as enclosed paradise; rather, it accords with a concept of the nation as a 'band of brothers'. Obviously, Ralegh's and Elizabeth's ideas about the English 'nation' and its westward expansion differed greatly, and that is why Ralegh repeatedly raises the spectre of Spanish Empire and world sovereignty, in order to convey the urgency of putting the Spaniards in their place and to confirm England's imperial rights: 'the shining glory of this conquest will eclipse all those so farre extended beames of the Spanish nation' (426).

Ideas of imperial monarchy might be quite useful when legitimizing claims to sovereignty, as the message of his text implies; but they need to be backed by imperialist action in order to yield any profit in terms of wealth and power:

> The West Indies were first offered her Majesties grandfather by Columbus a stranger … This Empire is made knowen to her Majestie by her owne vassall, and by him that oweth to her more duetie then an ordinary subject, so that it shall ill sort with the many graces and benefits which I have received to abuse her Highnesse, either with fables or imaginations. The countrey is alreadie discovered, many nations wonne to her Majesties love and obedience, and those Spaniardes which have latest and longest laboured about the

conquest, beaten out, discouraged and disgraced, which among
these nations were thought invincible. (430)

Interweaving symbolic and referential discourses in a way that legit-
imizes English conquest and settlement as well as masculine subjectivity,
Ralegh in this furious finale endeavours to present Guiana as a country
that 'answer(s) every mans longing, a better Indies for her Majestie
then the King of Spaine hath any' (342), tacitly glossing over the fact
that the description of the Spanish as 'beaten out, discouraged and disgraced' quite accurately reflects his own position at court. His attempts
to aggrandize himself by writing the body of the New World are
thwarted time and again by the Queen's reluctance to embark on this
venture. Subtly hinting at the fact that he is not alone in his frustration with courtly life and the female monarch, he suggests that '(h)er
Majestie may in this enterprize employ all those souldiers and gentlemen that are younger brethren, and all captaines and chieftaines
that want employment' (430), thus containing these potential malcontents by displacing them onto foreign territory in the service of
England's greatness. He concludes this passage with a vision of
England's imperial power in the New World that conveys a strong air
of contingency, in that it no longer depends on moral superiority and
divine sanction but on competitive, market-oriented action: 'For whatsoever Prince shall possesse it, shall be greatest, and if the king of
Spaine enjoy it, he will become unresistable. Her Majestie hereby shall
confirme and strengthen the opinions of all nations, as touching her
great and princely actions.' (431)

The *Discovery* is pervaded by a strong sense of competition (and thus
equality) between English and Spanish; but Ralegh insinuates that the
English, by claiming the country not from private interest but in the
name of their national community, have a superior right to it. By
extending the notion of his Queen's virgin body to Guiana, he includes
the prospective colony in the concept of national – that is, domestic –
space. Representing the as-yet untouched Guiana as a female body, the
text enables two different readings of the English approach to the
country, one inclusive and the other exclusive. On the one hand,
the extension of the paradigm of the virginal realm to Guiana conceptualizes the country as part of the English national territory, while, on
the other hand, its representation as a commodifiable female body
textualizes the country as the 'other' of the inviolable English body
politic, which is then to be appropriated in the service of individual
and national self-empowerment. Ralegh's text oscillates between the
two, endeavouring to integrate individual strivings for autonomy with

imperial demands for subjection. That this might not be his personal problem but a symptom of the anxieties besetting his whole generation is indicated by the frequency with which these images appear. George Chapman's *De Guiana Carmen Epicum*, which is incorporated in Keymis' relation of the voyage, also strives to establish the relationship of England and Guiana, by rendering them as female allegories while at the same time drafting a definitely masculinist subjectivity:

> That worke of honour and eternall name,
> For all the world t'envie and us t'atchieve,
> Filles me with furie, and gives armed hands
> To my hearts peace, that els would gladly turne
> My limmes and every sense into my thoughts
> Rapt with the thirsted action of my mind?
> O Clio, Honors Muse, sing in my voyce,
> Tell the attempt, and prophecie th'exploit
> Of his Eliza-consecrated sworde,
> That in this peacefull charme of Englands sleepe,
> Opens most tenderly her aged throte,
> Offring to powre fresh youth through all her vaines,
> That flesh of brasse and ribs of steele retaines.
> Riches, and Conquest, and Renowme I sing,
> Riches with honour, Conquest, without blood,
> Enough to seat the Monarchie of earth,
> Like to Joves Eagle on Elizas hand. (446/7)

While operating fully within the representational paradigm of imperial monarchy, associating Elizabeth with Jove and, through allusion to the sword of justice, with Astraea, the poem at the same time textualizes a masculine subjectivity emerging from the matrix of the new-found land. Clearly modelled on the Aeneid's 'arma virumque cano', this epic poem renders militancy as a precondition for national greatness, figured as 'riches, conquest, and renowne'. Imperial conquest, 'that worke of honour and eternall name' which is to be performed in the name of the English nation, can only be accomplished by martial action. In Chapman's poem, the youth of England venturing into the New World to acquire riches and honour are made of 'brasse and...steele'. The wealth of the new continent, however, is represented in the image of a female body:

> Guiana, whose rich feete are mines of golde,
> Whose forehead knockes against the roofe of Starres,

> Stands on her tip-toes at faire England looking,
> Kissing her hand, bowing her mightie breast,
> And every signe of all submission making,
> To be her sister, and the daughter both
> Of our most sacred Maide: whose barrennesse
> Is the true fruite of vertue, that may get,
> Beare and bring forth anew in all perfection,
> What heretofore savage corruption held
> In barbarous Chaos; and in this affaire
> Become her father, mother, and her heire. (447)

The militant Englishmen have now disappeared from sight, while the relationship of England, here unequivocally identified with the Queen, to Guiana is established as a family connection. This proves to be problematic due to the Queen's refusal to provide an heir of her own body, and thus maternity is transferred to a metaphorical level. Guiana is established as similar yet inferior to Elizabeth-England, whose superiority and perfection is rendered in an overdetermined cluster of familial relations: Elizabeth is sister, father, mother, and heir to Guiana. The image draws on the paradoxical notion of the virginal mother that is employed frequently in rendering Elizabeth as England, and stretches it almost beyond its semantic limits: in an image of divine perfection, Elizabeth-England, in addition to her female body, now assumes masculine power to inseminate as well as paternal power to command obedience. All these relations of 'kinship' and consanguinity, especially the final 'heir', effect a naturalization of claims to submission and possession, and, in their paradox combination, elevate the Queen into heavenly spheres. Elizabeth, then, Astraea-like, is exhorted to 'let your breath/Goe foorth upon the waters, and create/A golden world in this our yron age' (447), a golden world that is clearly associated with profit made by the conquest of the New World.

Obviously, the use of the image of the female body in these discourses negotiates different approaches to the new continent that, from historical hindsight, seem mutually exclusive. In the imagery employed here they are conjoined by the signifier 'desire', which is aimed at gold and honour alternately, both being representable as female bodies. In the course of time, however, the desire aimed at the body of the aristocratic woman, which, in a feudal paradigm of honour, is always already deferred, was replaced by the desire for gold and profit which was also represented as a female body, but one which could be appropriated by the male subject. The changing configuration of the image of the female body which stood in close conjunction with shifting 'class' and gender boundaries thus contributed immensely to the production of knowledge about New World inhabitants, as well as about European concepts of gender difference. New World anthropology and scientific reconceptualization of body discourses emerged as two sides of the same coin.

Notes

Introduction

1. 'The Extasie', in Herbert J. C. Grierson, ed., *Poetical Works* (Oxford: Oxford University Press, 1987), p. 47.
2. John Donne, 'Divine Poems', V. *Poetical Works*, p. 295.
3. See Judith Butler, *Bodies That Matter. On the Discursive Limits of 'Sex'* (New York and London: Routledge, 1993), p. 9, where she speaks of the materiality of the body as 'a process of materialization that stabilizes over time to produce the effect of boundary, fixity, and surface we call matter'.
4. I am here referring to the works of Michel Foucault, especially the *History of Sexuality*, 3 vols. (Harmondsworth: Penguin, 1990, 1990, and 1992), Thomas Laqueur, *Making Sex. Body and Gender from the Greeks to Freud* (Cambridge, Mass.: Harvard University Press, 1990), Barbara Duden, *The Woman Beneath the Skin* (Cambridge, Mass.: Harvard University Press, 1991), and to Claudia Honegger's *Die Ordnung der Geschlechter. Die Wissenschaft vom Menschen und das Weib* (Frankfurt a.M.: Campus, 1991).
5. Karl Figlio describes the transition as a 'degradation of the notion of a self extended into a unique and inviolable corporeal volume, to one in which the self only loosely possessed a body'. 'The Historiography of Scientific Medicine: an Invitation to the Human Sciences', *Comparative Studies in Society and History*, 19 (1977), p. 277.
6. Laqueur, *Making Sex*, p. 62.
7. G. R. Elton, *The Tudor Revolution in Government: Administrative Changes in the Reign of Henry VIII* (Cambridge: Cambridge University Press, 1953), p. 3.
8. Ernst H. Kantorowicz, *The King's Two Bodies. A Study in Mediaeval Political Theology* (Princeton: Princeton University Press, 1957). For the Elizabethan uses of the concept see pp. 7–41.
9. Richard Helgerson, *Forms of Nationhood. The Elizabethan Writing of England* (Chicago: Chicago University Press, 1992), p. 2.
10. I am drawing here on Homi Bhabha's notion of the nation as narration as put forward in *Nation and Narration* (London and New York: Routledge, 1992) and *The Location of Culture* (London and New York: Routledge, 1994).
11. Bhabha, *Nation and Narration*, p. 2.
12. Helgerson, *Forms of Nationhood*, p. 4.
13. Benedict Anderson, *Imagined Communities. Reflections on the Origins and Spread of Nationalism* (London: Verso, rev. ed., 1991), p. 204.
14. Louis A. Montrose, 'Professing the Renaissance: The Poetics and Politics of Culture', in H. Aram Veeser, ed., *The New Historicism* (London and New York: Routledge, 1989), p. 20.
15. Norbert Elias, *The Civilizing Process* (New York: Pantheon, 1982).
16. Mary Douglas, *Purity and Danger. An Analysis of the Concepts of Pollution and Taboo* (London and New York: Routledge, 1994).

17. Michel Foucault, *The History of Sexuality,* vols. 2 and 3 (Harmondsworth: Penguin, 1990 and 1992).
18. Ibid., vol. 2, pp. 76–7.
19. Philip Sidney, *An Apology for Poetry,* ed. Geoffrey Shepherd (Manchester: Manchester University Press, 1984), p. 119.
20. Helen Hackett, *Virgin Mother, Maiden Queen. Elizabeth I and the Cult of the Virgin Mary* (Basingstoke and London: Macmillan, 1995), p. 237.

1   Well-Tempered Bodies: Self-Government and Subjectivity

1. Elias, *The Civilizing Process.*
2. Linda Gregerson, *The Reformation of the Subject. Spenser, Milton and the English Protestant Epic* (Cambridge: Cambridge University Press, 1995), p. 82.
3. Stephen Greenblatt, *Renaissance Self-Fashioning. From More to Shakespeare* (Chicago and London: Chicago University Press, 1984), p. 9.
4. On the humanist curriculum on moral philosophy see Paul Oskar Kristeller, *Renaissance Thought and the Arts* (Princeton: Princeton University Press, rev. ed., 1990), pp. 20–68 and 228–46.
5. 'Self-mastery was a way of being a man with respect to oneself.' Foucault, *The History of Sexuality,* vol. 2, pp. 82–3. I would like to emphasize, however, that masculinity in this sense is not directly tied to a male body morphology. A masculine self-relation can also be established by women, for whom it then entails a doubly fractured sense of self: there is no possibility of establishing a relation to themselves as a woman, but only the basically authoritarian, 'masculine' model of subjectivity.
6. Hugh Rhodes, *The Book of Nurture for menseruants and Children (with Stans puer ad mensam) newly corrected, very vtile and necessary vnto all youth* (London, 1550) [BL C.39.e.52], C3^r.
7. *Galateo of Maister John Della Casa, Archebishop of Beneventa. Or rather, A treatise of the manners and behaviours, it behoueth a man to vse and eschewe, in his familiar conversation. A worke very necessary and profitable for all Gentlemen, or other.* Done into English by Robert Peterson, of Lincoln's Inn (London, 1576) [BL C.121.a.13]. All quotations are from this version (abbreviated as G); page numbers are given in the text.
8. Anna Bryson, 'The Rhetoric of Status: Gesture, Demeanour and the Image of the Gentleman in Sixteenth- and Seventeenth-Century England', in Lucy Gent and Nigel Llewellyn, eds., *Renaissance Bodies. The Human Figure in English Culture c. 1540–1660* (London: Reaktion Books, 1990), p. 139.
9. Ibid., p. 145.
10. David Kuchta, 'The Semiotics of Masculinity in Renaissance England', in James Grantham Turner, ed., *Sexuality and Gender in Early Modern Europe. Institutions, Texts, Images* (Cambridge: Cambridge University Press, 1993), pp. 235–6.
11. Ibid., p. 239.
12. [Francis Seager,] *The School of Vertue, and booke of good Nourture for chyldren, and youth to learne theyr dutie by. Newely perused, corrected, and augmented by the fyrst Auctor.* F.S. with a brief declaration of the dutie of eche degree (London, 1557) [BL 232.a.45], A8^r.

13. Mikhail Bakthin, *Rabelais and his World*, transl. Hélène Iswolski (Bloomington: Indiana University Press, 1984), pp. 308–9.

14. Jan Bremmer, 'Walking, Standing, and Sitting in Ancient Greek Culture', in Bremmer and Herman Roodenburg, eds., *A Cultural History of Gesture* (Ithaca, N.Y.: Cornell University Press, 1992), p. 23.

15. Ibid., p. 29.

16. [Ludovico Vives] *A very frutefull and pleasant boke called the Instruction of a Christen Woman made fyrst in Laten and dedicated vnto the quenes good grace by the right famous clerke master Lewes Viues and turned out of Laten into Englysshe by Richard Byrd* (London, 1529) [BL G.11884], sig. I3^v–I4^r.

17. On the analogies between women, servants, and pets, the inhabitants of the 'domestic' sphere, in the discourses of male selfhood see Juliana Schiesari, 'The Face of Domestication: Physiognomy, Gender Politics, and Humanism's Others', in Margo Hendricks and Patricia Parker, eds., *Women, 'Race', and Writing in the Early Modern Period* (London and New York: Routledge, 1994), pp. 55–70.

18. Edmund Spenser, 'A Letter of the Authors...to Sir Walter Raleigh knight', *The Faerie Queene*, ed. A. C. Hamilton (London and New York: Longman, 1987), p. 737.

19. Greenblatt, *Renaissance Self-Fashioning*.

20. Aristotle teaches that 'temperance...has to do with the pleasures of the body'. *Nicomachean Ethics,* transl. H. Rackham (London: Heinemann, 1926), III.x.3, pp. 174–5.

21. James Nohrnberg, *The Analogy of 'The Faerie Queene'* (Princeton: Princeton University Press, 1980), p. 327.

22. The (ideally) victorious mind or soul is depicted as a captain, as, for example, in Hoby's *Courtier*, where he distinguishes between continence (dealing with the sensual passions) and temperance: '(C)ontinencie may be compared to a Captaine that fighteth manlie, and though his enemies be stronge and well appointed, yet geveth he them the overthrow, but for al that not without much a do and daunger. But temperance free from all disquietinge, is like the Captain that without resistance overcommeth and reigneth.' [Thomas Hoby] *The Book of the Courtier from the Italian of Count Baldassare Castiglione: Done into English by Sir Thomas Hoby Anno 1561* (Rpt. New York: AMS Press, 1967) p. 308. Claudio's comment that 'the body public be/A horse whereon the governor doth ride' in Shakespeare's *Measure for Measure* also draws on the link between body natural and body politic. Ed. J. W. Lever (London and New York: Routledge, 1994) 1.2.149, p. 17.

23. Thomas Aquinas considers sensuality to be an effect of the Fall, which has impaired the human power to act according to reason: 'when man turned his back on God, he fell under the influence of his sensual impulses: in fact this happens to each one individually, the more he deviates from the path of reason, so that, after a fashion, he is likened to the beasts that are led by the impulse of sensuality'. *The 'Summa Theologica' of St. Thomas Aquinas in 22 Volumes*, literally transl. by Fathers of the English Dominican Province (London: Burns Oates & Washbourne, 1942), vol. 8, part II/1 quest.91 art.6, p. 20.

24. Hamilton explains in his note to 2.8.17 that 'the rider on his horse signifies the control of the passions by reason', which explains why Guyon does not

regain his horse, stolen by Braggadochio, before he has learned to govern his passions.

25. 'What is its [virtue's] occupation save to wage perpetual war with vices – not those that are outside of us, but within; not other men's, but our own – a war which is waged especially by that virtue which the Greeks call *sophro-sune*, and we temperance, and which bridles carnal lusts and prevents them from winning the consent of the spirit to wicked deeds?' Quoted from Nohrnberg, p. 291.

26. Aristotle, *Nicomachean Ethics,* III.xi.8, pp. 182–3.

27. Philip Sidney, *An Apology for Poetry,* p. 101. Sidney's statement comes in the context of the question of whether poetry is able to present visions of perfection which, due to humankind's fallen condition, can never be reached: 'since our erected wit maketh us know what perfection is, and yet our infected will keepeth us from reaching unto it'. Later in the same text he points to the function of learning, 'the final end [of which] is to lead and draw us to as high a perfection as our degenerate souls, made worse by their clayey lodgings, can be capable of', p. 104.

28. Ibid., p. 104.

29. See David Lee Miller, *The Poem's Two Bodies. The Poetics of the 1590 Faerie Queene* (Princeton: Princeton University Press, 1988), pp. 164–214 ('Alma's Nought') and James Nohrnberg, part III (pp. 283–425) *passim.*

30. Anthea Hume, *Edmund Spenser: Protestant Poet* (Cambridge: Cambridge University Press, 1984), p. 121.

31. This parallel is pointed out by Nohrnberg, p. 290.

32. Traditional 'medical' assumptions about temperaments and humours underlie this description. The idea of digestion as concoction is basically Galenic: food is transformed into chyle in the stomach under the influence of heat and then refined into blood and the other body fluids.

33. Bakhtin, *Rabelais and his World,* pp. 303–67.

34. *History of Sexuality,* vol. 2, p. 72.

35. David Lee Miller comments on this elision as follows: 'The urinary tract and bowels bring us just to the point at which we should encounter the genitals, but instead they are treated as "nought" – naughty, and therefore nothing; they are "auoided quite", excluded "priuily", and so become the figurative excrementa of this first "digestion" of the body into allegory. The body is thus doubly refigured: as flesh – for which the genitals are a kind of negative metonymy – the body is repudiated, refigured as excrement; while as coherent form (synecdoche, symbolic wholeness, phallic self-sufficiency) it is displaced into an open-ended series of transformations.' *The Poem's Two Bodies,* p. 180.

36. My thanks to Margaret Healy for pointing out this connection to me.

37. Miller, *The Poem's Two Bodies,* p. 174.

38. The centrality of this 'parlour of the heart' is also emphasized by the fact that Guyon and Arthur here find allegories of exactly those virtues which dominate in their own dynamic of passions, Prays-desire and Shamefastnesse. 'Shamefastness' here apparently means as much as self-consciousness, that is, the idea of *nosce teipsum* combined with a certain self-relation that is necessary to fashion oneself as a subject. It seems that the ideals of the virtues have been displaced, from the (Platonic) sphere of

ideas, into the core of the subject itself, there to temper Cupid and to help fashion the subject.

39. See Foucault, *History of Sexuality,* vol. 1, pp. 15–49. This is also the point where a 'natural' sexual difference can be introduced into body discourses. Judith Butler has argued that the sexual dimorphism purportedly based on the 'hard' facts of anatomical discoveries is implicitly heterosexual, and that it is the result of performance rather than essentially unchangeable facts. The subject thus emerges as having one of two possible sexes which he or she constantly reaffirms through participating in culturally determined discourses and practices. He or she is thus always already gendered and constantly performing his or her gender at the same time: *Gender Trouble. Feminism and the Subversion of Identity* (New York and London: Routledge, 1990), *passim.*

40. Patricia Parker, 'Suspended Instruments: Lyric and Power in the Bower of Bliss', in Marjorie Garber, ed., *Cannibals, Witches, and Divorce. Estranging the Renaissance* (Baltimore and London: Johns Hopkins University Press, 1987), p. 25.

2   Imagined Individuals: A Body of One's Own

1. Greenblatt, *Renaissance Self-Fashioning*, p. 162.
2. Ibid., p. 9.
3. In the introduction to *Allegory and Representation*, Greenblatt claims, 'Allegory may dream of presenting the thing itself but its deeper purpose and its actual effect is to acknowledge the darkness, the arbitrariness, and the void that underlie, and paradoxically make possible, all representation of realms of light, order, and presence. Insofar as the project of mimesis is the direct representation of a stable, objective reality, allegory, in attempting and always failing to present reality, inevitably reveals the impossibility of this project. This impossibility is precisely the foundation upon which all representation, indeed, all discourse, is constructed.' (Baltimore and London: Johns Hopkins University Press, Selected Papers of the English Institute 5, 1981), p. viii.
4. Parker, 'Suspended Instruments', p. 29.
5. *The Faerie Queene*, p. 739.
6. See John Freccero, 'The Fig Tree and the Laurel: Petrarch's Poetics', in Patricia Parker and David Quint, eds., *Literary Theory/Renaissance Texts* (Baltimore and London: Johns Hopkins University Press, 1986), pp. 20–32, Nancy J. Vickers, 'Diana Described: Scattered Woman and Scattered Rhyme', in Elizabeth Abel, ed., *Writing and Sexual Difference* (Brighton: Harvester, 1982), pp. 95–109, and Naomi Yavneh, 'The Ambiguity of Beauty in Tasso and Petrarch', in Turner, ed., *Sexuality and Gender in Early Modern Europe*, pp. 133–57.
7. Gregerson, *The Reformation of the Subject*, p. 127.
8. It is this reversal that is at the core of Petrarch's and Spenser's use of the Actaeon-myth from Ovid's *Metamorphoses*. See Chapter 3.
9. Castiglione/Hoby, *The Book of the Courtier*. Page numbers are given in the text.

10. Joan Kelly, *Women, History and Theory. The Essays of Joan Kelly* (Chicago: Chicago University Press, 1984), p. 45.
11. Hoby, *The Book of the Courtier*, p. 46.
12. Butler, *Bodies That Matter*, pp. 1–23.
13. Gregerson, *The Reformation of the Subject*, p. 6.
14. Kuchta, 'The Semiotics of Masculinity', p. 236.
15. See also the characterization of 'Tellus' in Lyly's *Endimion*: in contrast to Endymion's own dissimulation, which is regarded as a proof of his courtliness, Tellus quasi-represents the negative aspects of courtly dissembling, unsurprisingly and, as I would argue, not coincidentally, in a female body form. See Chapter 5.
16. Greenblatt, *Self-Fashioning*, p. 162.
17. Ibid.
18. On Spenser's 'idolatry' and his efforts to disclaim the artificiality (and thus the contingency) of his writings, see Kenneth Gross, *Spenserian Poetics: Idolatry, Iconoclasm, and Magic* (Ithaca and London: Cornell University Press, 1985).
19. Gregerson, *The Reformation of the Subject*, p. 82.
20. Kuchta, 'The Semiotics of Masculinity', p. 242.
21. On the courtly vice of slander see also Lyly's *Endimion*, where the Goddess Cynthia is obsessed with controlling the tongues of her subjects. I discuss the play in Chapter 5.
22. Parker, 'Suspended Instruments', pp. 21–39. See my reading of the Bower of Bliss in Chapter 3.
23. On the *Shepheardes Calender's* vision of court and pastoral world and their influence on the poet-subject see Hume, *Edmund Spenser, Protestant Poet*, pp. 13–56.
24. Quoted in Alan Sinfield, 'Protestantism: Questions of Subjectivity and Control', in *Faultlines. Cultural Materialism and the Politics of Dissident Reading* (Oxford: Clarendon, 1992), p. 163.
25. Ibid., p. 160.
26. See Foucault's commentary on the construction of the self by practices of confession and self-examination: 'The confession is a ritual of discourse in which the speaking subject is also the subject of the statement; it is also a ritual that unfolds within a power relationship, for one does not confess without the presence (or virtual presence) of a partner who is not simply the interlocutor but the authority who requires the confession, prescribes and appreciates it, and intervenes in order to judge, punish, forgive, console, and reconcile; a ritual in which the truth is corroborated by the obstacles and resistances it has had to surmount in order to be formulated, and finally a ritual in which the expression alone, independently of its external consequences, produces intrinsic modifications in the person who articulates it: it exonerates, redeems, and purifies him; it unburdens him of wrongs, liberates him, and promises him salvation.' *The History of Sexuality*, vol. 1, pp. 61–2.

3 Gendered Objects: Sexualizing the Female Body

1. It is obvious that this entails a high degree of self-alienation for women: the *Faerie Queene's* prime instance of a female subject is Britomart, who lives in

a male body habitus (bodily behaviour as inflected and produced by cultural discourses). See Chapter 1, n. 5.

2. Introduction to 'Amoretti and Epithalamion', in William A. Oram *et al.*, *The Yale Edition of the Shorter Poems of Edmund Spenser* (New Haven and London: Yale University Press, 1989), p. 587. All quotations from *Amoretti* and *Epithalamion* are from this edition; references are given in brackets.

3. *Shorter Poems*, p. 588.

4. Jonathan Sawday, *The Body Emblazoned: Dissection and the Human Body in Renaissance Culture* (London and New York: Routledge, 1995), p. 198.

5. Nancy Vickers, ' "The blazon of sweet beauty's best": Shakespeare's "Lucrece" ', in Patricia Parker and Geoffrey Hartman, eds., *Shakespeare and the Question of Theory* (New York and London: Methuen, 1985), p. 95.

6. Sawday, *The Body Emblazoned*, pp. 192–5.

7. William Shakespeare, *The Sonnets and A Lover's Complaint*, ed. John Kerrigan (Harmondsworth: Penguin, 1986), p. 129.

8. Sawday, *The Body Emblazoned*, p. 198.

9. Ibid., p. 199.

10. On the readership of Elizabethan sonnet cycles see Clark Hulse, 'Stella's Wit: Penelope Rich as Reader of Sidney's Sonnets', in Margaret W. Ferguson *et al.*, eds., *Rewriting the Renaissance. The Discourses of Sexual Difference in Early Modern Europe* (Chicago and London: Chicago University Press, 1987), pp. 272–86.

11. 'The inventory or itemizing impulse of the blazon … would seem to be part of the motif of taking control of a woman's body by making it, precisely, the engaging 'matter' of male discourse, a passive commodity in a homosocial discourse of male exchange in which the woman herself, traditionally absent, does not speak. The "inventory" of parts becomes a way of taking possession by the very act of naming or accounting.' Patricia Parker, 'Rhetorics of Property: Exploration, Inventory, Blazon', in *Literary Fat Ladies: Rhetoric, Gender, Property* (London and New York: Methuen, 1987), p. 131.

12. See Sonnets 13, 17, and 24, *Shorter Poems*, pp. 608–14.

13. See Sonnet 64: 'Comming to kisse her lyps, (such grace I found)/Me seemd I smelt a gardin of sweet flowres'. *Shorter Poems*, p. 638.

14. Gregerson, *Reformation of the Subject*, p. 138.

15. See my discussion of Una's encounter with the 'salvage nation' in Chapter 4.

16. Francesco Petrarca, *Canzoniere*, ed. Alberto Chiari (Rome: Mondadori, 1992), p. 83. Translation by Nancy Vickers, 'Diana Described', p. 98.

17. Vickers, 'Diana Described', pp. 102–3.

18. Parker, 'Suspended Instruments', p. 30.

19. Bakhtin, *Rabelais and his World*, p. 303.

20. The question imposes itself of whether this might have also included Elizabeth, hinting at an implicit conflict between her female body and political rule, which are here represented as incompatible. Even if different paradigms are at work in the representation of the Queen and her adversaries, the essentialist implications of the notion of incommensurable anatomies of men and women, that emerged coextensively with the kind of masculine identity advocated here, also taint the Queen's right to rule.

21. Gail Kern Paster, *The Body Embarrassed: Drama and the Disciplines of Shame in Early Modern England* (Ithaca: Cornell University Press, 1993), pp. 23–63.

22. Greenblatt, *Renaissance Self-Fashioning*, p. 176.
23. Parker, 'Suspended Instruments', p. 26.
24. Walter Ralegh, 'The Discoverie of … Guiana', in Richard Hakluyt, *The Principal Navigations, Voyages, Traffiques & Discoveries of the English Nation (1600)* (Glasgow: John MacLehose, 1903–5), vol. X, p. 388. On the parallels between the two texts see my article 'Pleasure Island, or: When Guyon discovered Guiana: Visions of the Female Body in English Renaissance Literature', *European Journal for English Studies*, 2 (1998), pp. 285–305.
25. Philippa Berry stresses the fact that, as the privy chamber of a Queen is a space to which males have only restricted access, the court could in fact be conceived as a female space. *Of Chastity and Power. Elizabethan Literature and the Unmarried Queen* (London and New York: Routledge, 1989), pp. 61–82 and 111–33.
26. Louis Montrose, 'The Work of Gender in the Discourse of Discovery', *Representations*, 33 (1991), pp. 25–6.

4 Time, Space, and the Body in the Narrative of the Nation

1. Of the 21 'gynaecological' tracts assembled in Israel Spachius' collection, *Gynaecia*, of 1597, only Ambroise Paré's text refers to the phenomenon of a physical sign of virginity. In this text, originally published in 1573 as the first part of his *Deux Livres de Chirurgie*, he argued that the existence of a hymen was an absolute exception: 'Pareillement il se trouve quelquefois en aucunes vierges une membrane à l'orifice du col de la matrice, appelée des anciens hymen, qui empeche d'avoir la compagnee de l'homme & faict la femme sterile. Or le vulgaire … cuydent et estiment qu'il n'y a nulle vierge qui n'ayt la dicte hymen, qui est la porte virginalle, mays ilz s'abusent, pour ce que bien rarement on la trouve.' Ambroise Paré, *Deux Livres de la Chirurgie* (Paris, 1573), p. 216.
2. Cf. Jocelyn Wogan-Browne, 'The Virgin's Tale', in Ruth Evans and Lesley Johnson, eds., *Feminist Readings in Middle English Literature* (London and New York: Routledge, 1994), p. 168, where she mentions recipes for the restoration of a lost hymen. She points out, however, that the hymen, which is composed of inner folds of flesh, is culturally constructed as imperforate (p. 168, n. 16).
3 Giulia Sissa points out that the mention of the hymen does not necessarily refer to physical virginity, arguing that there was no connection between 'hymen' and *Hymenaios* for the ancient Greeks: 'L'accident qui provoque la mort d'un jeune époux ne symbolise pas, pour les Grecs, la fracture d'un hymen féminin.' Soranus mentions the hymen but does not connect it to a notion of virginity. Sissa attributes this connection to popular prejudice, Christian gynaecology, and 'notions imprécises partagées par les sages femmes'. *Le corps virginal. La virginité feminine en Grèce ancienne* (Paris: J. Vrin, 1987), pp. 129 and 134–5.
4. Not only Paré but also Andreas Vesalius and Charles Estienne still drew on the notion of the one body in two versions while in fact laying the roots for a scientific separation of the sexes according to their different anatomies. See Laqueur, *Making Sex*, pp. 63–113. Although describing the

female 'reproductive' organs in detail and only occasionally evoking the analogy with the respective male organs, Vesalius did not mention the hymen at all, and Estienne dedicated one sentence to it: 'Mais de la membrane que l'on apelle hymen & que l'on dit se pouvoir trouver aux vierges qui n'ont encor eu leurs menstrues: cela croyons piteusement & n'y adioustons pas grand foy: Nous en raportans ad ce qui en est.' Charles Estienne, *La dissection des parties du corps humain* (Paris, 1545), p. 314. Andreas Vesalius, *De humani corporis fabrica libri septem* (Basel, 1543).

5. Helkiah Crooke, *Microcosmographia: A Description of the Body of Man* (London, 1615), p. 256.
6. A clear conceptual differentiation of virginity and chastity is impossible at a time when virginity did not yet denote a physical state. In my discussion of the concepts I therefore use virginity as a somewhat divine state of perfection, mostly in connection with the Queen, while chastity denotes a body practice, that is, a continual fashioning of the female body in accordance with an ideal of containment that is considered to be normative for all women. In Chapter 7 I discuss the gradual reconceptualization of the notion of virginity.
7. Kelly, 'Did Women have a Renaissance?', pp. 19–50.
8. Elias, *The Civilizing Process*.
9. On the political uses of body imagery, see Leonard Barkan, *Nature's Work of Art. The Human Body as Image of the World* (New Haven and London: Yale University Press, 1977). On the concept of the 'King's Two Bodies' and its Elizabethan uses, see Marie Axton, *The Queen's Two Bodies. Drama and the Elizabethan Succession* (London: Royal Historical Society, 1977), Carole Levin, *The Heart and Stomach of a King. Elizabeth I and the Politics of Sex and Power* (Philadelphia: Pennsylvania University Press, 1994), and of course Kantorowicz, *The King's Two Bodies*.
10. Douglas, *Purity and Danger*, pp. 122–3.
11. On Elizabeth's marriage policies see Levin, *The Heart and Stomach of a King*, pp. 39–65, and Hackett, *Virgin Mother, Maiden Queen*, pp. 52–5 and 72–4.
12. Staley Johnson, summing up the instances of (continental and domestic) Catholicism threatening the integrity of the English Protestant community, such as the Norfolk rebellion in 1569, the Ridolfi plot 1571/72 leading to the execution of the Duke of Norfolk, the Treaty of Blois in April 1572, and the Bartholomew massacre in August of the same year (and the appearance of a new star in November), concludes that 'these tensions and problems perhaps reinforced Protestant England's sense of itself as an elect nation. Much of the national and religious rhetoric of the period is a result of what can only be called an "exile mentality"'. J. Staley Johnson, 'Elizabeth, Bride and Queen: A Study of Spenser's "April Eclogue" and the Metaphors of English Protestantism', *Spenser Studies*, 2 (1981), pp. 76–7.
13. John Stubbs, *The Discoverie of a Gaping Gulf whereinto England is like to be swallowed by an other French marriage, if the Lord forbid not the banes, by letting her Maiestie see the sin and punishment thereof* (London, 1579), fol. C2^r.
14. Stubbs changes the genders here to fit Elizabeth in: Genesis 6 is about the sons of God and the daughters of men.
15. Hackett, *Virgin Mother, Maiden Queen*, especially pp. 94–127.
16. Ibid., p. 55, also Johnson, 'Elizebeth, Bride and Queen', *passim*.

17. She is also described in imagery which conjoins the Song of Solomon and Revelation: 'As bright as doth the morning starre appeare/Out of the East, with flaming lockes bedight' (1.12.21). See Song of Solomon 6: 10 and Rev. 22: 16.

18. The English pastoral of the sixteenth century, as Helen Cooper has pointed out, was a combination of two different genres, one being the scholarly eclogue, drawing on the Virgilian type of Arcadia, the other being the traditional May game. The Virgilian prototype is important here as it brings with it the structural components which make pastoral an appropriate genre for courtly panegyrics. Virgil's version of Arcadia, drawing on the even older imagery of the *locus amoenus,* with its structural features of remoteness from the outside world and perpetual fertility, has deeply influenced the development of bucolic literature, which often projected its version of Arcadia back into a mythical Golden Age. From the earliest times bucolic literature has been used in praise of the powerful, depicting the respective sovereign's or emperor's reign as a Golden Age. Some of the central motives of pastoral literature have been transformed by Christian thought, such as the persona of the shepherd, which became spiritualized by conflation with the image of the *pastor bonus* which was frequently employed in representations of Christ, and with Pan, the shepherd God, who was now taken to be a type of Christ. The pasture on which the shepherd grazes his flock was transformed into a paradise garden, which in turn was depicted as hedged in by a wall from the High Middle Ages onward. This identification of the pastoral setting with the imagery of the *hortus conclusus* achieved particular importance in depictions of Elizabeth in pastoral literature. Elizabethan pastoral drew heavily on the (spiritualized) Virgilian pattern of Arcadia, but there was another tradition of pastoral pageantry which combined with the scholarly eclogue to form the decidedly Elizabethan version of pastoral as represented, for example, by Spenser's *Shepheardes Calender.* This was the tradition of the May game with its stock figures of the Wild Man, the Shepherd, and the Lady of May, which was quite popular in sixteenth-century England, maybe owing to its strong anti-clerical and anti-papal element. Spenser's *Shepheardes Calender* combined this satirical tradition of religious commentary with the Virgilian tradition of courtly panegyrics through reference to a Golden Age of peace and plenty. On the topic of Elizabethan pastoral see Louis A. Montrose, ' "Eliza, Queen of Shepheards" and the Pastoral of Power', *English Literary Renaissance,* 10 (1980), pp. 153–82, and 'Of Gentlemen and Shepherds: The Politics of Elizabethan Pastoral Form', *Journal of English Literary History,* 50 (1983), pp. 415–60, Annabel Patterson, 'Re-Opening the Green Cabinet: Clément Marot and Edmund Spenser', *ELR* 16 (1986), pp. 44–70, and *Pastoral and Ideology. Virgil to Valéry* (Oxford: Oxford University Press, 1988), Helen Cooper, *Pastoral: Medieval into Renaissance* (Ipswich: D. S. Brewer, 1977), Petra Maisak, *Arkadien. Genese und Typologie einer idyllischen Wunschwelt* (Frankfurt and Bern: Lang, 1981), Sukanta Chaudhuri, *Renaissance Pastoral and its English Developments* (Oxford: Oxford University Press, 1989), and Paul Alpers, 'What is Pastoral?' *Critical Inquiry,* 8 (1982), pp. 437–60.

19. This implicitly draws on a legal logic of just conquest. Andrew Hadfield, who reads *The Faerie Queene* against the background of Spenser's colonialist

experience, comments on the ambiguities inherent in the various construc-
tions of 'sa(l)vage' personages in the poem: no clear distinctions seem possible between civilized and savage, destabilizing one of the basic polarities of
colonial discourse. *Spenser's Irish Experience. Wilde Fruit and Salvage Soyl*
(Oxford: Clarendon, 1997), pp. 130–4.

20. St George had been venerated in England since the time of Richard I and
became the patron saint of the newly founded Order of the Garter in 1348.
The figure of George combines the ideal of the *militia Christi* with the
adoration of the Immaculate Virgin; he was the patron saint of harbours
and city gates, and was invoked against the Saracens as well as against the
plague, leprosy, syphilis, poisonous snakes, and witches. See the entry
'Georg' in the *Lexikon der Christlichen Ikonographie*, ed. Wolfgang Braunfels
(Freiburg: Herder, 1968), vol. 6, cols. 365–90.

21. *Sermons, or Homilies, appointed to be read in Churches in the Time of Elizabeth
of Famous Memory. To which are added the Articles of Religion* (London:
C. Best, 1840), p. 119.

22. Louis Montrose, 'Celebration and Insinuation: Sir Philip Sidney and the
Motives of Elizabethan Courtiership', *Renaissance Drama*, n.s. VIII (1977),
p. 24.

23. I am following Jean Wilson's text in *Entertainments for Elizabeth I*
(Woodbridge: D. S. Brewer, 1980), which varies slightly from Nichols' version and which is based on the copy in the BL [C.33.a.38]. All quotations
are from this edition; page numbers are given in the text.

24. Jean Wilson, Louis Montrose, and Norman Concil assume that Sidney was
the principal author of this entertainment, as its position in relation to the
Anjou marriage is that of the Leicester–Sidney–Walsingham faction; it is
not, however, included in Katherine Duncan-Jones's and Jan Van Dorsten's
edition of Sidney's *Miscellaneous Prose* (Oxford: Oxford University Press,
1973), although the editors concede that he might have had a hand in
devising this entertainment. Wilson, *Entertainments for Elizabeth I*, pp. 62–3,
Montrose, 'Celebration and Insinuation', p. 24, Norman Council, ' "O Dea
Certe": The Allegory of "The Fortress of Perfect Beauty" ', *Huntington Library
Quarterly*, 39 (1976), pp. 332–3.

25. Francis de Valois was Duc d'Alençon until 1574, when he became Duc
d'Anjou upon his elder brother Henry's accession to the French throne.

26. I am drawing on Montrose's identification of the 'Foster Children' in
'Celebration and Insinuation' p. 25, n. 31.

27. Philip Sidney, 'Discourse of Syr Ph. S. to the Queenes Majesty touching
hir marriage with monsieur', in Albert Feuillerat, ed., *Complete Works*
(Cambridge: Cambridge University Press, 1923), vol. 3, pp. 51–60.

28. Jean Wilson points out that 'the prospective marriage was generally unpop-
ular, most strongly opposed by the party of the Earl of Leicester, who
sympathized with those Protestants who were firmly against a Catholic
marriage,' *Entertainments for Elizabeth I*, p. 61.

29. Council, p. 331; he quotes from 'O Dea Certe', *Calendar of State Papers and
Manuscripts: Venice*, ed. R. Browne and G. C. Bentinck (London, 1890),
vol. VII (1558–80), nr. 782 (Oct. 23, 1579).

30. On the Neoplatonic concept of love and beauty, see Thomas Hyde, *The
Poetic Theology of Love. Cupid in Renaissance Literature* (Newark: University

of Delaware Press, 1986), A. J. Smith, 'The Metaphysic of Love', *Review of English Studies*, n.s., 9 (1958), pp. 362–75, Paul Oskar Kristeller, *Renaissance Thought and the Arts* (Princeton: Princeton University Press, 1990), pp. 89–118.

31. Sidney, 'Astrophil and Stella', sonnet 4, in Katherine Duncan-Jones, ed., *The Major Works* (Oxford: Oxford University Press, 1992), p. 154.

32. Giovanni Pico della Mirandola, *Commentary on a Canzone of Benivieni*, transl. Sears Jane (New York, Bern *et al*.: Lang, 1984), p. 105.

33. Sidney, 'Discourse', p. 56.

34. Ibid., p. 58.

35. Montrose points out that because of his political position in the marriage question and his daughter Lettice's clandestine marriage to Leicester, Francis Knollys and his sons had an 'urgent need to impress the queen with a romantic display of their own adoration, obedience, and utility,' 'Celebration and Insinuation', p. 27.

36. Most recently in Susan Frye, 'The Myth of Elizabeth at Tilbury', *Sixteenth-Century Journal*, 23/1 (1992), pp. 95–114 and Levin, *The Heart and Stomach of a King*, pp. 1 and 143–4.

37. In most cases, the 'state' can be identified with a dynasty or the legal fiction of the 'crown' as analysed by Kantorowicz, *The King's Two Bodies*, pp. 314–450. On this identification see also Helgerson, *Forms of Nationhood*, pp. 295–301.

38. Jacques Lacan, 'The Mirror-Stage as Formative of the Function of the I', in *Ecrits. A Selection*, transl. Alan Sheridan (New York and London: W.W. Norton, 1977), pp. 1–7.

39. 'Chronicle was the Ur-genre of national self-representation. More than any other discursive form, chronicle gave Tudor Englishmen a sense of their national identity.' Helgerson, *Forms of Nationhood*, p. 11.

40. Kantorowicz, *The King's Two Bodies*, pp. 314–450.

41. Bhabha, *Nation and Narration*, pp. 1–7, and *The Location of Culture*, pp. 139–70.

42. 'Nations, like narratives, lose their origins in the myths of time, and only realize their horizons in the mind's eye.' Bhabha, *Nation and Narration*, p. 2. Though Bhabha does not analyse the beginnings of nationhood, some of his theories are very well applicable to the formation of the English nation in the early modern period. In particular, the idea that the 'future perfect' is the appropriate tense for writing the nation ties in directly with Spenser's temporal conception of his Elizabeth-as-England personae.

43. Hadfield, *Spenser's Irish Experience*, p. 140.

44. See Jane Aptekar, *Icons of Justice. Iconography and Thematic Imagery in Book V of 'The Faerie Queene'* (New York and London: Columbia University Press, 1969), pp. 87–107, where she points out that 'the heroes of justice do tend to be over-forceful; they have just as much recourse to "forged guile" as does the crocodile which is a very symbol of fraud', p. 88.

45. Mihoko Suzuki, 'Scapegoating Radigund', in Suzuki, ed., *Critical Essays on Edmund Spenser* (New York: G.K. Hall, 1996), pp. 183–98.

46. See my interpretation of this episode in Chapter 3.

47. Suzuki, 'Scapegoating Radegund', p. 190.

5 Internal Imperialism: Domestic Loyalties

1. Claire McEachern, ' "Henry V": The Paradox of the Body Politic', *Shakespeare Quarterly*, 45/1 (1994), p. 42.
2. Edward Forset, *A Comparative Discourse of the Bodies Natural and Politique. Wherein out of the Principles of Nature, is set forth the true form of a Commonweale, with the dutie of Subiects, and the right of the Soueraigne: together with manie good points of Politicall learning, mentioned in Brief after the Preface* (London, 1606, rpt. Meisenheim: Hain, 1969), p. 16.
3. Anderson, *Imagined Communities*, p. 7.
4. William H. Sherman, *John Dee: The Politics of Reading and Writing in the English Renaissance* (Amherst, Mass.: University of Massachusetts Press, 1995), p. 152.
5. On the level of domestic diplomacy, the anxiety about the loyalty of the landed élites in times of crisis led to the drafting of a document concerning the safety of the Queen's person, the *Instrument of an Association for the preservation of the Queen's Majesty's royal person* of 1584. The assassination of William of Orange and the success of the Spanish army under the Duke of Parma, the claims to the throne of Mary Queen of Scots, the discovery of Catholic conspiracies and Spanish invasion plans in the interrogations of Francis Throckmorton and the Jesuit William Creighton led to a feeling of imminent danger to the Queen and realm. After approval by the Privy Chamber, the *Instrument* was circulated throughout the country to win members to the Association. As Christopher Haigh points out, besides testifying to an enormous anxiety about England's safety from invasion by the Catholic powers of the continent, the document was also 'a gigantic propaganda exercise, designed to unify the ruling order in the face of internal divisions and foreign challenges'. Christopher Haigh, 'The Governance of the Realm: Bureaucracy and Aristocracy', in Simon Adams, ed., *Queen Elizabeth I: Most Politick Princess* (Special Issue of *History Today*, 1984), p. 9. I am grateful to Dr Adams for providing me with a copy of the *Most Politick Princess*.
6. Frances A. Yates, *Astraea. The Imperial Theme in the Sixteenth Century* (London: Pimlico, 1993), pp. 58–9.
7. We should not forget that panegyric can be employed retrospectively and prospectively, as a praise of deeds already achieved by the monarch as well as an outline of ideals to be aspired to. I here prefer to read representations of Elizabeth as 'imperial' monarch as belonging to the second category.
8. I would not, however, completely dismiss the idea that actual plans for imperialist action were being voiced in Elizabethan England. Although never adopted by official policy, there were propositions for colonial ventures which were legitimized by the idea of imperial monarchy. Fuelled by the ideas of John Dee and Giordano Bruno, who both took up the central tenets of the imperial idea and politicized them in the current situation, the 'imperial' doctrine was used to legitimize a policy of expansion. The adherents of Dee and Bruno, however, were a tiny minority, and during Elizabeth's reign their proposals were never seriously considered as realizable by those in power. On John Dee's imperialistic ideas, see Sherman, *John Dee*, pp. 148–200.
9. Hackett, *Virgin Mother, Maiden Queen*, p. 182.

10. Catherine Bates, *The Rhetoric of Courtship in Elizabethan Language and Literature* (Cambridge: Cambridge University Press, 1992), p. 2.
11. Ibid., p. 7.
12. Linda Gregerson, 'Narcissus Interrupted: Specularity and the Subject of the Tudor State', *Criticism*, 35/1 (1993), p. 1. My thanks to Gisela Engel for bringing this article to my attention.
13. 'Write thy Queene anew', ran Walter Ralegh's suggestion to Edmund Spenser in his commendatory sonnet accompanying the first instalment of the *Faerie Queene*. Longman ed., p. 739.
14. Montrose, 'The Elizabethan Subject and the Spenserian Text', in Parker and Quint, *Literary Theory/Renaissance Texts*, p. 325.
15. Andrew Hadfield, *Literature, Politics and National Identity. Reformation to Renaissance* (Cambridge: Cambridge University Press, 1994), p. 149.
16. Helgerson, *Forms of Nationhood*, p. 14.
17. Hadfield, *Literature, Politics and National Identity*, p. 152.
18. I use the poem's edition in David Norbrook and H. R. Woudhuysen, eds., sel., *The Penguin Book of Renaissance Verse 1509–1659* (Harmondsworth: Penguin, 1993), pp. 102–16; line numbers are given in the text.
19. The following quotation from Ralegh's poem contains two intertextual references that determine the way it is to be read. The classical source for the image of the stream is certainly Virgil's *Aeneid* II, 496–99, where it refers to the anarchy of war. The more immediate source might be Book 2 of Spenser's *The Faerie Queene* published in 1590, where it refers to the anarchic power of the passions and deadly sins attacking Arthur (2.11.18). The image reappears in a similar context of a struggle of nature and culture in 6.1.21, where Calidore's fury is described in terms of a natural power temporarily unloosened. Ralegh's use of the image evokes traditional images of war and anarchy in order to describe the lover's effort to ensure a woman's love and favour.
20. Although I admit that the frequency of Ralegh's allusions to 'long arections' and consecutive 'sudden falls' is rather tempting, I will refrain from reading the text as too blunt an enactment of Ralegh's sexual frustrations with his beloved. In fact, I find Philippa Berry's approach to the poem as a conflict of the 'apparently ever-erect phallus' with the 'overwhelming experience of female sexual desire' rather problematic in that it presupposes a notion of sexuality that in my opinion is only just emerging in Ralegh's time. *Of Chastity and Power*, p. 151.
21. Stephen Greenblatt, *Sir Walter Ralegh. The Renaissance Man and His Roles* (New Haven and London: Yale University Press, 1973), p. 93.
22. Wilson, *Entertainments for Elizabeth*, p. 97; the text of the entertainment is documented on pp. 99–118.
23. I would not, however, agree with Hackett that the entertainment primarily uses its Cynthia-imagery as a vehicle to 'assert English claims to imperial power', *Virgin Mother, Maiden Queen*, p. 176.
24. See my discussion of this episode in the previous chapter.
25. See G. R. Elton, *England under the Tudors* (London and New York: Methuen, 1974), p. 281.
26. David Lindley, *The Trials of Frances Howard. Fact and Fiction at the Court of King James* (London and New York: Routledge, 1996), pp. 13–42.

27. The editor of the Clarendon edition of Lyly's *Complete Works*, R. Warwick Bond, gives Feb. 2, 1585/6 as the most probable date for the first performance. It was entered into the Stationer's Register on October 4, 1591. John Lyly, *Complete Works*, ed. R. Warwick Bond (Oxford: Clarendon, 1902), vol. 3, p. 11.

28. The Burghley faction in the privy council consisted of William Cecil, Lord Burghley and his son Robert, Edward de Vere, earl of Oxford, Lord Henry Howard and Charles Arundel (who were Catholics), Sir Edward Stafford, the earl of Sussex, and, more obscurely, Sir James Croft and Sir Christopher Hatton. Patrick Collinson points out that 'a common interest in the destruction of Leicester was perhaps the strongest force holding these elements together', *The Elizabethan Puritan Movement* (London: Cape, 1971), p. 198. Though being in the minority in the privy council, this group's politics of non-intervention was approved of by the Queen.

29. Robert Graves, *The Greek Myths*, 2 vols. (Harmondsworth: Penguin, 1955), vol. 1, pp. 210–11.

30. As Catherine Bates points out, this is the very essence of the 'rhetoric of courtship': 'Courtship is … a mode which puts sincerity and deception in a teasing and often inextricable juxtaposition.' *Rhetoric of Courtship*, p. 2.

31. See my discussion of the gendered positions in the discourse of *sprezzatura* in Chapter 2.

32. Berry is probably right in assuming that this representation of courtly life suited Elizabeth more than the visions of the Leicester–Walsingham faction; *Of Chastity and Power*, p. 129.

33. Lyly, *Complete Works*, p. 7.

34. On the countryside as a locus of truth see Book 6 of *The Faerie Queene*, which I discuss in Chapter 2.

35. See Lisa Jardine, *Still Harping on Daughters. Women and Drama in the Age of Shakespeare* (Brighton: Harvester, 1983), pp. 121–33.

36. See George Puttenham's explanation of the 'Courtly figure *Allegoria*, which is when we speake one thing and thinke another, and that our wordes and our meanings meete not. The vse of this figure is so large, and his vertue of so great efficacie as it is supposed no man can pleasantly vtter and perswade without it, but in effect is sure neuer or very seldome to thriue and prosper in the world, that cannot skilfully put in vse, in somuch as not onely euery common Courtier but also the grauest Counsellor, yea and the most noble and wisest Prince of them all are many times enforced to use it. … Of this figure therefore which for his duplicitie we call the figure of [*false semblant or dissimulation*] we will speake first.' *The Arte of English Poesie* (1589), ed. Edward Arber (Westminster: Constable, 1895), pp. 196–7.

6   Astraea's Substitute: Ireland and the Quest for National Unity

1. Yates, *Astraea*, especially pp. 29–87.

2. 'Virgo caede madentis, ultima caelestum, terras Astraea reliquit.' Ovid, *Metamorphoses*, 2 vols., transl. Frank Justus Miller. 2nd rev. ed. (Cambridge, Mass. and London: Harvard University Press, 1984), I, 149–50, p. 12.

3. Virgil, *The Eclogues*. IV, 6. Ed. and transl. Guy Lee (Harmondsworth: Penguin, 1984), p. 56.
4. See John Davies' acrostic *Hymns of Astraea:*

> Eternal virgin, goddess true,
> Let me presume to sing to you:
> Iove, even great Jove, hath leisure
> Sometimes to hear the vulgar crew,
> And hears them oft with pleasure.

> Blessed Astraea, I in part
> Enjoy the blessings you impart,
> The peace, the milk and honey,
> Humanity, and civil art,
> A richer dower than money.

> Right glad am I that now I live
> Even in these days whereto you give
> Great happiness and glory:
> If after you I should be born
> No doubt I should my birth day scorn,
> Admiring your sweet story.

In Douglas Brooks-Davies, ed., *Silver Poets of the Sixteenth Century* (London: Everyman, 1992), Hymn 2, p. 341.
5. Bhabha, *Location of Culture*, p. 145.
6. Ibid., p. 151.
7. I have pointed out before the parallels of this construction with Lacan's notion of identity formation. In Lacanian terms, this could be called the establishment of identity in a 'fictional direction', where wholeness only exists 'in the mind's eye' as an unreachable goal while the present is conceived in terms of fragmentation and lack. See 'The mirror stage as formative of the function of the I', in *Ecrits*, p. 2. As a rhetorical and representational strategy, this dialectical relationship of wholeness and fragmentation is of course well-known to the Renaissance, since it is a basic feature of any kind of 'utopian' or Golden-Age imagery and, as Greenblatt has pointed out, of allegory; see Chapter 2, n. 3.
8. *The Faerie Queene*, 7.6.38–55.
9. Edmund Spenser, 'A View of the Present State of Ireland', in *Complete Works* (variorum ed.), ed. R. B. Gottfried (Baltimore: Johns Hopkins University Press, 1949), vol. IX, pp. 40–231. Quotations are from this edition, lines are given in the text.
10. Anne Fogarty, 'The Colonization of Language: Narrative Strategy in "A View of the Present State of Ireland" and "The Faerie Queene"', in Patricia Coughlan, ed., *Spenser and Ireland. An Interdisciplinary Perspective* (Cork: Cork University Press, 1989), p. 77.
11. See Andrew Hadfield, 'The Course of Justice: Spenser, Ireland and Political Discourse', *Studia Neophilologica*, 65 (1993), pp. 187–96.
12. See David Beers Quinn, *The Elizabethans and the Irish* (Ithaca: Cornell University Press, 1966), Nicholas Canny, 'The Ideology of English Colonization: From Ireland to America', *William and Mary Quarterly*, 30

(1973), pp. 575–98, Nicholas Canny and Anthony Pagden, eds., *Colonial Identity in the Atlantic World 1500–1800* (Princeton: Princeton University Press, 1987).

13. On the terminology and the problem of identity formation in Ireland see Canny, 'Edmund Spenser and the Development of an Anglo-Irish Identity', *Yearbook of English Studies*, 13 (1983), pp. 1–19, Canny and Pagden, eds., *Colonial Identity in the Atlantic World*, Ciaran Brady, 'Spenser's Irish Crisis: Humanism and Experience in the 1590s', *Past and Present*, 111 (1986), pp. 17–49, Nicholas Canny and Ciaran Brady, 'Debate: Spenser's Irish Crisis: Humanism and Experience in the 1590s', *Past and Present*, 120 (1988), pp. 201–15, and Joseph Leersen, *Mere Irish and Fior-Ghael* (Amsterdam and Philadelphia: Benjamins, 1986).

14. Canny, 'Edmund Spenser and the Development of an Anglo-Irish Identity', pp. 12–13.

15. Andrew Murphy, 'Reviewing the Paradigm: A New Look at Early-Modern Ireland', *Eire-Ireland*, 31, 3/4 (1996), pp. 13–40. My thanks to Bernhard Klein for bringing this article to my attention.

16. Forset, *Comparative Discourse*, p. 78. The Ovidian 'original' reads 'militat omnis amans', *Amores* I, 9.

17. Forset, *Comparative Discourse*, p. 75.

18. 'Wherefore, if thine hand or thy fote cause thee to offende, cut them of, & cast them from thee: it is better for thee to enter into life, halt, or maimed, then hauing two hands or two fete, to be cast into euerlasting fyre.' Mt. 18: 8, Geneva Bible.

19. 'Where a disease is particular only to one part, as to the eye, the hand, foot, or such like, the losse whereof inferreth not the destruction of the whole; there, rather than a continuall molesting & annoying grieuance should encumber the ioyes of life, the part wherunto such paine sticketh & is so affixed, as that it cannot be remoued or remedied, were better to be pulled out, cut of, & disseuered from the bodie', Forset, *Comparative Discourse*, p. 84.

20. Eamon Grennan, 'Language and Politics: A Note on Spenser's "A View of the Present State of Ireland"', *Spenser Studies*, 3 (1982), pp. 99–100.

21. Hadfield, *Spenser's Irish Experience*, p. 2.

22. See Chapters 3 and 4.

23. Andrew Hadfield, 'English Colonialism and National Identity in Early Modern Ireland', *Eire-Ireland*, 28/1 (1993), p. 77.

24. Hayden White, 'The Forms of Wildness: Archaeology of an Idea', in *Tropics of Discourse* (Baltimore: Johns Hopkins University Press, 1987), pp. 150–82, and Homi K. Bhabha, 'Difference, Discrimination and the Discourse of Colonialism', in Francis Barker *et al.*, eds., *The Politics of Theory* (Colchester: University of Essex, 1983), pp. 194–211.

25. White, 'The Forms of Wildness', pp. 165–6.

26. Canny, 'Edmund Spenser', p. 2.

27. On the issue of anxieties about English 'barbarism' and the necessity of self-alienation in order to achieve national identity see Helgerson, *Forms of Nationhood*, especially, pp. 19–62.

28. Hadfield, 'English Colonialism and National Identity', pp. 78–9, quotes a piece of doggerel from Derrike's *The Image of Ireland* (London, 1581) to

illustrate this position:

> But Irishe karne unlike these foules,
> in burthe and high degree:
> No chaunglyngs are thei nowhit,
> In civill state to bee.
> Thei passe not for civilitie,
> Nor care for wisdomes lore:
> Sinne is their cheef felicitie,
> whereof thei have the store. (...)
> Yea though thei were in Courte trained up,
> and yeres there lived tenne:
> Yet doe thei loke to shaking boggs,
> scarce provyng honest menne.
> And when thei have wonne the Boggs,
> suche vertue hath that grounde:
> that they are wurse than wildest Karne,
> And more in sinne abounde.

29. See Peter Hulme, *Colonial Encounters. Europe and the Native Caribbean 1492–1797* (London and New York: Routledge, 1986), p. 86, where he defines cannibalism as the 'image of ferocious consumption of human flesh frequently used to mark the boundary between one community and its others.' I here read representations of Irish 'cannibalism' as a trope with a certain function in fashioning the identity of the English 'national' community.

30.
> Who came at length, with proud presumpteous gate,
> Into the field, as if he fearelesse were,
> All armed in cote of yron plate,
> Of great defence to ward the deadly feare,
> And on his head a steele cap he did weare
> Of colour rustie browne, but sure and strong;
> And in his hand an huge Polaxe did beare,
> Whose steale was yron studded, but not long,
> With which he wont to fight, to iustifie his wrong. (5.12.14)

The corresponding passage in the *View* reads: [The Irish foot soldier is] 'armed in a longhe shirte of mayle downe to the Caulfe of his legge with a longe, broade Axe in his hande' (2217–18).

31. See Nohrnberg, *Analogy*, Part III: 'Books of the Governors', pp. 283–425.
32. Thomas Healy, *New Latitudes. Theory and English Renaissance Literature* (London: Edward Arnold, 1992), p. 95.
33. Sheila Cavanagh, *Wanton Eyes and Chaste Desires. Female Sexuality in 'The Faerie Queene'* (Bloomington and Indianapolis: Indiana University Press, 1994), p. 1.

7 Female Territories: Textualizing the Body of the Other

1. Walter Ralegh, 'The discoverie of the large, rich, and beautifull Empire of Guiana...Performed in the yeere 1595', in Richard Hakluyt, *The Principal*

Navigations, Voyages, Traffiques & Discoveries of the English Nation (1600), ed. Walter Raleigh, 12 vols. (Glasgow: John MacLehose, 1903–05), vol. 10 (1904), pp. 338–431. All further quotations are taken from this edition; page numbers are given in the text.

2. Hulme, *Colonial Encounters*, p. 86. On Columbus' accounts of the inhabitants of the native Caribbean and the dissemination of the signifier 'canibal' see pp. 13–44.

3. Sigrid Brauner, 'Cannibals, Witches, and Shrews in the "Civilizing Process"', *Mitteilungen des Zentrums zur Erforschung der Frühen Neuzeit*, 2 (1994), p. 45.

4. Even though ideas of marriage changed in the early modern period, the fact that the state of the woman's body was of central concern did not. Whether a marriage was contracted to 'cement together two politically important males', as David Lindley puts it, or whether it was a contract between two people attached to each other by a romantic rather than a diplomatic bond, the 'untouched' condition of the woman's body was a central factor in the transaction. It became even more so during the transformation to what Lawrence Stone has called the 'patriarchal nuclear family', since in times of increasingly capitalist economic structures only the privileged access of one man to his wife's body could guarantee the legitimacy of his offspring intended to inherit his property. Lawrence Stone, *The Family, Sex and Marriage in England 1500–1800* (Harmondsworth: Penguin, 1988), pp. 93–146; Lindley, *The Trials of Francis Howard*, p. 85; Karen Newman, 'The Crown Conjugal: Marriage in Early Modern England', in *Fashioning Femininity and English Renaissance Drama* (Chicago: Chicago University Press, 1991), pp. 13–31.

5. I am not arguing that women were generally victimized by these processes of commodification, and the self-affirmative acceptance of discourses of chastity by Protestant women of the emerging 'middling sort' in order to distinguish themselves from aristocratic women is well-known. The fact remains, however, that this way of conceptualizing women and their bodies entails an objectifying impetus that facilitated its adaptation into capitalist modes of organization. See Chapter 3.

6. Donne, *Poetical Works*, p. 107.

7. Montrose, 'The Work of Gender in the Discourse of Discovery', p. 22.

8. Gesa Mackenthun, *Metaphors of Dispossession: American Beginnings and the Translation of Empire, 1492–1637* (Oklahoma: Oklahoma University Press, 1997), p. 164, n. 13.

9. Vives teaches that 'a woman hath no power of her owne body but her husbande'. *Instruction of a Christen Woman*, fol. X1^r.

10. Montrose argues that 'Elizabethan perception and speculation were structured by the cognitive operations of hierarchy and inversion, analogy and antithesis. By the logic of these operations, a conceptual space for reversal and negation was constructed within the world picture of a patriarchal society.' 'The Work of Gender in the Discourse of Discovery', p. 26.

11. Amerigo Vespucci, 'Mundus Novus. Letter to Lorenzo Pietro di Medici', in *Vespucci Reprints, Texts and Studies*, vol. 5, transl. George Tyler Northup (Princeton: Princeton University Press, 1916), pp. 5–6.

12. Sander Gilman, *Sexuality: An Illustrated History* (New York: John Wiley, 1989), p. 50; see also Leo Steinberg, *The Sexuality of Christ in Renaissance Art and in Modern Oblivion* (New York: Random House, 1986).

13. On the mechanism of this transfer, see Helen Carr, 'Woman/Indian. "The American" and his others', in Francis Barker *et al.*, eds., *Europe and Its Others* (Colchester: University of Essex, 1985), vol. 2, pp. 46–60.

14. Montrose, 'The Work of Gender in the Discourse of Discovery', p. 23.

15. See, for example, Luke Gernon's *A Discourse of Ireland* of 1620, which draws on the same representational matrix: 'This Nymph of Ireland is at all points like a young wench that hath the green sickness for want of occupying. She is very fair of visage and hath a smooth skin of tender grass. Indeed, she is somewhat freckled (as the Irish are) – some parts darker than other. Her flesh is of a soft and delicate mold of earth, and her blue veins trailing through every part of her like rivulets. She hath one master vein called the Shannon, which passeth quite through her, and if it were not for one knot (one main rock), it were navigable from head to foot. (...) Her bones are of polished marble, the gray marble, the black, the red, and the speckled, so fair for building that their houses show like colleges, and being polished is most rarely embellished. Her breasts are round hillocks of milk-yielding grass, and that so fertile that they contend with the valleys. And betwixt her legs (for Ireland is full of havens) she hath an open harbor, but not much frequented. (...) It is now since she was drawn out of the womb of rebellion about sixteen years... and yet she wants a husband: she is not embraced; she is not hedged and ditched; there is no quickset put into her.' In James P. Myers, Jr., ed., *Elizabethan Ireland. A Selection of Writings by Elizabethan Writers on Ireland* (Hamden, CT.: Archon, 1983), pp. 242–3.

16. On the 'colonial romance' imagery and the eroticization of landscape in early modern travel literature, see Sabine Schülting, *Wilde Frauen, Fremde Welten. Kolonisierungsgeschichten aus Amerika* (Reinbek: Rowohlt, 1997), pp. 21–78.

17. Francis Bacon, 'The Masculine Birth of Time', in Benjamin Farrington, *The Philosophy of Francis Bacon. With New Translations of Fundamental Texts* (Liverpool: Liverpool University Press, 1964), p. 72, and 'Novum Organum', in *The Works of Francis Bacon in 14 Vols*, ed. James Spedding *et al.* (London: Longman's Green, 1857–74), vol. 4, p. 42.

18. Michel Foucault has shown that male bodies are being objectified as well, through military drill and the commodification of labour. The fundamental difference, however, rests in the fact that women are exclusively identified with their bodies, thus conceptually unable to acquire the status of subjects. *Discipline and Punish. The Birth of the Prison* (Harmondsworth: Penguin, 1977).

19. See Montrose, 'The Work of Gender', Brauner, 'Witches, Cannibals', Annette Kolodny, *The Lay of the Land. Metaphor as Experience and History in American Life and Letters* (Chapel Hill: University of North Carolina Press, 1975), Carr, 'Woman / Indian', and Peter Hulme, 'Polytropic Man: Tropes of Sexuality and Mobility in Early Colonial Discourse', in Barker *et al.*, eds., *Europe and its Others*, pp. 17–32.

20. Montrose, 'The Work of Gender', p. 18.

21. Hakluyt, *The Principal Navigations*, vol. viii, p. 290. Emphasis added.

22. See my discussion of temperance in Chapter 1.

23. Juliana Schiesari points out that the rhetoric of domestication analogized women, servants, and pets as domestic 'others' of the subject, who had to prove his capability to rule in the public sphere by governing his private

domain, thus excluding from his concept of humanity those ostensibly in need of domestication. 'The Face of Domestication', pp. 55–70.

24. Apparently there is as yet no conceptual difference in the terminology describing aristocratic behaviour and that of the emergent merchant class. Helgerson, quoting a study on the representation of merchants in sixteenth-century popular literature by Laura Stevenson, points out that there was no conceptual vocabulary assigning any special value to merchants' activities. Rather, 'the labels Elizabethan authors attached to men of trade... reveal that they never sought to consolidate the social consciousness of these men by appealing to bourgeois values. Elizabethan praise of bourgeois men was expressed in the rhetoric – and by extension, in terms of social paradigms – of the aristocracy.' Laura Caroline Stevenson, *Praise and Paradox: Merchants and Craftsmen in Elizabethan Popular Literature* (Cambridge: Cambridge University Press, 1984), p. 6; see also Helgerson, *Forms of Nationhood*, pp. 168–9.

25. Montrose, 'The Work of Gender', p. 19.

26. *The Faerie Queene*, 2.7; see my discussion of Guyon as the paradigm for masculine subjectivity in Chapter 1.

27. Laurence Keymis, 'A Relation of the second Voyage to Guiana, performed and written in the yeere 1596', in Hakluyt, *The Principal Navigations*, vol. x, p. 473.

28. Ralegh is indeed a good example for the kind of strategic, cunningly intelligent, mobile, and eloquent colonial subject whom Hulme has called 'polytropic man'. Ralegh, like polytropic man, 'not only lies without compunction, he is proud to present himself as a consummate improviser, master of discourse'. Hulme, 'Polytropic man', in Barker *et al.*, *Europe and Its Others*, vol. 2, p. 21.

29. Mary C. Fuller, 'Ralegh's Fugitive Gold: Reference and Deferral in "The Discoverie of Guiana"', *Representations*, 33 (1991), p. 57.

30 In the *Mammon* episode, Guyon retorts to the money god's boastful claim 'Do not I kings create': 'Ne thine be kingdomes, ne the scepters thine; / But realmes and rulers thou doest both confound, / And loyall truth to treason doest incline' (*Faerie Queene* 2.7.11 and 13).

31. Richard Hakluyt, 'The Epistle Dedicatorie to Sir Francis Walsingham' (First ed. 1589), in *The Principal Navigations*, vol. 1, p. xviii.

32. Mackenthun points out that '[Ralegh] did not "discover" the "large, rich, and beautifull Empire of Guiana,"...his party had instead merely cruised along the Orinoco for about four hundred miles, made a few friendly contacts with the neighboring native groups and returned in a hurry to escape the dangers of the rainy season. Even this was no discovery at all as Ralegh's Spanish prisoner and informant, Don Antonio de Berrio, had already "discovered" the whole area before him. Ralegh's venture thus deserves the name only insofar as he dis-covered Guiana for Queen Elizabeth and the English nation.' *Metaphors of Dispossession*, p. 170.

Bibliography

Primary sources

[Aquinas, Thomas] *The 'Summa Theologica' of St. Thomas Aquinas in 22 Volumes*, literally transl. by Fathers of the English Dominican Province (London: Burns Oates & Washbourne, 1942).

Aristotle, *Nicomachean Ethics*, transl. H. Rackham (London: Heinemann, 1926).

Bacon, 'Novum Organum', in *The Works of Francis Bacon in 14 vols*, ed. James Spedding *et al.* (London: Longman's Green, 1857–74), vol. 4, pp. 39–248.

Bacon, Francis, 'The Masculine Birth of Time', in Benjamin Farrington, *The Philosophy of Francis Bacon. With New Translations of Fundamental Texts* (Liverpool: Liverpool University Press, 1964), pp. 60–72.

Brooks-Davies, Douglas, ed., *Silver Poets of the Sixteenth Century* (London: Everyman, 1992).

Calendar of State Papers and Manuscripts: Venice, ed. R. Browne and G. C. Bentinck (London, 1890).

Crooke, Helkiah, *Microcosmographia: A Description of the Body of Man* (London, 1615).

Donne, John, *Poetical Works*, ed. Herbert J. C. Grierson (Oxford: Oxford University Press, 1987).

Estienne, Charles, *La dissection des parties du corps humain* (Paris, 1545).

Forset, Edward, *A Comparative Discourse of the Bodies Natural and Politique. Wherein out of the Principles of Nature, is set forth the true form of a Commonweale, with the dutie of Subiects, and the right of the Soueraigne: together with manie good points of Politicall learning, mentioned in Brief after the Preface* (London, 1606, rpt. Meisenheim: Hain, 1969).

Galateo of Maister John Della Casa, Archebishop of Beneventa. Or rather, A treatise of the manners and behaviours, it behoueth a man to vse and eschewe, in his familiar conversation. A worke very necessary and profitable for all Gentlemen, or other. Done into English by Robert Peterson, of Lincoln's Inn (London, 1576) [BL C.121.a.13].

Geneva Bible (1560), facs., introd. Lloyd Berry (Madison: University of Wisconsin Press, 1969).

Gernon, Luke, 'A Discourse of Ireland' (1620), in James P. Myers, Jr., ed., *Elizabethan Ireland. A Selection of Writings by Elizabethan Writers on Ireland* (Hamden, CT.: Archon, 1983), pp. 241–57.

Graves, Robert, *The Greek Myths*, 2 vols. (Harmondsworth: Penguin, 1955).

Hakluyt, Richard, *The Principal Navigations, Voyages, Traffiques & Discoveries of the English Nation (1600)*, ed. Walter Raleigh, 12 vols. (Glasgow: John MacLehose, 1903–5).

Hakluyt, Richard, 'The Epistle Dedicatorie to Sir Francis Walsingham' (first ed. 1589), in *The Principal Navigations, Voyages, Traffiques & Discoveries of the English Nation (1600)*, ed. Walter Raleigh, 12 vols. (Glasgow: John MacLehose, 1903–5), vol. i, p. xviii.

[Hoby, Thomas] *The Book of the Courtier from the Italian of Count Baldassare Castiglione: Done into English by Sir Thomas Hoby Anno 1561* (rpt. New York: AMS Press, 1967).

Keymis, Laurence, 'A Relation of the second Voyage to Guiana, performed and written in the yeere 1596', in Hakluyt, Richard, *The Principal Navigations, Voyages, Traffiques & Discoveries of the English Nation (1600)*, ed. Walter Raleigh, 12 vols. (Glasgow: John MacLehose, 1903–5), vol. x, pp. 441–501.

Lexikon der Christlichen Ikonographie, ed. Wolfgang Braunfels *et al.* (Freiburg: Herder, 1968).

Lyly, John, *Complete Works*, ed. R. Warwick Bond (Oxford: Clarendon, 1902).

Norbrook, David, select. and introd. Henry Woudhuysen, ed., *The Penguin Book of Renaissance Verse 1509–1659* (Harmondsworth: Penguin, 1993).

Ovid, *Metamorphoses*, 2 vols., transl. Frank Justus Miller, 2nd rev. ed. (Cambridge, Mass. and London: Harvard University Press, 1984).

Paré, Ambroise, *Deux Livres de la Chirurgie* (Paris, 1573).

Petrarca, Francesco, *Canzoniere*, ed. Alberto Chiari (Rome: Mondadori, 1992).

Pico della Mirandola, Giovanni, *Commentary on a Canzone of Benivieni*, transl. Sears Jane (New York, Bern *et al.*: Lang, 1984).

Puttenham, George, *The Arte of English Poesie* (1589), ed. Edward Arber (Westminster: Constable, 1895).

Ralegh, Walter, 'The discoverie of the large, rich, and beautifull Empire of Guiana...Performed in the yeere 1595', in Richard Hakluyt, *The Principal Navigations, Voyages, Traffiques & Discoveries of the English Nation (1600)*, ed. Walter Raleigh, 12 vols. (Glasgow: John MacLehose, 1903–5), vol. x (1904), pp. 338–431.

Rhodes, Hugh, *The Book of Nurture for menseruants and Children (with Stans puer ad mensam) newly corrected, very vtile and necessary vnto all youth* (London, 1550) [BL C.39.e.52].

[Seager, Francis] *The School of Vertue, and booke of good Nourture for chyldren, and youth to learne theyr dutie by. Newely perused, corrected, and augmented by the fyrst Auctor. F.S. with a brief declaration of the dutie of eche degree* (London, 1557) [BL 232.a.45].

Sermons, or Homilies, appointed to be read in Churches in the Time of Elizabeth of Famous Memory. To which are added the Articles of Religion (London: C. Best, 1840).

Shakespeare, William, *Measure for Measure*, ed. J. W. Lever (London and New York: Routledge, 1994).

Shakespeare, William, *The Sonnets and A Lover's Complaint*, ed. John Kerrigan (Harmondsworth: Penguin, 1986).

Sidney, Philip, *An Apology for Poetry*, ed. Geoffrey Shepherd (Manchester: Manchester University Press, 1984).

Sidney, Philip, 'Discourse of Syr Ph. S. to the Queenes Majesty touching hir marriage with monsieur', in *Complete Works*, ed. Albert Feuillerat (Cambridge: Cambridge University Press, 1923), vol. 3, pp. 51–60.

Sidney, Philip, *Miscellaneous Prose*, ed. Katherine Duncan-Jones and Jan Van Dorsten (Oxford: Oxford University Press, 1973).

Sidney, Philip, *The Major Works*, ed. Katherine Duncan-Jones (Oxford: Oxford University Press, 1992).

Spachius, Israel, *Gynaecia* (London, 1597).

Spenser, Edmund, 'A View of the Present State of Ireland', in *Complete Works* (variorum ed.), ed. R. B. Gottfried (Baltimore: Johns Hopkins University Press, 1949), vol. ix, pp. 40–231.

Spenser, Edmund, *The Faerie Queene*, ed. A. C. Hamilton (London and New York: Longman, 1987).

Spenser, Edmund, *The Yale Edition of the Shorter Poems of Edmund Spenser*, ed. William A. Oram *et al.* (New Haven and London: Yale University Press, 1989).

Stubbs, John, *The Discoverie of a Gaping Gulf whereinto England is like to be swallowed by an other French marriage, if the Lord forbid not the banes, by letting her Maiestie see the sin and punishment thereof* (London, 1579).

Vesalius, Andreas, *De humani corporis fabrica libri septem* (Basel, 1543).

Vespucci, Amerigo, 'Mundus Novus. Letter to Lorenzo Pietro di Medici', in *Vespucci Reprints, Texts and Studies*, vol. 5, transl. George Tyler Northup (Princeton: Princeton University Press, 1916), pp. 5–6.

Virgil, *The Eclogues*, ed. and transl. Guy Lee (Harmondsworth: Penguin, 1984).

[Vives, Ludovico] *A very frutefull and pleasant boke called the Instruction of a Christen Woman made fyrst in Laten and dedicated vnto the quenes good grace by the right famous clerke master Lewes Viues and turned out of Laten into Englysshe by Richard Byrd* (London, 1529) [BL G.11884].

Secondary sources

Abel, Elizabeth, ed., *Writing and Sexual Difference* (Brighton: Harvester, 1982).

Adams, Simon, ed., *Queen Elizabeth I: Most Politick Princess* (special issue of *History Today*, 1984).

Alpers, Paul, 'What is Pastoral?', *Critical Inquiry*, 8 (1982), pp. 437–60.

Anderson, Benedict, *Imagined Communities. Reflections on the Origins and Spread of Nationalism* (London: Verso, rev. ed. 1991).

Aptekar, Jane, *Icons of Justice. Iconography and Thematic Imagery in Book V of 'The Faerie Queene'* (New York and London: Columbia University Press, 1969).

Axton, Marie, *The Queen's Two Bodies. Drama and the Elizabethan Succession* (London: Royal Historical Society, 1977).

Bakhtin, Mikhail, *Rabelais and his World*, transl. Hélène Iswolski (Bloomington: Indiana University Press, 1984).

Barkan, Leonard, *Nature's Work of Art. The Human Body as Image of the World* (New Haven and London: Yale University Press, 1977).

Barker, Francis *et al.*, eds., *Europe and Its Others*, 2 vols. (Colchester: University of Essex, 1985).

—— *et al.*, eds., *The Politics of Theory* (Colchester: University of Essex, 1983).

Bates, Catherine, *The Rhetoric of Courtship in Elizabethan Language and Literature* (Cambridge: Cambridge University Press, 1992).

Berry, Philippa, *Of Chastity and Power. Elizabethan Literature and the Unmarried Queen* (London and New York: Routledge, 1989).

Bhabha, Homi K., 'Difference, Discrimination and the Discourse of Colonialism', in Francis Barker *et al.*, eds., *The Politics of Theory* (Colchester: University of Essex, 1983), pp. 194–211.

—— *Nation and Narration* (London and New York: Routledge, 1992).

Bhabha, Homi K., *The Location of Culture* (London and New York: Routledge, 1994).

Brady, Ciaran, 'Spenser's Irish Crisis: Humanism and Experience in the 1590s', *Past and Present*, 111 (1986), pp. 17–49.

Brauner, Sigrid, 'Cannibals, Witches, and Shrews in the "Civilizing Process"', *Mitteilungen des Zentrums zur Erforschung der Frühen Neuzeit*, 2 (1994), pp. 29–54.

Bremmer, Jan, 'Walking, Standing, and Sitting in Ancient Greek Culture', in Jan Bremmer and Herman Roodenburg, eds., *A Cultural History of Gesture* (Ithaca: Cornell University Press, 1992), pp. 15–35.

—— and Herman Roodenburg, eds., *A Cultural History of Gesture* (Ithaca: Cornell University Press, 1992).

Bryson, Anna, 'The Rhetoric of Status: Gesture, Demeanour and the Image of the Gentleman in Sixteenth- and Seventeenth-Century England', in Lucy Gent and Nigel Llewellyn, eds., *Renaissance Bodies. The Human Figure in English Culture c. 1540–1660* (London: Reaktion Books 1990), pp. 136–53.

Butler, Judith, *Bodies That Matter. On the Discursive Limits of 'Sex'* (New York and London: Routledge, 1993).

—— *Gender Trouble. Feminism and the Subversion of Identity* (New York and London: Routledge, 1990).

Canny, Nicholas and Ciaran Brady, 'Debate: Spenser's Irish Crisis: Humanism and Experience in the 1590s', *Past and Present*, 120 (1988), pp. 201–15.

—— and Anthony Pagden, eds., *Colonial Identity in the Atlantic World 1500–1800* (Princeton: Princeton University Press, 1987).

—— 'Edmund Spenser and the Development of an Anglo-Irish Identity', *Yearbook of English Studies*, 13 (1983), pp. 1–19.

—— 'The Ideology of English Colonization: From Ireland to America', *William and Mary Quarterly*, 30 (1973), pp. 575–98.

Carr, Helen, 'Woman/Indian. "The American" and his others', in Francis Barker *et al.*, eds., *Europe and Its Others* (Colchester: University of Essex, 1985), vol. 2, pp. 46–60.

Cavanagh, Sheila, *Wanton Eyes and Chaste Desires. Female Sexuality in 'The Faerie Queene'* (Bloomington and Indianapolis: Indiana University Press, 1994).

Chaudhuri, Sukanta, *Renaissance Pastoral and its English Developments* (Oxford: Oxford University Press, 1989).

Collinson, Patrick, *The Elizabethan Puritan Movement* (London: Cape, 1971).

Cooper, Helen, *Pastoral: Medieval into Renaissance* (Ipswich: D. S. Brewer, 1977).

Council, Norman, '"O Dea Certe": The Allegory of "The Fortress of Perfect Beauty"', *Huntington Library Quarterly*, 39 (1976), pp. 328–42.

Douglas, Mary, *Purity and Danger. An Analysis of the Concepts of Pollution and Taboo* (London and New York: Routledge, 1994).

Duden, Barbara, *The Woman Beneath the Skin*, transl. Lee Hoinacki (Cambridge, Mass.: Harvard University Press, 1991).

Elias, Norbert, *The Civilizing Process. The History of Manners* (New York: Pantheon, 1982).

Elton, G. R., *England under the Tudors* (London and New York: Methuen, 1974).

—— *The Tudor Revolution in Government: Administrative Changes in the Reign of Henry VIII* (Cambridge: Cambridge University Press, 1953).

Evans, Ruth and Lesley Johnson, eds., *Feminist Readings in Middle English Literature* (London and New York: Routledge, 1994).

Ferguson, Margaret W. *et al.*, eds., *Rewriting the Renaissance. The Discourses of Sexual Difference in Early Modern Europe* (Chicago and London: Chicago University Press, 1987).

Figlio, Karl, 'The Historiography of Scientific Medicine: an Invitation to the Human Sciences', *Comparative Studies in Society and History*, 19 (1977), pp. 262–86.

Fogarty, Anne, 'The Colonization of Language: Narrative Strategy in "A View of the Present State of Ireland" and "The Faerie Queene"', in Patricia Coughlan, ed., *Spenser and Ireland. An Interdisciplinary Perspective* (Cork: Cork University Press, 1989), pp. 75–108.

Foucault, Michel, *Discipline and Punish. The Birth of the Prison* (Harmondsworth: Penguin, 1977).

——*The History of Sexuality, vol. 1: An Introduction*, transl. Robert Hurley (Harmondsworth: Penguin, 1990).

——*The History of Sexuality, vol. 2: The Use of Pleasure*, transl. Robert Hurley (Harmondsworth: Penguin, 1990).

——*The History of Sexuality, vol. 3: The Care of the Self*, transl. Robert Hurley (Harmondsworth: Penguin, 1992).

Freccero, John, 'The Fig Tree and the Laurel: Petrarch's Poetics', in Patricia Parker and David Quint, eds., *Literary Theory/Renaissance Texts* (Baltimore and London: Johns Hopkins University Press, 1986), pp. 20–32.

Frye, Susan, 'The Myth of Elizabeth at Tilbury', *Sixteenth-Century Journal*, 23/1 (1992), pp. 95–114.

Fuller, Mary C., 'Ralegh's Fugitive Gold: Reference and Deferral in "The Discoverie of Guiana"', *Representations*, 33 (1991), pp. 42–66.

Garber, Marjorie, ed., *Cannibals, Witches, and Divorce. Estranging the Renaissance* (Baltimore and London: Johns Hopkins University Press, 1987).

Gent, Lucy and Nigel Llewellyn, eds., *Renaissance Bodies. The Human Figure in English Culture c. 1540–1660* (London: Reaktion Books, 1990).

Gilman, Sander, *Sexuality: An Illustrated History* (New York: John Wiley, 1989).

Greenblatt, Stephen, ed., *Allegory and Representation* (Baltimore and London: Johns Hopkins University Press, Selected Papers of the English Institute 5, 1981).

——*Renaissance Self Fashioning. From More to Shakespeare* (Chicago and London: Chicago University Press, 1984).

——*Sir Walter Ralegh. The Renaissance Man and His Roles* (New Haven and London: Yale University Press, 1973).

Gregerson, Linda, 'Narcissus Interrupted: Specularity and the Subject of the Tudor State', *Criticism*, 35/1 (1993), pp. 1–40.

—— *The Reformation of the Subject. Spenser, Milton and the English Protestant Epic* (Cambridge: Cambridge University Press, 1995).

Grennan, Eamon, 'Language and Politics: A Note on Spenser's "A View of the Present State of Ireland"', *Spenser Studies*, 3 (1982), pp. 99–110.

Gross, Kenneth, *Spenserian Poetics: Idolatry, Iconoclasm, and Magic* (Ithaca and London: Cornell University Press, 1985).

Hackett, Helen, *Virgin Mother, Maiden Queen. Elizabeth I and the Cult of the Virgin Mary* (Basingstoke and London: Macmillan, 1995).

Hadfield, Andrew, 'English Colonialism and National Identity in Early Modern Ireland', *Eire-Ireland*, 28/1 (1993), pp. 69–86.

Hadfield, Andrew, *Literature, Politics and National Identity. Reformation to Renaissance* (Cambridge: Cambridge University Press, 1994).
——*Spenser's Irish Experience. Wilde Fruit and Salvage Soyl* (Oxford: Clarendon, 1997).
——'The Course of Justice: Spenser, Ireland and Political Discourse', *Studia Neophilologica*, 65 (1993), pp. 187–96.
Haigh, Christopher, 'The Governance of the Realm: Bureaucracy and Aristocracy', in Simon Adams, ed., *Queen Elizabeth I: Most Politick Princess.* (Special Issue of *History Today*, 1984), pp. 9–12.
Healy, Thomas, *New Latitudes. Theory and English Renaissance Literature* (London: Edward Arnold, 1992).
Helgerson, Richard, *Forms of Nationhood. The Elizabethan Writing of England* (Chicago: Chicago University Press, 1992).
Hendricks, Margo and Patricia Parker, eds., *Women, 'Race', and Writing in the Early Modern Period* (London and New York: Routledge, 1994).
Honegger, Claudia, *Die Ordnung der Geschlechter. Die Wissenschaft vom Menschen und das Weib* (Frankfurt: Campus, 1991).
Hulme, Peter, *Colonial Encounters. Europe and the Native Caribbean 1492–1797* (London and New York: Routledge, 1986).
——'Polytropic Man: Tropes of Sexuality and Mobility in Early Colonial Discourse', in Francis Barker *et al.*, eds., *Europe and its Others* (Colchester: University of Essex, 1985), vol. 2, pp. 17–32.
Hulse, Clark, 'Stella's Wit: Penelope Rich as Reader of Sidney's Sonnets', in Margaret W. Ferguson *et al.*, eds., *Rewriting the Renaissance. The Discourses of Sexual Difference in Early Modern Europe* (Chicago and London: Chicago University Press, 1987), pp. 272–86.
Hume, Anthea, *Edmund Spenser: Protestant Poet* (Cambridge: Cambridge University Press, 1984).
Hyde, Thomas, *The Poetic Theology of Love. Cupid in Renaissance Literature* (Newark: University of Delaware Press, 1986).
Jardine, Lisa, *Still Harping on Daughters. Women and Drama in the Age of Shakespeare* (Brighton: Harvester, 1983).
Johnson, J. Staley, 'Elizabeth, Bride and Queen: A Study of Spenser's "April Eclogue" and the Metaphors of English Protestantism', *Spenser Studies*, 2 (1981), pp. 75–91.
Kantorowicz, Ernst H., *The King's Two Bodies. A Study in Mediaeval Political Theology* (Princeton: Princeton University Press, 1957).
Kelly, Joan, *Women, History and Theory. The Essays of Joan Kelly* (Chicago: Chicago University Press, 1984).
Kolodny, Annette, *The Lay of the Land. Metaphor as Experience and History in American Life and Letters* (Chapel Hill: University of North Carolina Press, 1975).
Kristeller, Paul Oskar, *Renaissance Thought and the Arts* (Princeton: Princeton University Press, 1990).
Kuchta, David, 'The Semiotics of Masculinity in Renaissance England', in James Grantham Turner, ed., *Sexuality and Gender in Early Modern Europe. Institutions, Texts, Images* (Cambridge: Cambridge University Press, 1993), pp. 233–46.
Lacan, Jacques, 'The Mirror-Stage as Formative of the Function of the I', in *Ecrits. A Selection,* transl. Alan Sheridan (New York and London: W. W. Norton, 1977), pp. 1–7.

Laqueur, Thomas, *Making Sex. Body and Gender from the Greeks to Freud* (Cambridge, Mass.: Harvard University Press, 1990).

Leersen, Joseph, *Mere Irish and Fíor-Ghael* (Amsterdam and Philadelphia: Benjamins, 1986).

Levin, Carole, *The Heart and Stomach of a King. Elizabeth I and the Politics of Sex and Power* (Philadelphia: Pennsylvania University Press, 1994).

Lindley, David, *The Trials of Frances Howard. Fact and Fiction at the Court of King James* (London and New York: Routledge, 1996).

Mackenthun, Gesa, *Metaphors of Dispossession: American Beginnings and the Translation of Empire, 1492–1637* (Oklahoma: Oklahoma University Press, 1997).

Maisak, Petra, *Arkadien. Genese und Typologie einer idyllischen Wunschwelt* (Frankfurt and Bern: Lang, 1981).

McEachern, Claire, ' "Henry V": The Paradox of the Body Politic', *Shakespeare Quarterly*, 45 / 1 (1994), pp. 33–56.

Miller, David Lee, *The Poem's Two Bodies. The Poetics of the 1590 Faerie Queene* (Princeton: Princeton University Press, 1988).

Montrose, Louis, ' "Eliza, Queen of Shepheards" and the Pastoral of Power', *English Literary Renaissance*, 10 (1980), pp. 153–82.

—— 'Professing the Renaissance: The Poetics and Politics of Culture', in H. Aram Veeser, ed., *The New Historicism* (London and New York: Routledge, 1989), pp. 15–37.

—— 'Of Gentlemen and Shepherds: The Politics of Elizabethan Pastoral Form', *Journal of English Literary History*, 50 (1983), pp. 415–60.

—— Celebration and Insinuation: Sir Philip Sidney and the Motives of Elizabethan Courtiership', *Renaissance Drama*, n.s., VIII (1977), pp. 3–35.

—— 'The Elizabethan Subject and the Spenserian Text', in Patricia Parker and David Quint, *Literary Theory/Renaissance Texts* (Baltimore: Johns Hopkins University Press, 1986), pp. 303–40.

—— 'The Work of Gender in the Discourse of Discovery', *Representations*, 33 (1991), pp. 1–41.

Murphy, Andrew, 'Reviewing the Paradigm: A New Look at Early-Modern Ireland', *Eire-Ireland*, 31, 3/4 (1996), pp. 13–40.

Newman, Karen, *Fashioning Femininity and English Renaissance Drama* (Chicago: Chicago University Press, 1991).

Nohrnberg, James, *The Analogy of 'The Faerie Queene'* (Princeton: Princeton University Press, 1980).

Parker, Patricia and David Quint, *Literary Theory/Renaissance Texts* (Baltimore: Johns Hopkins University Press, 1986).

—— and Geoffrey Hartman, eds., *Shakespeare and the Question of Theory* (New York and London: Methuen, 1985).

—— *Literary Fat Ladies: Rhetoric, Gender, Property* (London and New York: Methuen, 1987).

—— 'Suspended Instruments: Lyric and Power in the Bower of Bliss', in Marjorie Garber, ed., *Cannibals, Witches, and Divorce. Estranging the Renaissance* (Baltimore and London: Johns Hopkins University Press, 1987), pp. 21–39.

Paster, Gail Kern, *The Body Embarrassed: Drama and the Disciplines of Shame in Early Modern England* (Ithaca: Cornell University Press, 1993).

Patricia Coughlan, ed., *Spenser and Ireland. An Interdisciplinary Perspective* (Cork: Cork University Press, 1989).

Patterson, Annabel, *Pastoral and Ideology. Virgil to Valéry* (Oxford: Oxford University Press, 1988).

——'Re-opening the Green Cabinet: Clément Marot and Edmund Spenser', *English Literary Renaissance*, 16 (1986), pp. 44–70.

Quinn, David Beers, *The Elizabethans and the Irish* (Ithaca: Cornell University Press, 1966).

Sawday, Jonathan, *The Body Emblazoned: Dissection and the Human Body in Renaissance Culture* (London and New York: Routledge, 1995).

Schiesari, Juliana, 'The Face of Domestication: Physiognomy, Gender Politics, and Humanism's Others', in Margo Hendricks and Patricia Parker, eds., *Women, 'Race', and Writing in the Early Modern Period* (London and New York: Routledge, 1994), pp. 55–70.

Scholz, Susanne, 'Pleasure Island, or: When Guyon Discovered Guiana: Visions of the Female Body in English Renaissance Literature', *European Journal for English Studies*, 2 (1998), pp. 285–305.

Schülting, Sabine, *Wilde Frauen, Fremde Welten. Kolonisierungsgeschichten aus Amerika* (Reinbek: Rowohlt, 1997).

Sherman, William H., *John Dee: The Politics of Reading and Writing in the English Renaissance* (Amherst, Mass.: University of Massachusetts Press, 1995).

Sinfield, Alan, *Faultlines. Cultural Materialism and the Politics of Dissident Reading* (Oxford: Clarendon, 1992).

Sissa, Giulia, *Le corps virginal. La virginité feminine en Grèce ancienne* (Paris: J. Vrin, 1987).

Smith, A. J., 'The Metaphysic of Love', *Review of English Studies*, n.s. 9 (1958), pp. 362–75.

Steinberg, Leo, *The Sexuality of Christ in Renaissance Art and in Modern Oblivion* (New York: Random House, 1986).

Stevenson, Laura Caroline, *Praise and Paradox: Merchants and Craftsmen in Elizabethan Popular Literature* (Cambridge: Cambridge University Press, 1984).

Stone, Lawrence, *The Family, Sex and Marriage in England 1500–1800* (Harmondsworth: Penguin, 1988).

Suzuki, Mihoko, ed., *Critical Essays on Edmund Spenser* (New York: G. K. Hall, 1996).

——'Scapegoating Radigund', in Mihoko Suzuki, ed., *Critical Essays on Edmund Spenser* (New York: G. K. Hall, 1996), pp. 183–98.

Turner, James Grantham, ed., *Sexuality and Gender in Early Modern Europe. Institutions, Texts, Images* (Cambridge: Cambridge University Press, 1993).

Veeser, H. Aram, ed., *The New Historicism* (London and New York: Routledge, 1989).

Vickers, Nancy J., 'Diana Described: Scattered Woman and Scattered Rhyme', in Elizabeth Abel, ed., *Writing and Sexual Difference* (Brighton: Harvester, 1982), pp. 95–109.

——' "The Blazon of Sweet Beauty's Best": Shakespeare's "Lucrece" ', in Patricia Parker and Geoffrey Hartman, eds., *Shakespeare and the Question of Theory* (New York and London: Methuen, 1985), pp. 95–115.

White, Hayden, *Tropics of Discourse* (Baltimore: Johns Hopkins University Press, 1987).

Wilson, Jean, *Entertainments for Elizabeth I* (Woodbridge: D. S. Brewer, 1980).

Wogan-Browne, Jocelyn, 'The Virgin's Tale', in Ruth Evans and Lesley Johnson, eds., *Feminist Readings in Middle English Literature* (London and New York: Routledge, 1994), pp. 165–94.

Yates, Frances A., *Astraea. The Imperial Theme in the Sixteenth Century* (London: Pimlico, 1993).

Yavneh, Naomi, 'The Ambiguity of Beauty in Tasso and Petrarch', in James Grantham Turner, ed., *Sexuality and Gender in Early Modern Europe* (Cambridge: Cambridge University Press, 1993), pp. 133–57.

Index